IMAGES
of America

Fox Township, Elk County

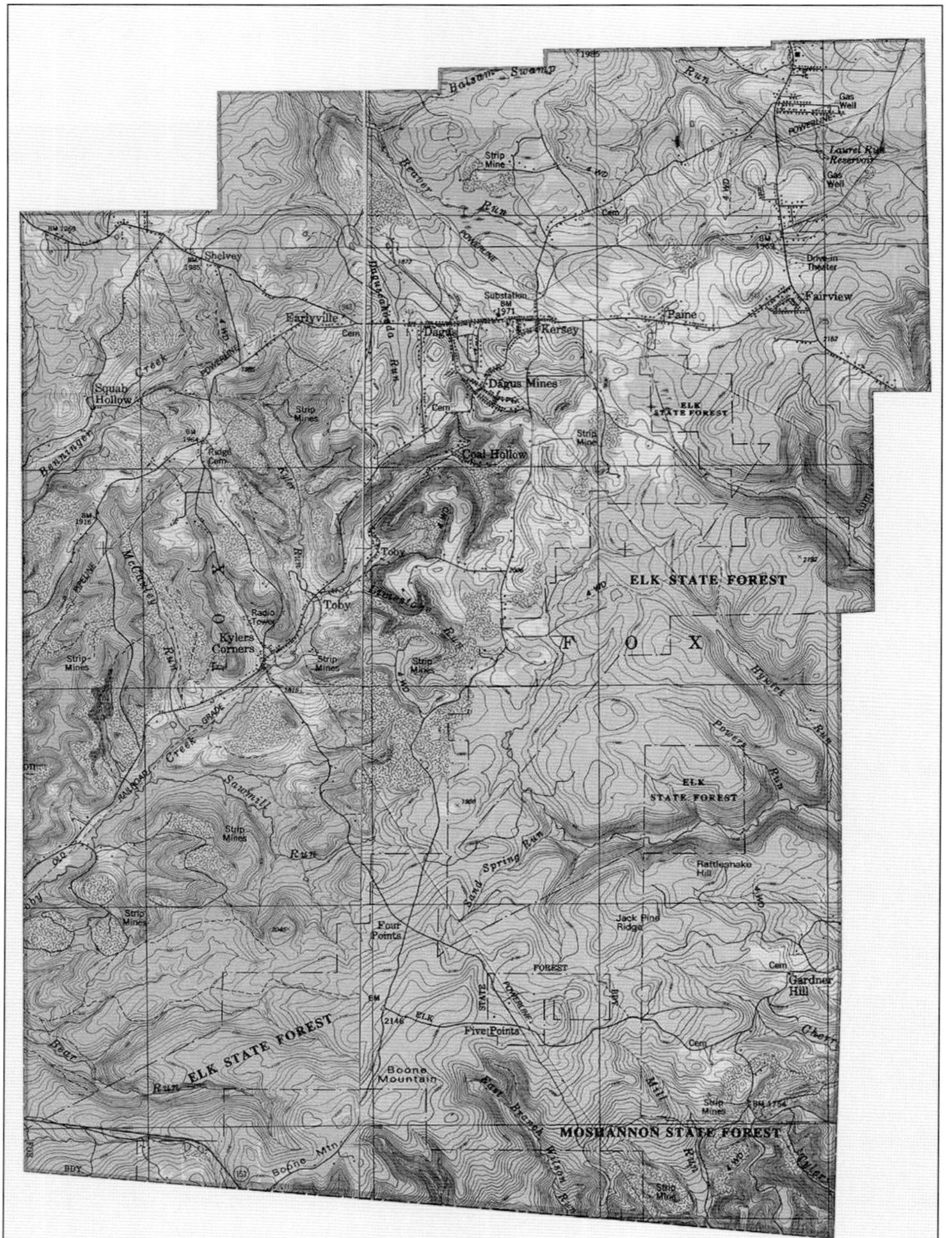

Fox Township is located in Elk County, in north-central Pennsylvania. It is a collection of small towns, each with a unique character. The township was named for Samuel Fox, of the Fox and Norris Land Company, and was originally established in 1814 as part of Clearfield County. (Courtesy of Jason Bolt.)

On the Cover: Beadle's Elk Filling Station, one of the first gas stations in the community, was located at the crossing in Kersey and is seen here in the 1920s. Notice the gas pump in the foreground, which permitted customers to make sure they were getting the amount of gas desired. The Beimel family was the last owner of the station. (Courtesy of Joan Verbka.)

IMAGES
of America

FOX TOWNSHIP, ELK COUNTY

Robert J. Schreiber Jr.

ARCADIA
PUBLISHING

ISBN 9978-0-7385-9907-6

Published by Arcadia Publishing
Charleston, South Carolina

Printed in the United States of America

Library of Congress Control Number: 2012951436

For all general information, please contact Arcadia Publishing:
Telephone 843-853-2070
Fax 843-853-0044
E-mail sales@arcadiapublishing.com
For customer service and orders:
Toll-Free 1-888-313-2665

Visit us on the Internet at www.arcadiapublishing.com

To my father, R.J. Schreiber, a truly good man.

Contents

Acknowledgments

I would like to thank all the people of Fox Township and vicinity who have helped me in the preparation of this book. Numerous individuals have submitted photographs and ideas. They have continuously encouraged and inspired me.

I would like, however, to single out Ken Anderson, Joan Verbka, Jason Bolt, Mike Belovesich, Chris Casey, William and Janice Haller, Kathy Dowie, Hazel Luchini, Ken Meredith, Barb Pistner, Debbie Agosti, Harriet Moyer, Jim Catalone, Anna Mae Short, the bicentennial committee, and the St. Boniface parish for all their images. Most of all, I would like to thank the love of my life, my editor and wife, Paulette, who still gets great pleasure out of correcting my mistakes.

Unless otherwise noted, all photographs belong to the author.

INTRODUCTION

Fox Township, located in the mountains of north-central Pennsylvania, was the first area settled in what is now Elk County. In 1798, the first white settlers, General Wade and his family, along with a friend identified as Slade, came and settled above Toby Valley, on Hogback Ridge. They moved, however, in 1803, to the mouth of the Little Toby River. The next early settlers were Amos Davis and his family, who arrived in 1807 and settled near Krise Road and what is now Earlyville. They sold out and moved in 1816.

The first permanent settlers came about 1812 in response to advertising and inducements made by the owners of much of the land, the Fox and Norris Land Company. These pioneer families settled throughout the current township: John Kyler at Kylers Corners in Toby, Elijah Meredith on Chicken Hill, Samuel Miller in Earlyville, Jacob Wilson near the Crossing, and Jonah Miller in present Kersey. By 1820, other families arrived with surnames such as Reesman, Taylor, McCauley, Meade, Green, and Shafer. In the 1820s, surnames such as Moyer, Rodgers, Clark, Coleman, Keller, and others began to appear. Many descendants of these first families still reside in the township, and their family names still resound.

Kersey is the common name used to describe much of what is now Fox Township. It is named for surveyor and Fox and Norris land agent William Kersey, who was charged with building the first road into the county. The road began between what are now Curwensville and Luthersburg, and came up Little Toby Creek and over Hogback Ridge to Earlyville. The 33-mile road opened about 1812 as little more than a path. The trees were cut as low as possible, but the stumps remained; subsequently, wagons intended for traveling this road needed high axles to overcome the uneven terrain. The path was just wide enough for an ox-drawn wagon to pass and had no bridges over the streams. Swamps were corduroyed, and the road was impassable when it rained, and almost as bad in the winter. Even so, the road did allow settlers to bring personal belongings, instead of just what could be carried on their backs or by horse. William Kersey also built the first gristmill in the county, on Daguscahonda Run near the end of Krise Road.

The next major development in the area was the construction of the first "good" road. The Milesburg-Smethport Turnpike, a privately owned road constructed with financial help from the state, was finished by 1828. The toll was high, but the pike never made money for investors and was declared abandoned by the company in about 1844. It did, however, benefit the communities along its path by opening the area to new settlers and investments. Today, the deeds of Main Street in Kersey all refer to the Milesburg-Smethport Turnpike.

Although the entire area is still called Kersey, the little settlements and communities of the area developed somewhat independently. Irishtown, Earlyville, Toby, South Kersey, Coal Hollow, and Centreville each had unique characteristics. In 1846, Centreville was platted by John Green, and lots were sold on both sides of the pike. As there were already several Centrevilles in Pennsylvania, the postal service officially changed the name to Kersey in 1876, even though residents still used the Centreville address for years to come.

Fox Township began to change from an agriculturally based economy with the development of the coal mining industry and the arrival of the railroads. Coal was discovered early in the township's history, but was initially only able to be used locally. As the Industrial Revolution took hold in America after the Civil War, demand for coal increased and a method of transportation was developed. The coal, steel, and railroad industries each contributed to the other's development and to the growth of Fox Township.

The Daguscahonda Branch of the Philadelphia & Erie Railroad was the first in the township. The six-mile line began operation about 1866, and moved coal from Dagus Mines via the Northwest Mining and Exchange mines to the main line in Daguscahonda. Another 11.4-mile line was opened in the mid-1880s, connecting Toby and Coal Hollow with Brockway; the St. Mary & Southwestern connected the community with St. Marys in 1894.

Both coal and steel directly provided work for hundreds of men. Other businesses grew to support the mines and miners. Lumbermen had markets for railroad ties, mine headings, and new housing for the growing population and new businesses. Farmers had more markets for their crops and meat.

Dagus Mines, Toby, and Coal Hollow practically became company towns. The Northwest Mining and Exchange provided company houses and a company store, doctor, and drugstore. They also donated land and materials for churches and, as well water was tainted, a public water system. All of this was, however, at great cost to the miners. There were several strikes and constant attempts to unionize. Originally, the miners were mainly Swedes and Scots, but by the late 1800s, many Italian immigrants arrived, leading to much conflict and prejudice against the Roman Catholic immigrants.

Kersey became the retail center for the township. The main street had, at times, six hotels, numerous taverns, general stores, liveries, doctor's and dentist's offices, a funeral home, cobblers, harness and wagon shops, blacksmith shops, tailor and millinery shops, bakeries, candy stores, butcher shops, slaughterhouses, a foundry, a brewery and bottling factory, and much more.

Other small little hamlets grew up around railroad stops such as Paine, Gillen, Shelvey Summit, and Squab Hollow, and still others surrounded lumbering and farming, such as the small settlements on Boones Mountain and in South Kersey. Many had one-room schools, churches, and other buildings, but the settlements declined when the railroads ceased operating and the timber had been cut.

Beginning before World War II, the coal mines began to decline. Though much coal was still available, the most easily obtainable coal, the cheapest to mine, was gone. Although deep mining was still profitable, larger profits could be made elsewhere. With the loss of the mines, so went the railroads, with the last line abandoned in the early 1970s. Consequently, most residents began to work in the growing carbon factories and newly developing powdered metal industries in nearby St. Marys. Today, the township is again growing and prosperous, with many small factories and shops opening regularly.

The township has always had a strong sense of community and pride, as expressed in township-wide groups such as service and fraternal organizations, churches, schools, and sports. The Fox Township Volunteer Fire Department, Fox Legion Post 511, Troop 94 of Boy Scouts of America, and the Fox Township Lions and Sportsman's Clubs, for example, have served the area for decades.

Community-wide festivities such as field days, parades, shooting matches, barbecues, and holiday activities have been enjoyed since the earliest days. The Fourth of July has been celebrated with food, speeches, fireworks, and parades since at least the 1860s, culminating with the present celebrations at the Fox Township Community Park. The park also has annual Halloween, Christmas, Easter, and summer activities for all residents. Baseball has drawn our towns together for more than 150 years, as have soccer, midget football, and high school sports.

As the 2013 bicentennial celebration approaches, residents take pride in the works of our predecessors and our rural advantages. All agree with the celebration's motto: "Built and preserved by community spirit."

One

Kersey and Vicinity

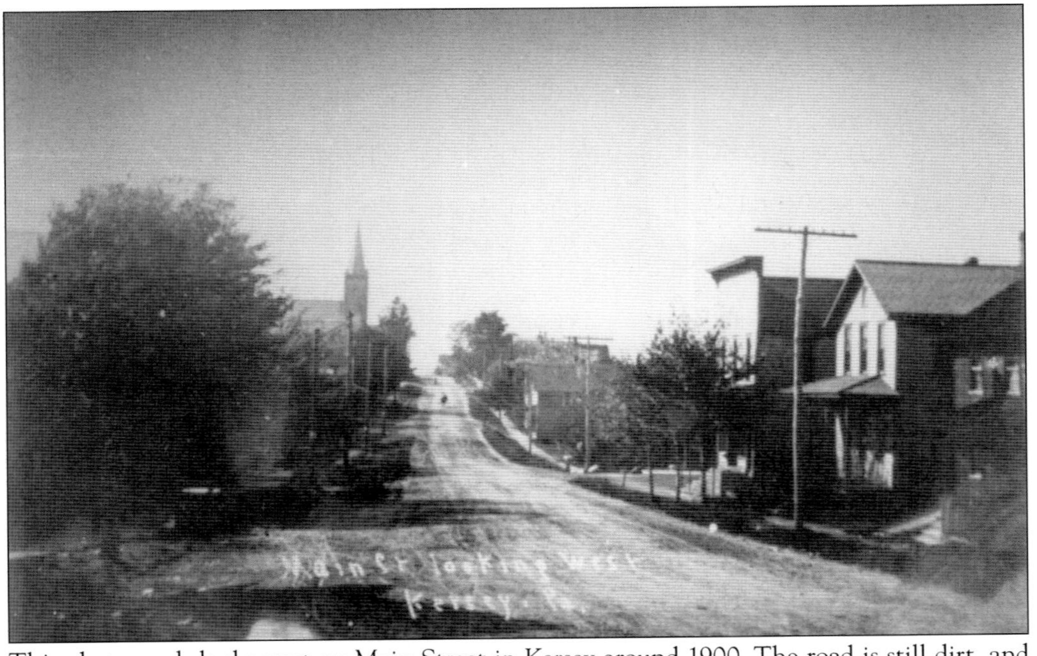

This photograph looks west on Main Street in Kersey around 1900. The road is still dirt, and was not paved until 1905. On the right is Urmann's bottling factory, which was later known as Hackerl's and then J.J. Malone's. In the distance is St. Boniface Church, with its original steeple. The steeple was removed in the 1930s for safety reasons, as slates continually fell off of it. (Courtesy of Chris Casey.)

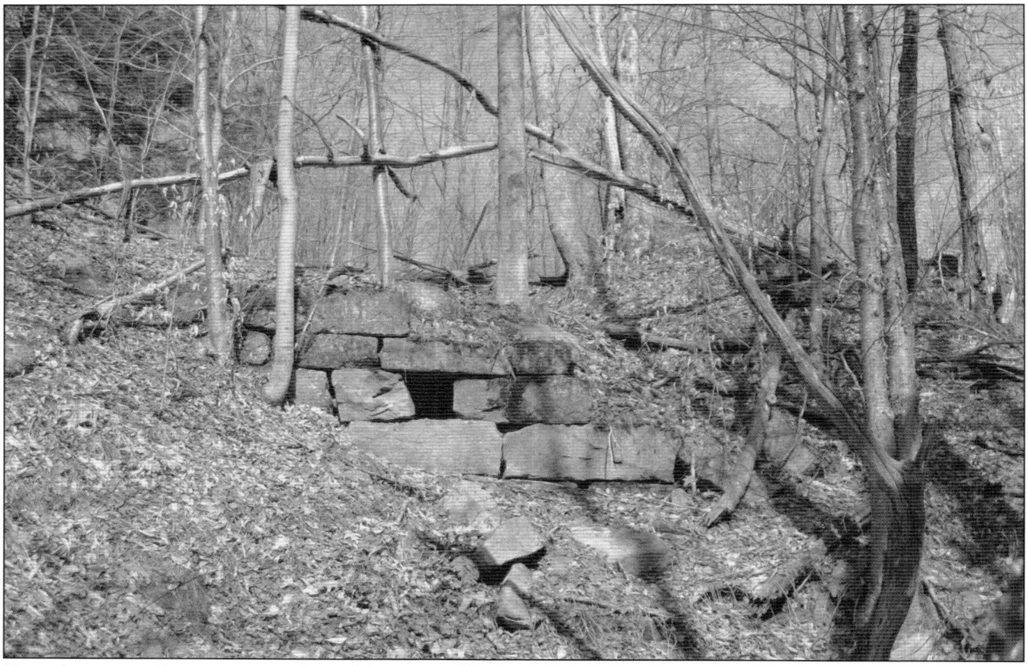

Seen here are the remains of an old gristmill at the site of William Kersey's original mill. The mill was essential to local farmers for grinding their grain. Kersey's mill was the first large machine of any sort in Elk County. Although it burned down several times, other mills were built at the site, and they remained in operation until well after the Civil War and the rise of steam power.

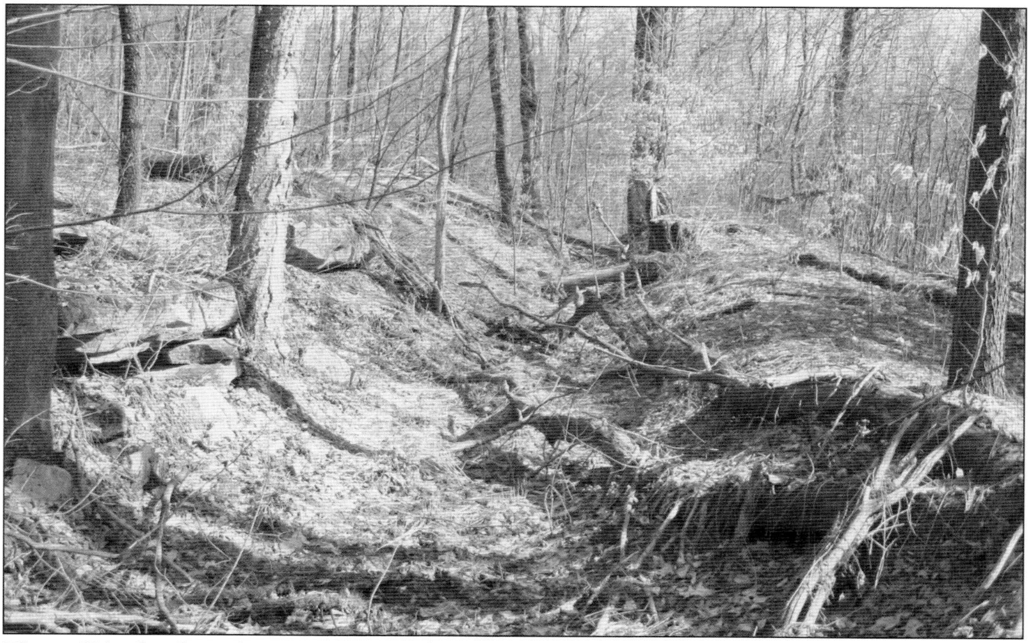

The mill had a dam about a quarter mile upstream and a raceway leading to the mill. This is a portion of the raceway channel, just before it turns 90 degrees toward the mill's waterwheel. The millpond and breastworks are still visible, although they are now covered with small trees.

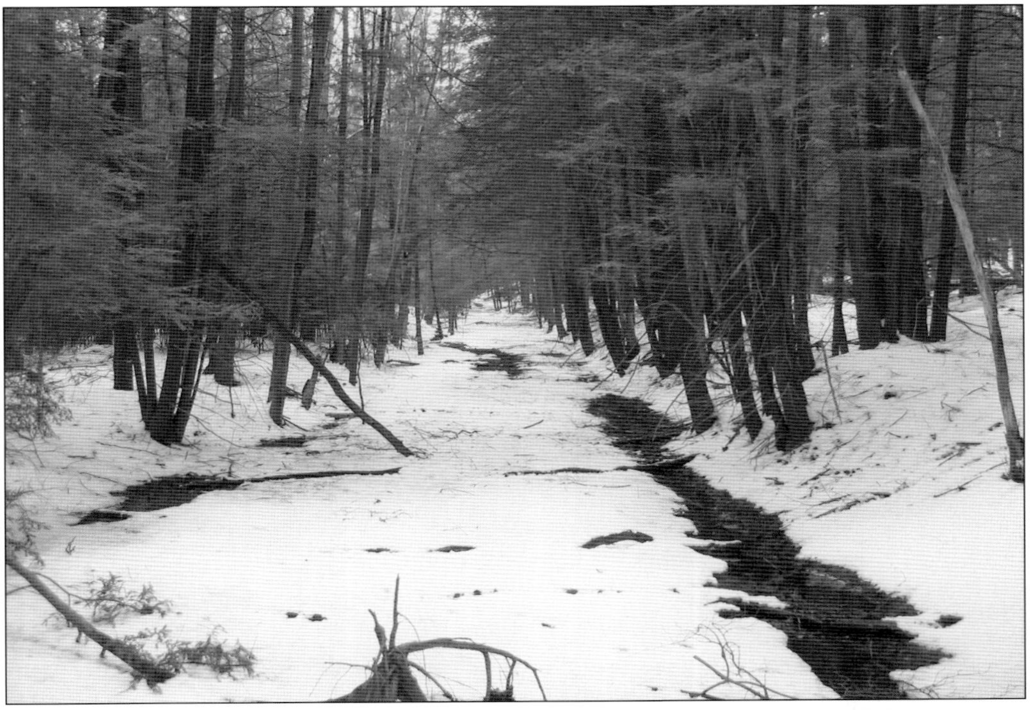

The Milesburg-Smethport Turnpike was the road most responsible for opening up north-central Pennsylvania. Incorporated in 1825, the privately owned 120-mile road was completed in 1828 with help from the state. Local farmers, paid from the tolls they collected, maintained sections of the road. The image above shows perhaps the last portion of the original road in Fox Township. It is located between Frey Road and present Route 948. Along this part of the road, a horse trough (right) still exists. Mail, stagecoaches, and freight traveled along this piece of road for nearly 100 years before current Route 948 connected directly to Route 255 at Fairview. Townsend Fall of Centreville charged 5¢ a mile for the twice-weekly, one-day stage trip to Smethport. He promised good horses and sober drivers.

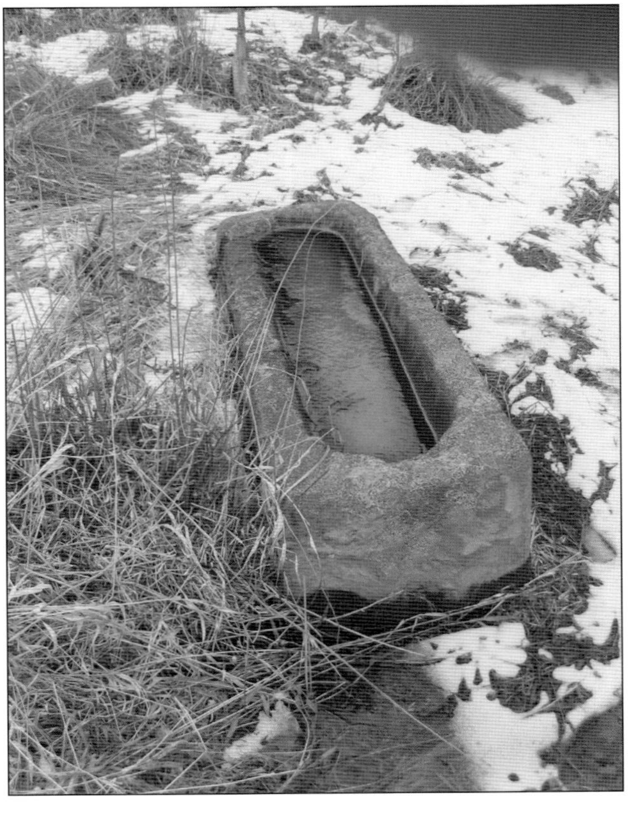

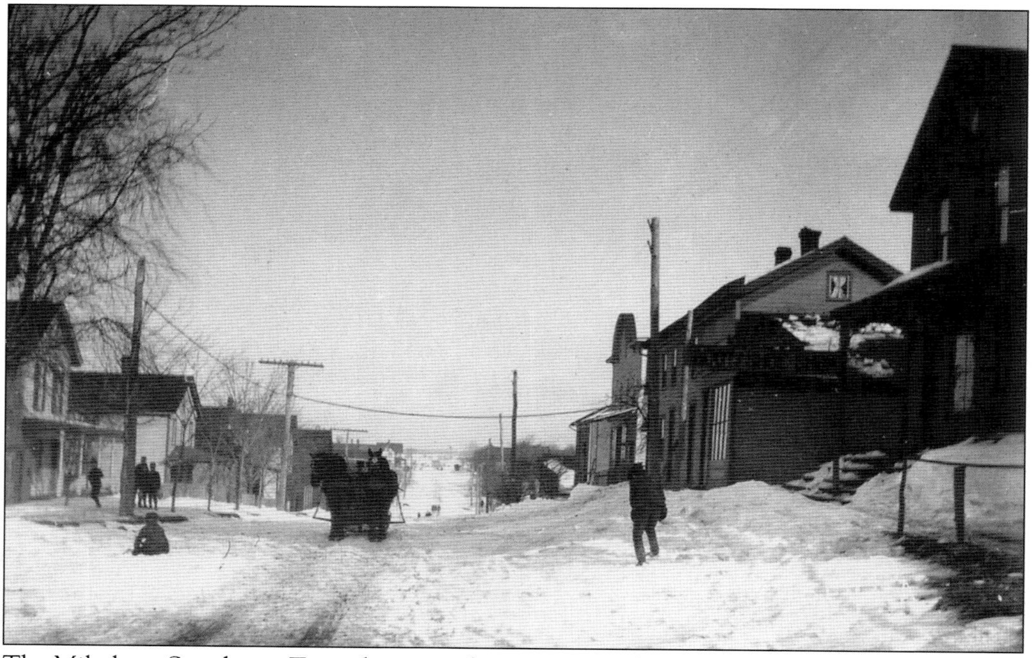

The Milesburg-Smethport Turnpike is seen here as it goes through Kersey. It was renamed Main Street when John Green platted Centreville and sold lots along the pike. Looking east from the hill in front of St. Boniface Church (right) is Miller's Fashionable Boot and Shoe Shop, then Klein's grocery, and then Beveridge's general merchandise. Across the street is the telephone exchange operated by the McMinn sisters. (Courtesy of Chris Casey.)

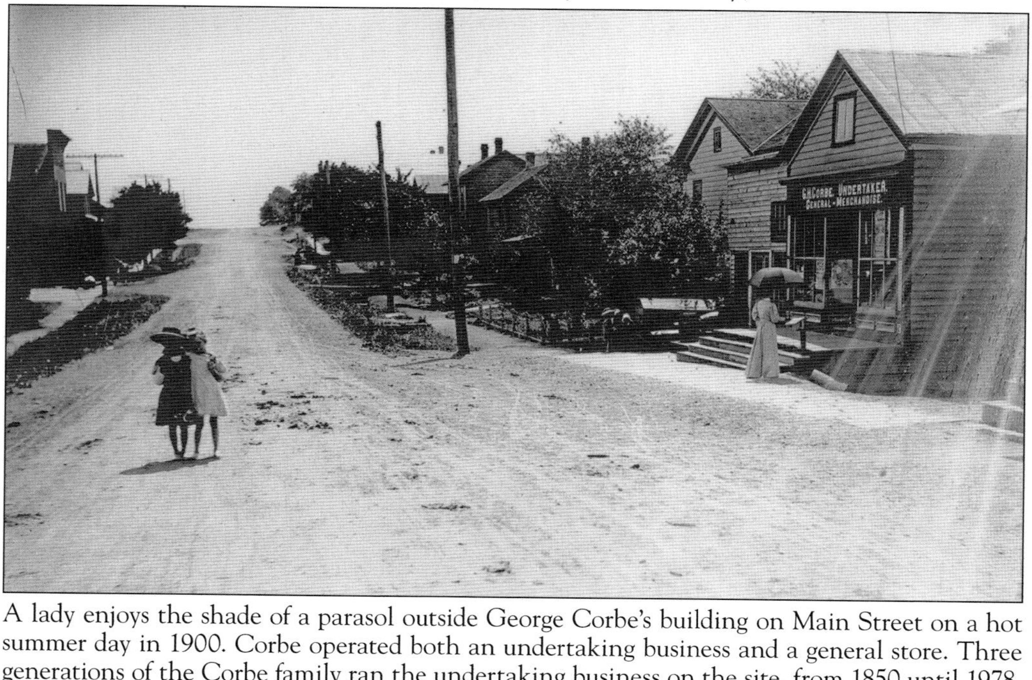

A lady enjoys the shade of a parasol outside George Corbe's building on Main Street on a hot summer day in 1900. Corbe operated both an undertaking business and a general store. Three generations of the Corbe family ran the undertaking business on the site, from 1850 until 1978. The large building on the left is Urmann's bottling works. (Courtesy of Chris Casey.)

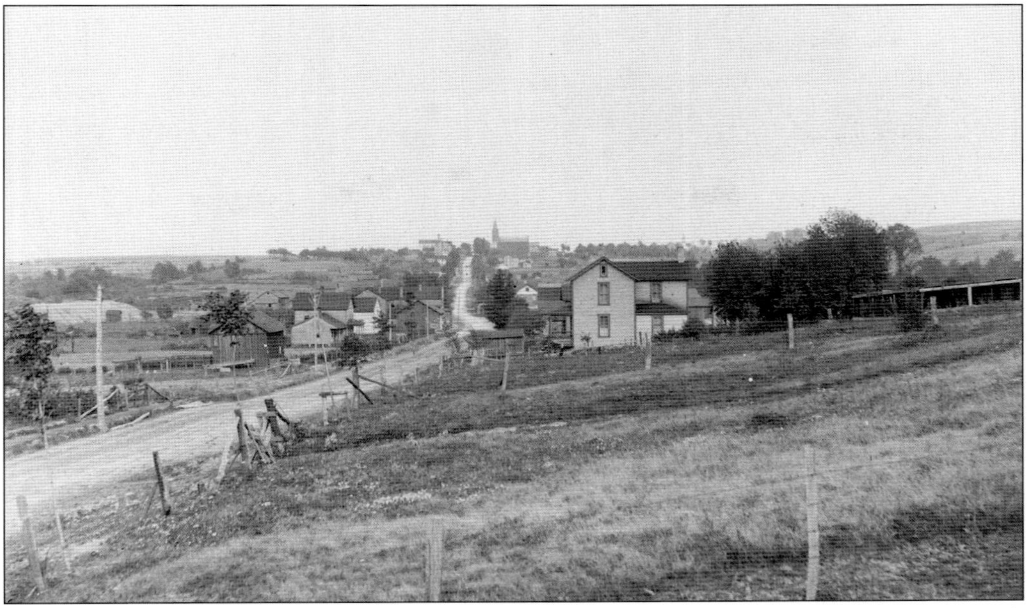

These views look east along Main Street (the Milesburg/Smethport Turnpike). The photograph above was taken from outside of town at Earlyville, with Koch Hotel and St. Boniface Church in the distance. The photograph below was taken from the Crossing, so named because the Erie Railroad crossed here on its way to the mines in Dagus. Eli Weinstein's general store is on the immediate left, and the Railroad Hotel, owned by Jacob Anderson, which was later Woodley's Sports Store, is on the right. The Railroad Hotel was at times known as "the bloody bucket" because of the many fights that occurred there. This view also shows, just beyond Weinstein's, the Jacob Musante (Mosier) candy store, famous for its hand-roasted peanuts, always done to perfection. George Foster's store, which rolled special cigars for Pres. Ulysses S. Grant, is on the immediate right. (Both, courtesy of Chris Casey.)

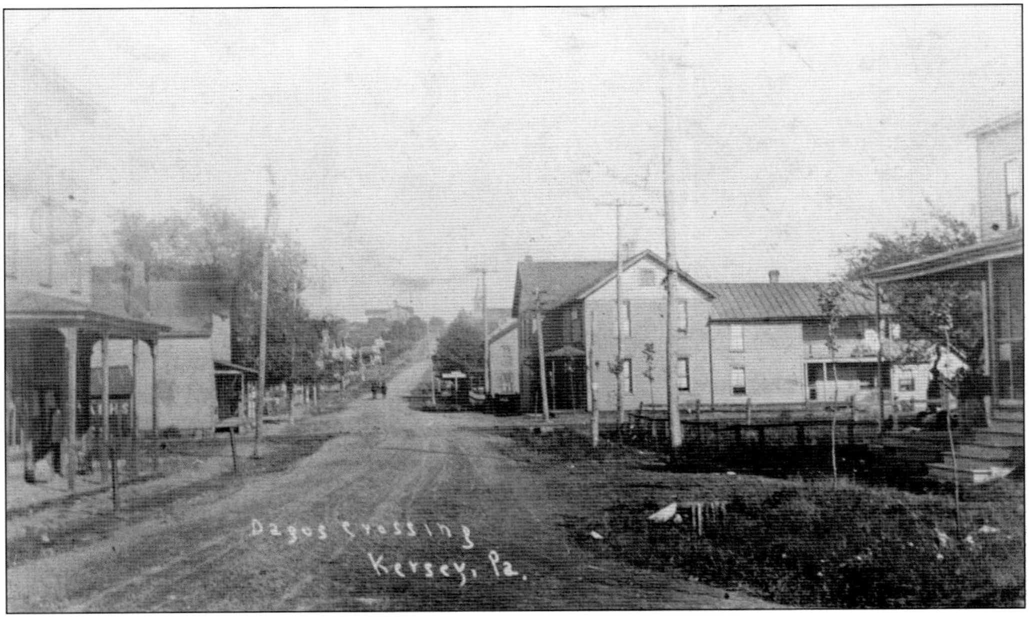

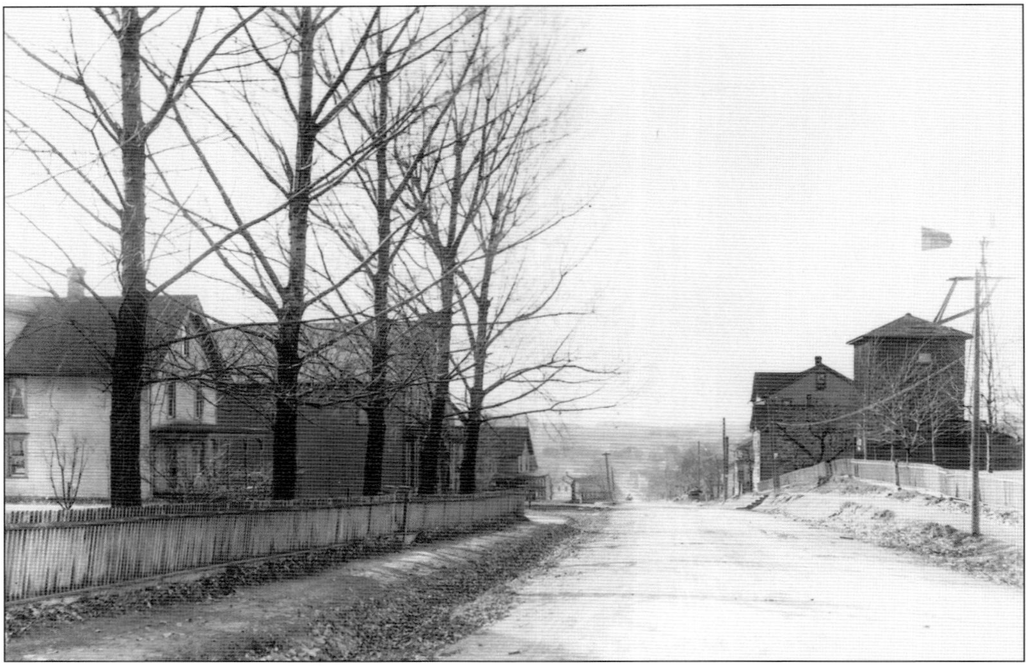

The photograph above, taken in front of where the Guardian Angels Center is today, looks down Main Street toward the Crossing. On the left is the Holjencin/Pop-in Video building, which was razed in 2012. Next is the Koch/Ubel building, on the site of the new Fox Township Senior Center. On the right is a windmill designed for pumping water into the tank to supply running water to the upper floors of the Koch Hotel. The photograph below was taken farther west down Main Street, in the summer, just beyond the Koch Hotel. Note that the telephone poles have only one or two wires. There is very little traffic on the street, which was very busy on most days. (Both, courtesy of Chris Casey.)

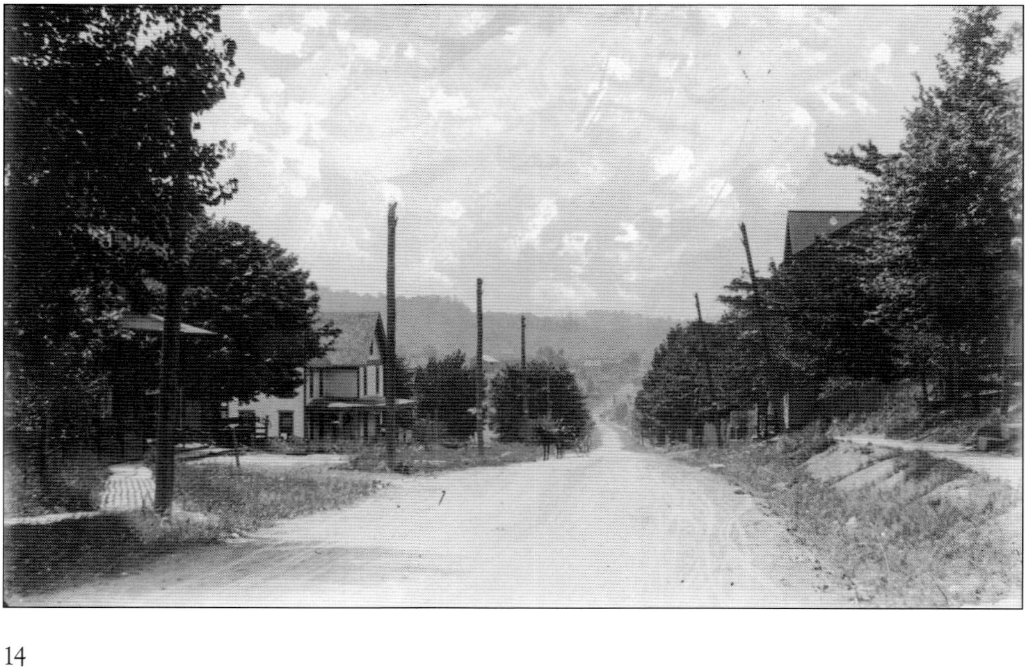

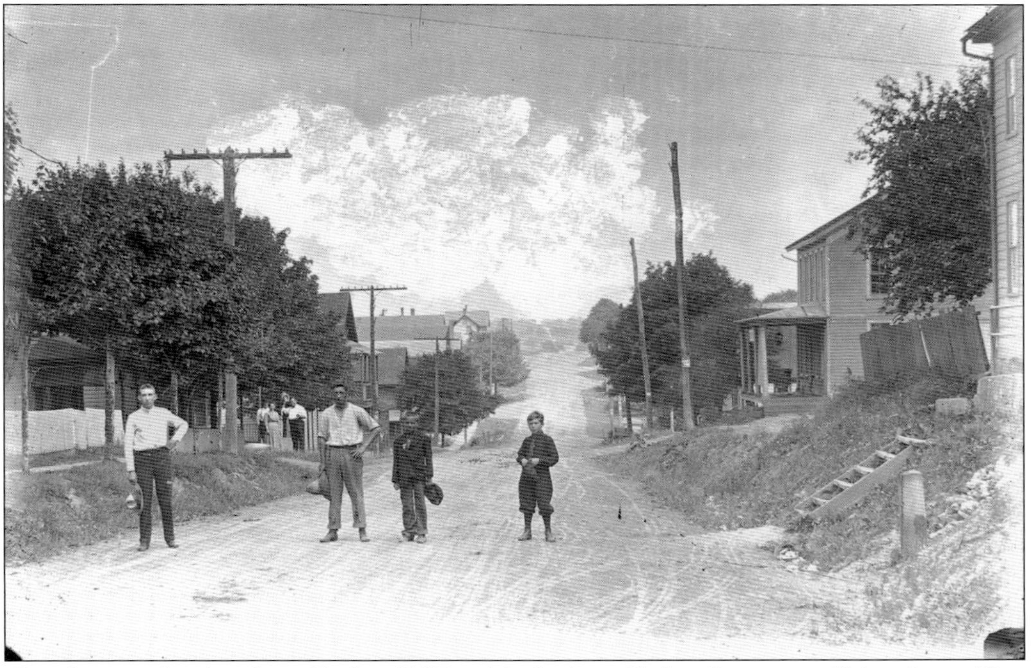

This photograph, taken from Chicken Hill Road, looks down Skyline Drive toward Main Street. This area was originally owned by pioneer James Green and his son John. The first post office was here, where elections were held. These are some of the oldest buildings in Fox Township. The young man at center with his hand on his hip is Jack "the Mighty Mo" Mosier. (Courtesy of Chris Casey.)

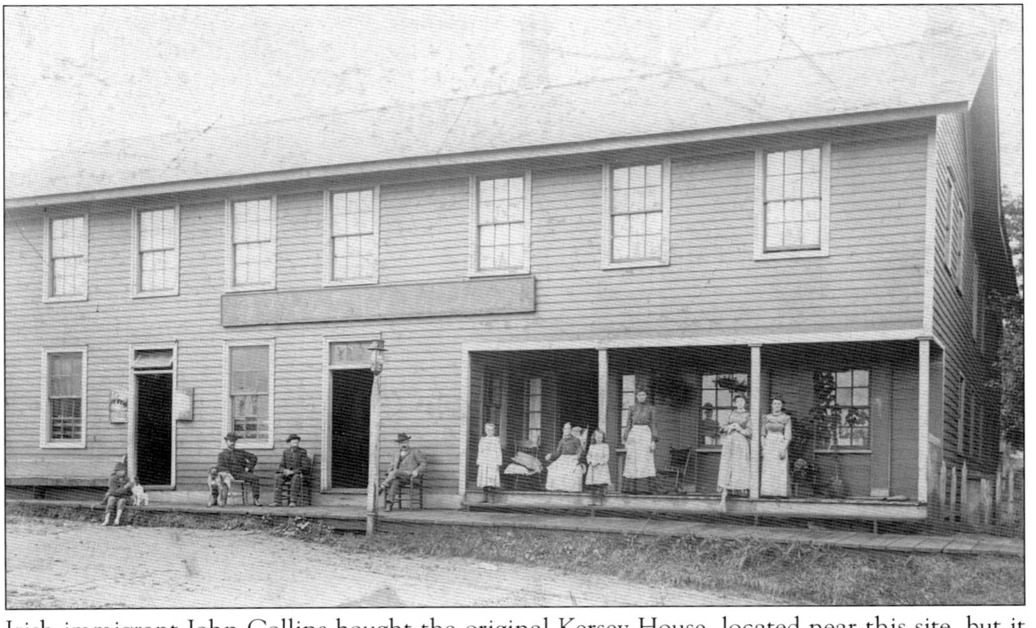

Irish immigrant John Collins bought the original Kersey House, located near this site, but it was destroyed by fire in 1880. He then quickly bought this building, the McCauley House, and reopened it as the Collins House. Numerous other residents operated taverns on this site. Michael Spangler owned and operated it until about 1950. (Courtesy of Ken Anderson.)

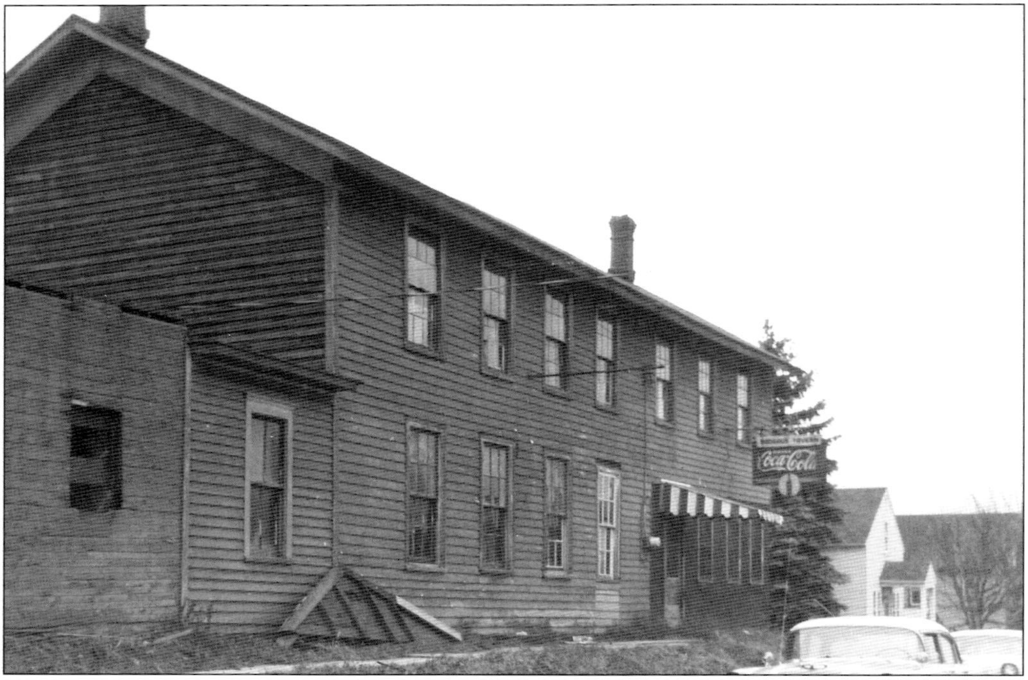

Badeau's Tavern was purchased from a Mr. Spangler by Al and Agnes "Ag" Badeau in 1951. The tavern was famous for its golden-brown, deep-fried chicken wings. Al added the freezer building to the left in this photograph. The Badeaus razed the building in 1962 and replaced it with the current block building. The building is now home to the First Chance Inn. (Courtesy of Ken Anderson.)

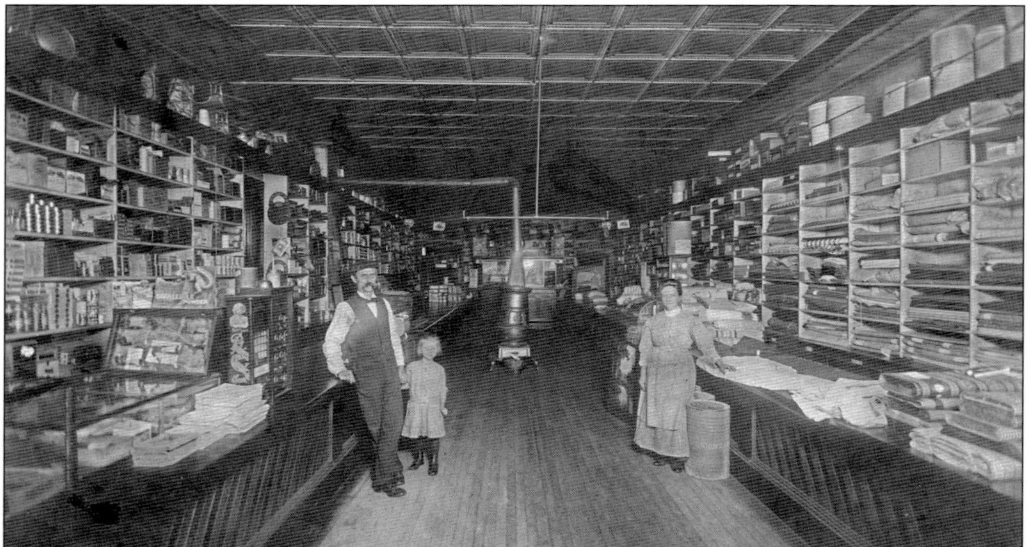

Fuenfinger's store, built by Michael "Five Fingers" Fuenfinger, was on the corner of Main Street and Skyline Drive. The store also had a branch of the Farmers and Merchants Bank inside, of which Fuenfinger was a director, as well as a bicycle repair shop on the side. Fuenfinger was a leading citizen, and was a founder of the Kersey Hook and Ladder Company in 1897, and the Centreville Cornet Band. (Courtesy of Joan Herbstritt.)

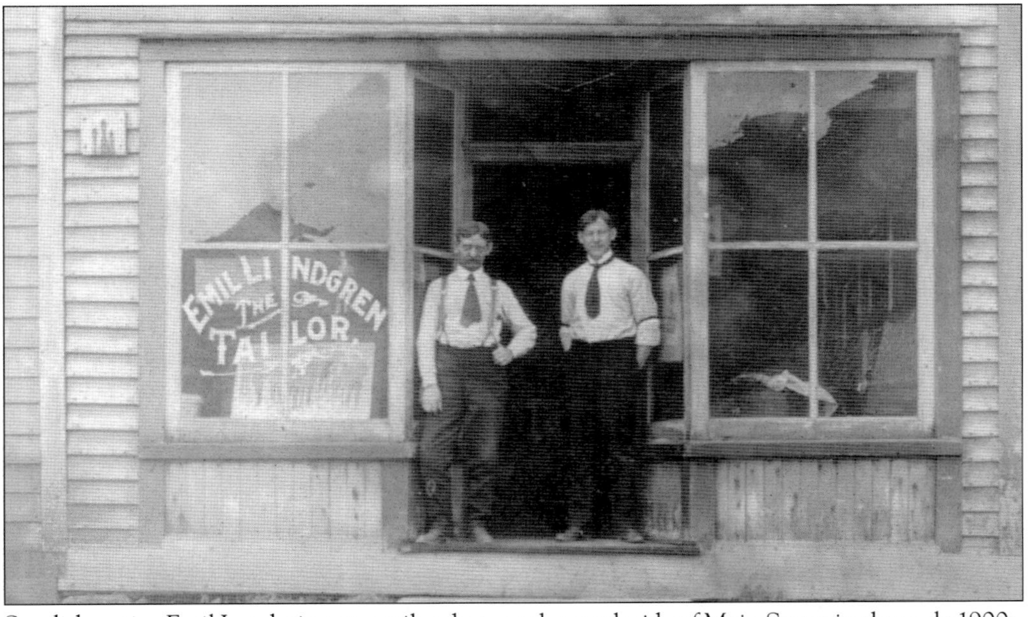

Swedish native Emil Lundgrin ran a tailor shop on the south side of Main Street in the early 1900s. It was near the intersection of Taylor and Main Streets, just west of Kie Schreiber's blacksmith shop. Across the street was another tailor shop, owned by John Hedburg, and Nellie Malone also ran a millinery nearby. Main Street was the booming retail section of the township around 1900.

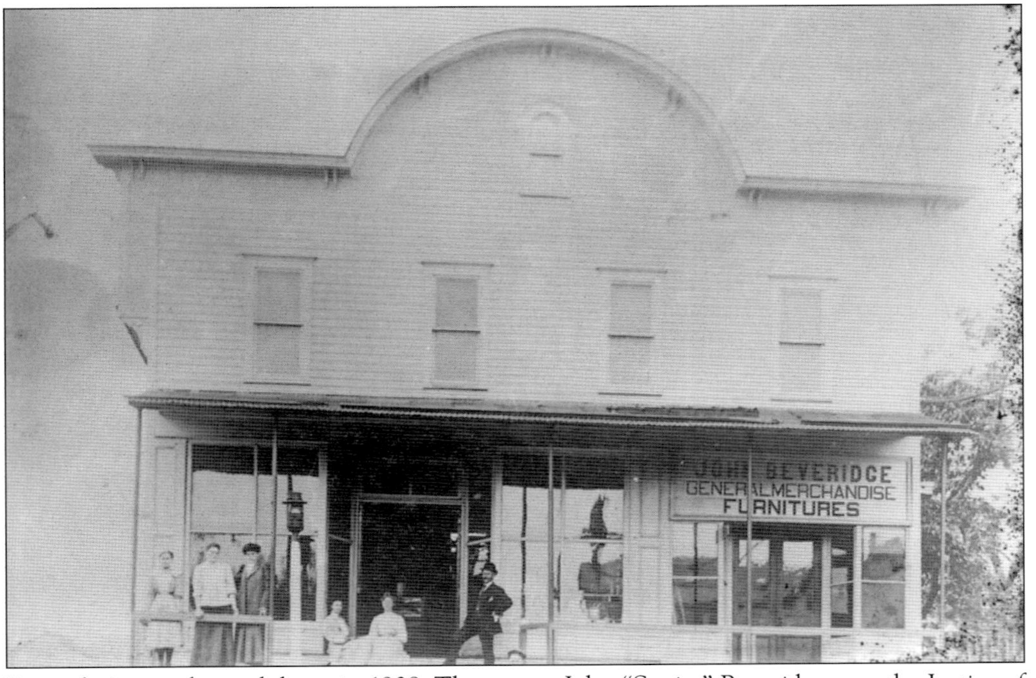

Beveridge's store burned down in 1908. The owner, John "Squire" Beveridge, was the Justice of the Peace and one of the most respected men in the community. His son Tom and his grandson Dick later operated a Gulf gas station and auto repair business at the same location, which closed in 1989. (Courtesy of Chris Casey.)

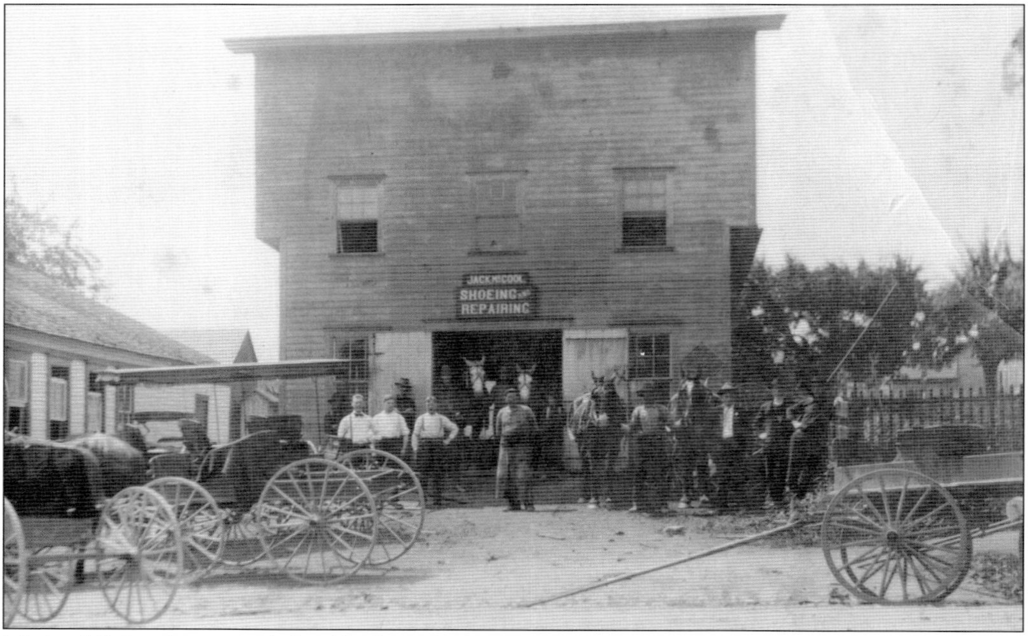

Michael Schreiber owned this blacksmith shop on Main Street in Kersey, near the Taylor Street intersection, until his death in 1906. Upon his death, Jack McCool operated the shop until Schreiber's son Kie was old enough to take over and run the business by himself. Below, inside the store, Kie Schreiber is leaning on the sledgehammer. Notice the horseshoes hanging from the rafters. Those were templates used to size the shoes for each horse, because horses, like humans, have differently sized feet. His grandson, also named Kie, currently owns and lives on the site. When these photographs were taken, around 1915, there were at least two other blacksmith shops on Main Street.

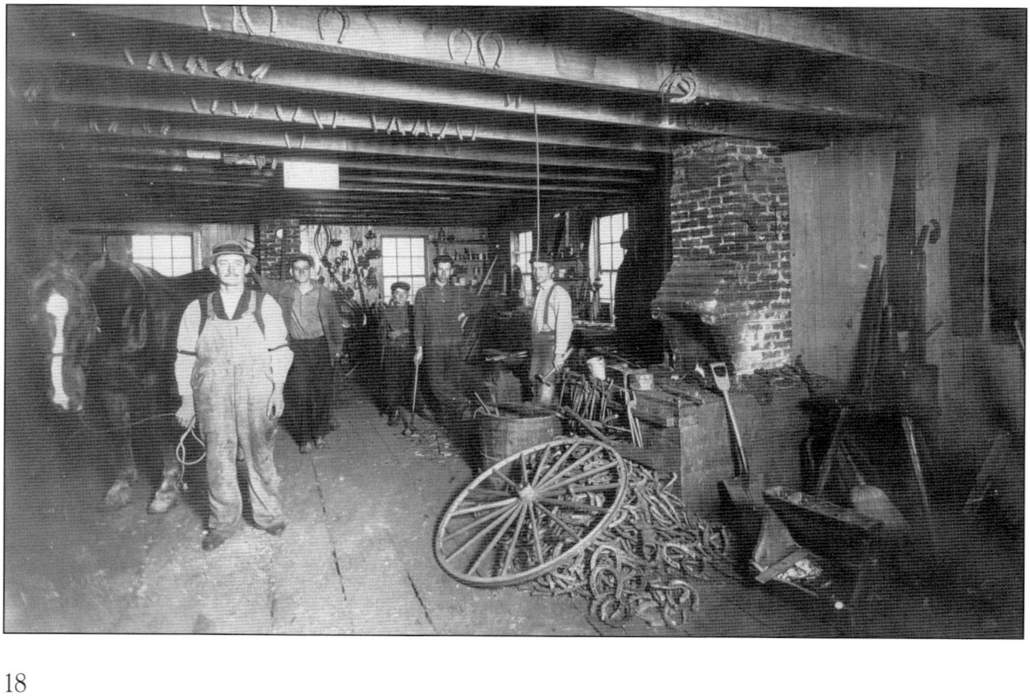

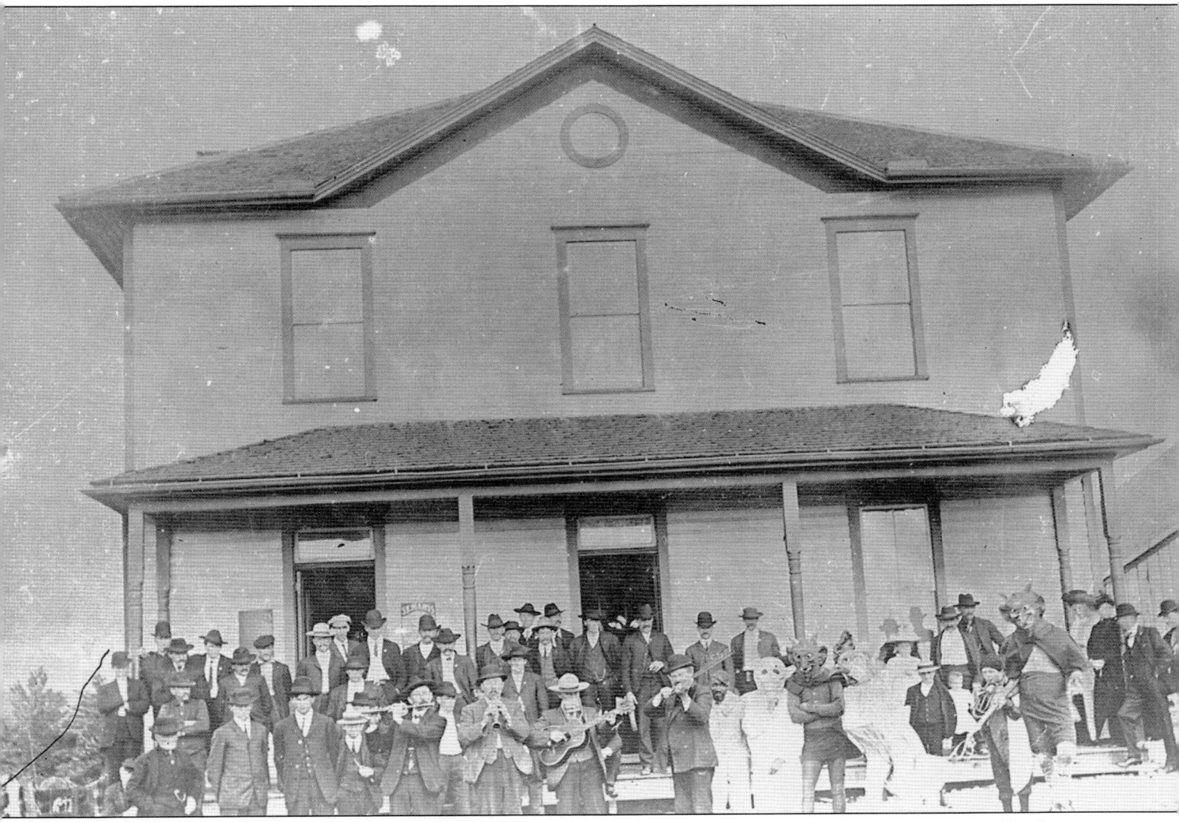

The German House was on Irishtown Road near the railroad depot. Andrew Hau was the first owner, and called it the Hau Hotel. He owned a small coal mine nearby and had contracts to sell coal to the Elk County Courthouse in Ridgway. He became an Elk County commissioner in the 1890s. Later, his son Bill owned and operated a tavern in Dagus Mines until he retired in the 1970s. It was known for having the coldest beer in town. This photograph shows a Halloween celebration at the German House around 1910, when N.A. Nelson owned it. The building was the starting point for many parades and celebrations. Nelson also had a photography studio on Main Street and took many of the photographs in this book. The hotel was on the site of the current Fox Township Municipal Building. (Courtesy of Chris Casey.)

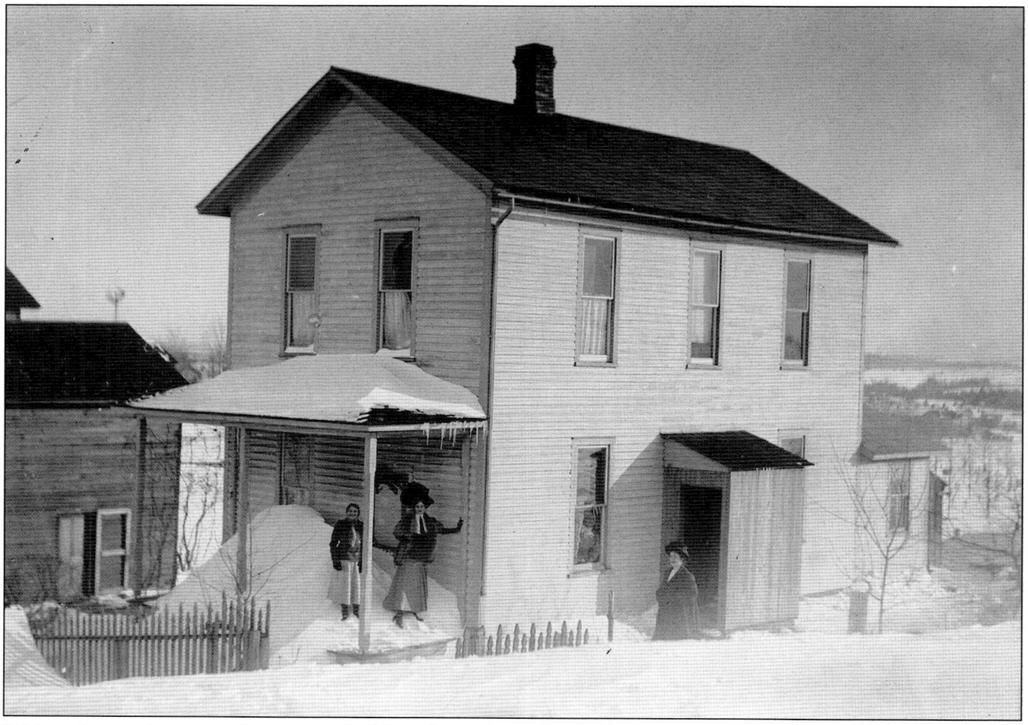

This winter photograph was probably taken from the hill just south of Kersey, near what is now Higgins Road. Notice the cemetery in the lower right and the distant windmill in the upper left, which was most likely the mill that pumped water to the three-story Koch Hotel. Note the girl looking out the lower window. (Courtesy of Chris Casey.)

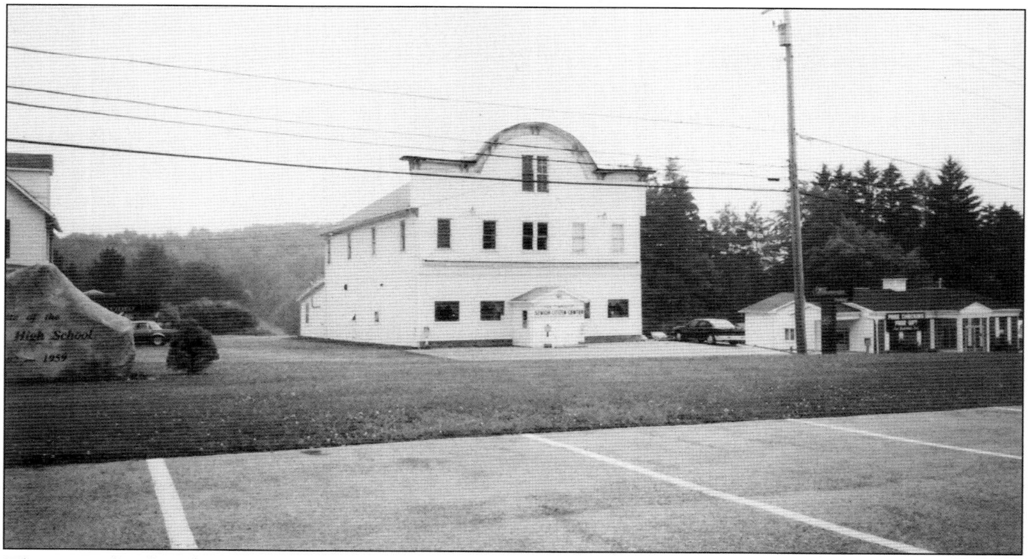

This was the first big store in Fox Township, built before the Civil War by James Green. Over the years, it also served as a bakery, a gunsmith shop, a towel factory, a furniture store, and a Knights of Columbus hall and senior center until 2003, when the current Fox Township Senior Center was built on the site. To the right is the First Commonwealth Bank. (Courtesy of Ken Anderson.)

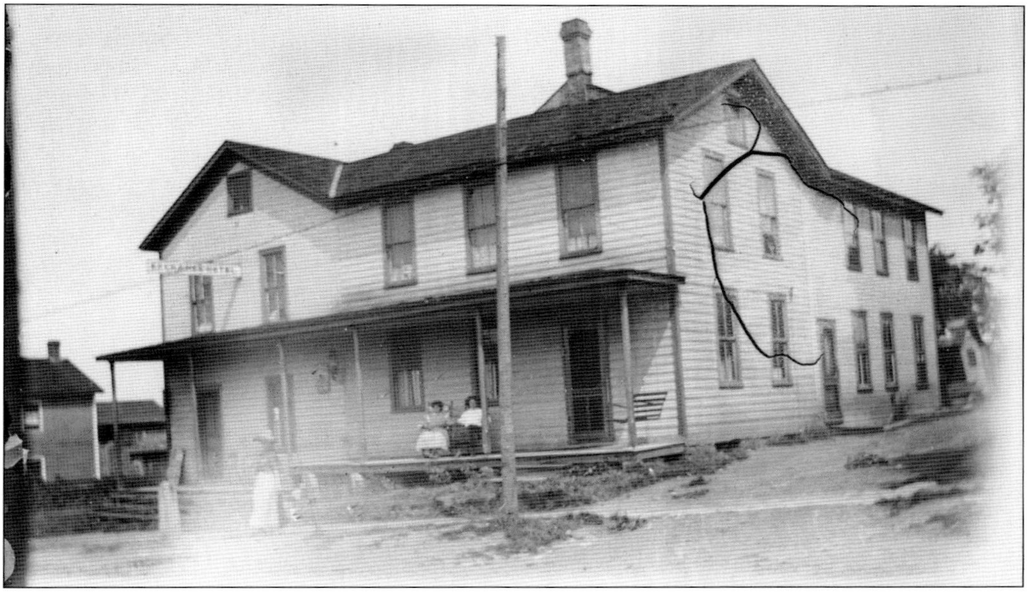

The Exchange Hotel, also known as the Thomas House, was owned and operated by Lewis Thomas from the time of the Civil War to at least 1890. It was down the hill from the Koch Hotel on Main Street, and was destroyed by fire in 1908 or 1909. Jonathan Davies owned it at the time. (Courtesy of Chris Casey.)

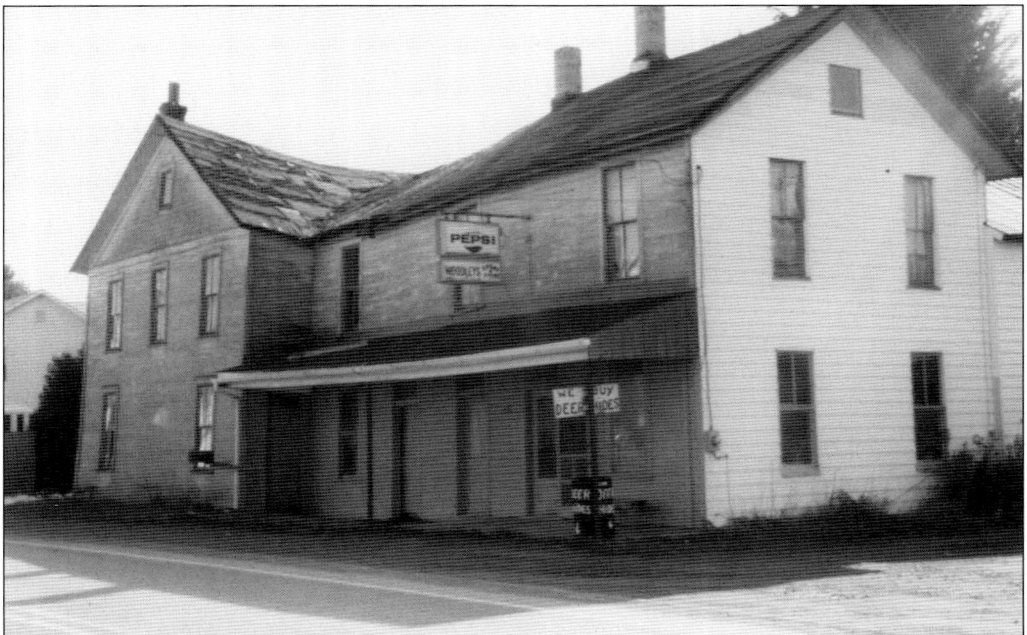

The Railroad Hotel was directly beside the railroad crossing on Main Street. It was sometimes known as "the bloody bucket" because of the many brawls that occurred there. For the second half of the 1900s, it was home to Woodley's Sport Store and barbershop, and was a famous place for people of all ages to hang out. Proprietor Clarence Woodley was a well-known figure around town. It was demolished in 2000. (Courtesy of Ken Anderson.)

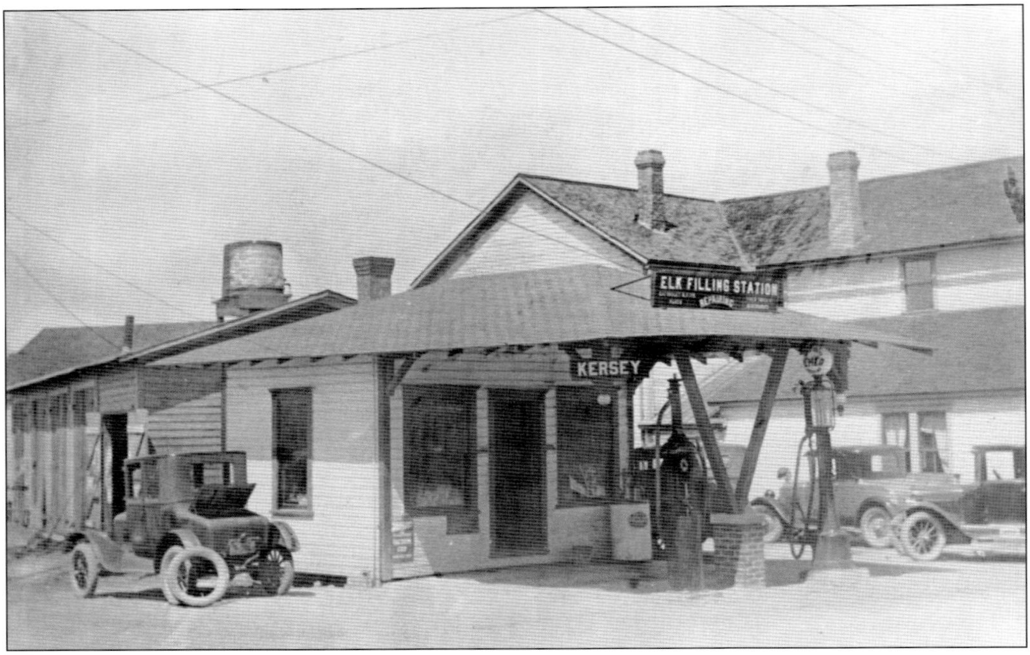

In August 1923, a gun battle between authorities and suspected bootlegger Serafine Fuente took place here. Numerous shots were fired between Fuente and Corporal Jones of the Pennsylvania State Police before Fuente, who had been hit at least three times, died. This photograph was taken a few years later, with Ford Model As parked nearby. (Courtesy of Joan Verbka.)

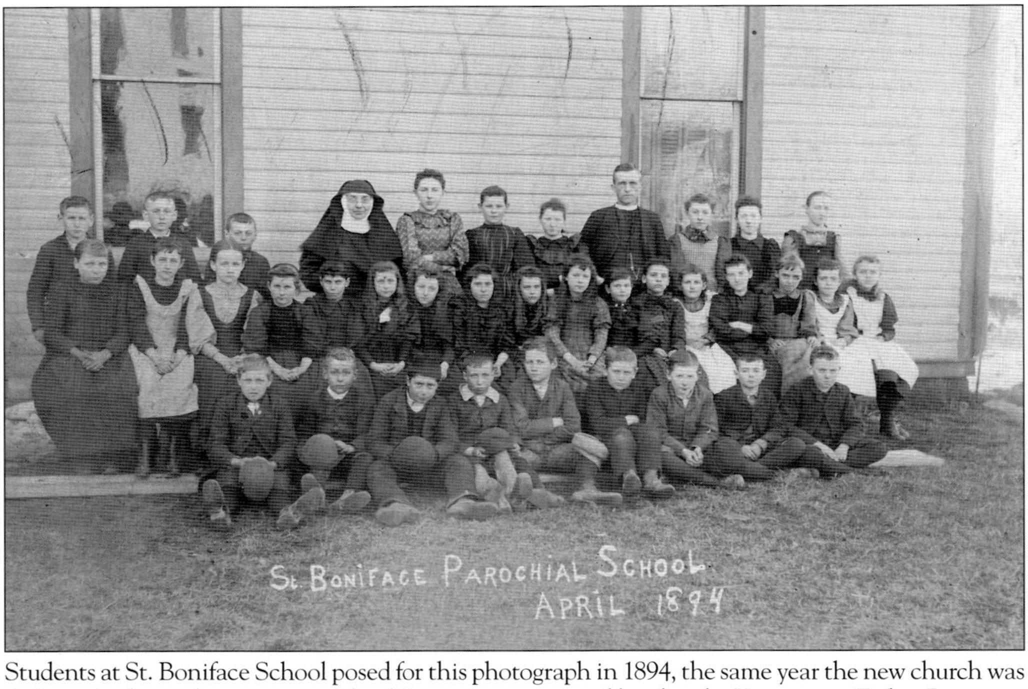

Students at St. Boniface School posed for this photograph in 1894, the same year the new church was dedicated. The students were mainly of German ancestry and lived in the Kersey area. Father Benjamin Raycroft was the priest, serving the community from 1890 to 1900. (Courtesy of St. Boniface.)

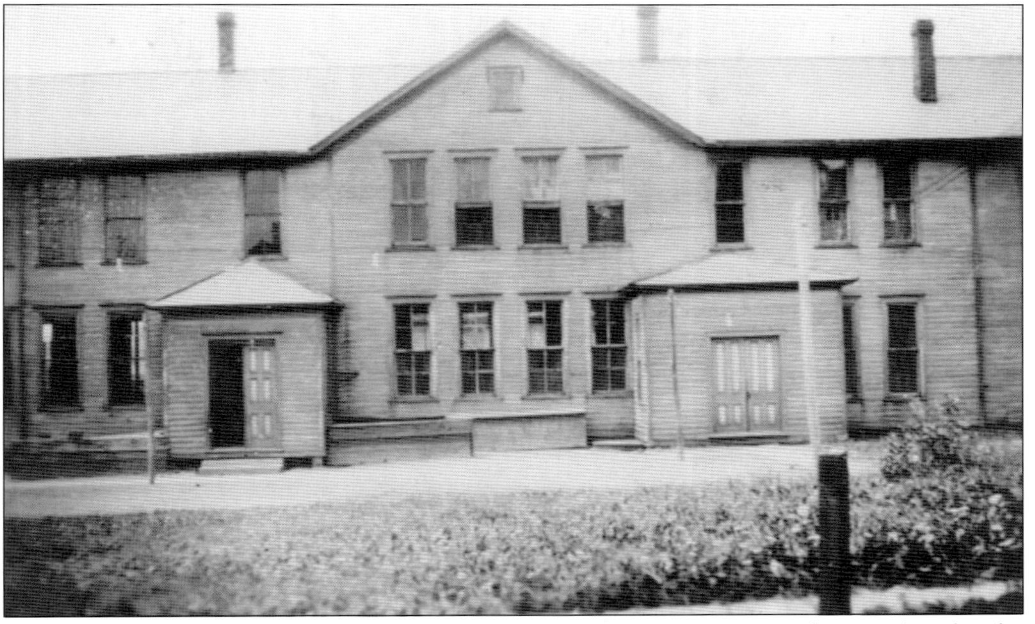

St. Boniface School, the first Catholic school in Elk County, was opened in 1885 under the direction of pastor Rev. John Link. Built at a cost of $5,000, it is the oldest operating parish school in the Erie Diocese. The building above was also a convent for the Benedictine nuns who taught there. The structure was razed and a new school opened in 1956. Below, volunteers pose outside the school. Fundraising was and still is fundamental to keeping this private school open. Fairs, raffles, dances, bazaars, and bingo have all been organized to raise money to support the school. (Both, courtesy of St. Boniface.)

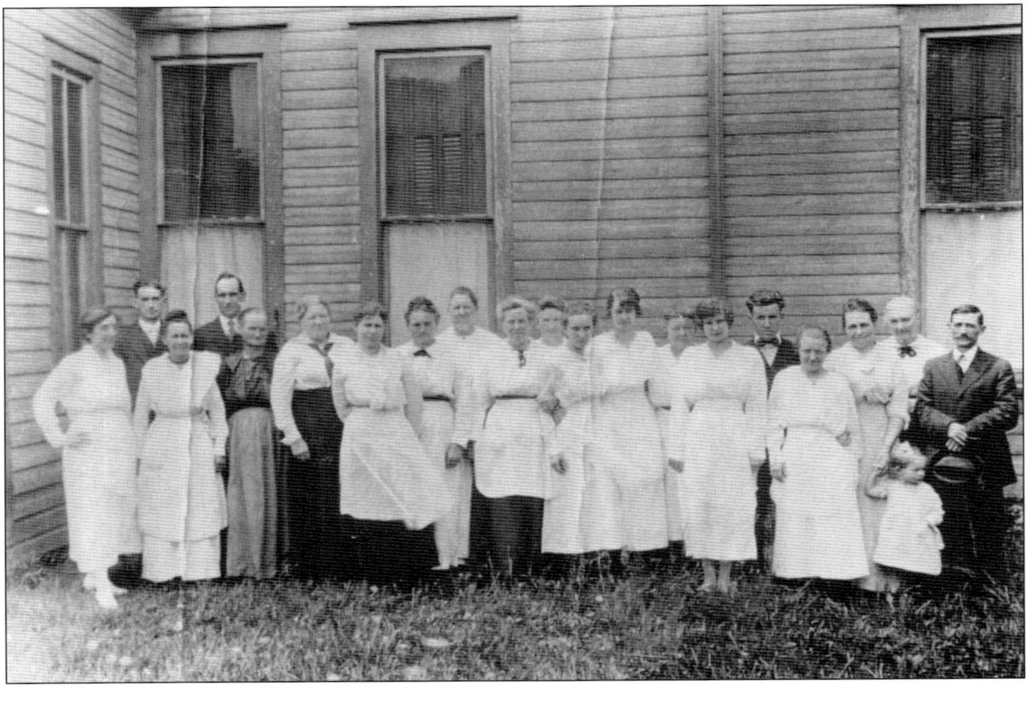

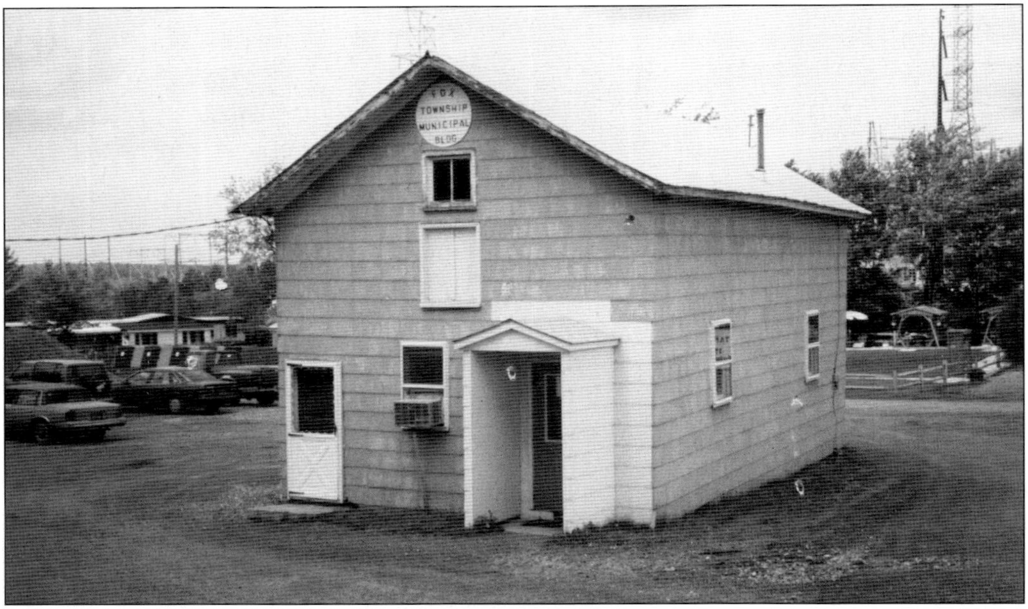

This is the old Fox Township Municipal Building, located across Irishtown Road from the current structure, which was built in 1994. There was much vocal opposition to the new building at the time, but today, everyone is very satisfied. The old building, originally a farmhouse, served the township for decades. It was mainly used for the storage of records, board of supervisors' meetings, and other board meetings.

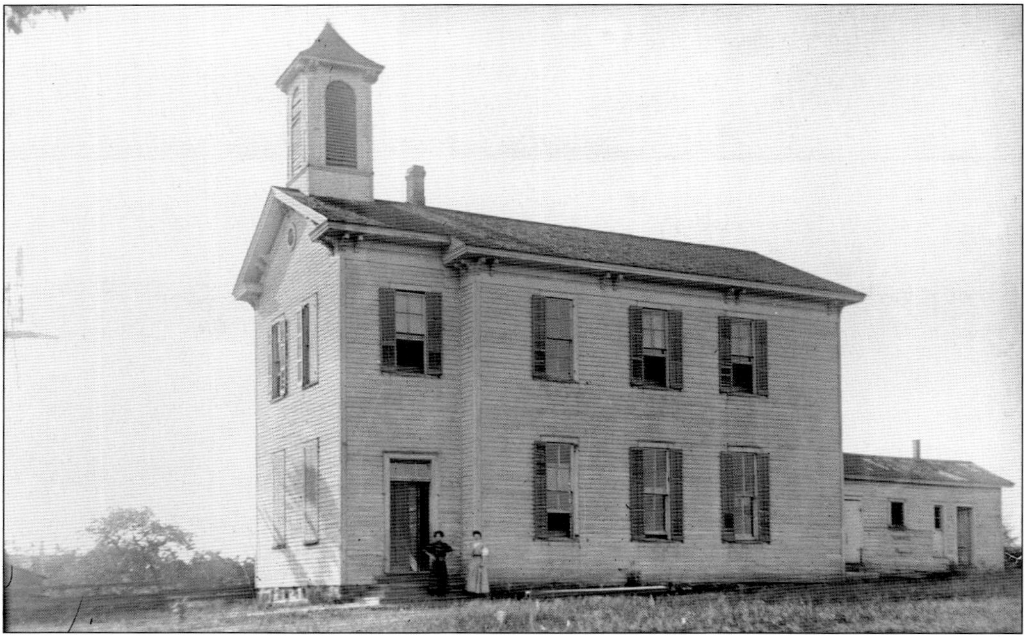

Fox Township High School's last graduating class was in 1913. It was on the same property as the new school, near the present community building. Because students had to walk from as far away as South Kersey or Toby, many in the township wanted a more central location, but, since the school board already owned the land, the new school was built in uptown Kersey.

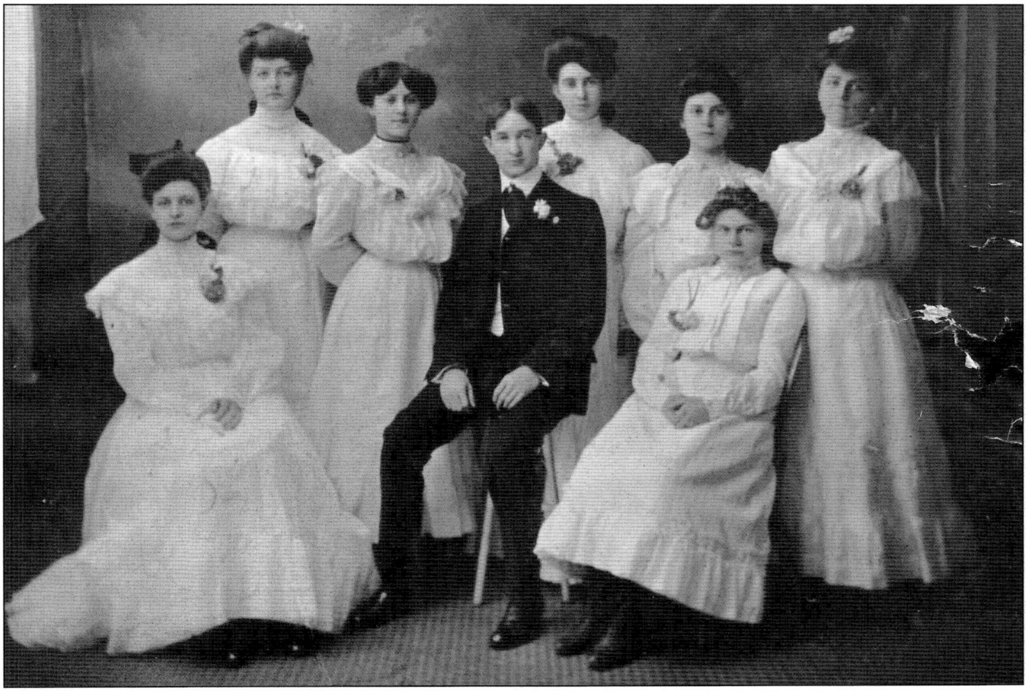

In 1904, the entire graduating class at Fox Township High School was female. Commencement was held in May at Anderson Hall in downtown Kersey. The graduates, with principal R.F. Bastian (seated, center), are, from left to right, (seated) Mayme Pfaff and Anna Hodgson; (standing) Tillie Dollinger, Anna Shuttleworth, Lizzie Brown, Ida Mae Hulet, and Theresa Dollinger.

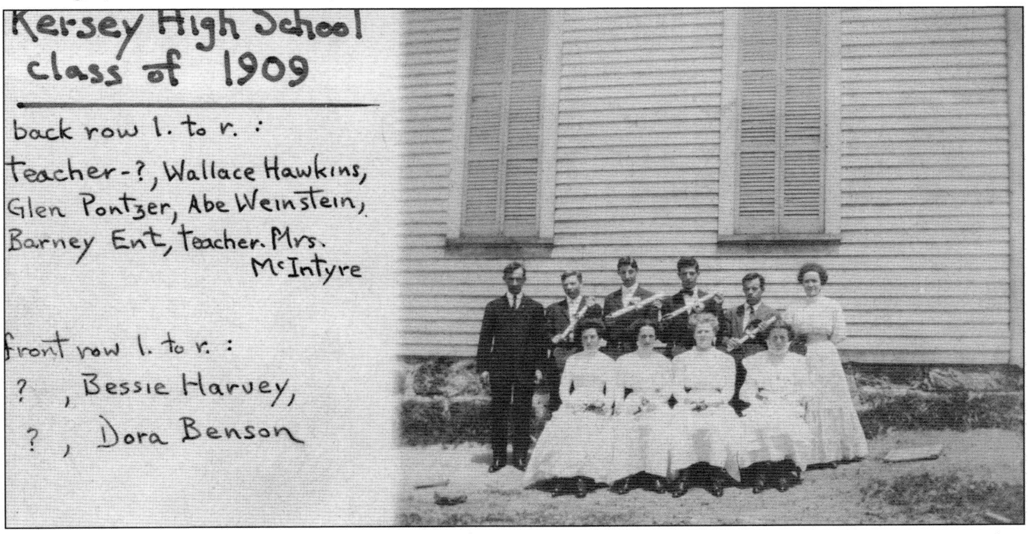

This 1909 graduation photograph, taken outside the old high school, includes, from left to right, (seated) unidentified, Bessie Harvey, unidentified, and Dora Benson; (standing) an unidentified teacher, Wallace Hawkins, Glen Pontzer, Abe Weinstein, Barney Ent, and teacher Mrs. Mcyntyre. Graduating classes were small, in part, because of transportation difficulties. Also, at the time, an education beyond primary school was not as essential as being physically strong in order to work on a farm or in a mine.

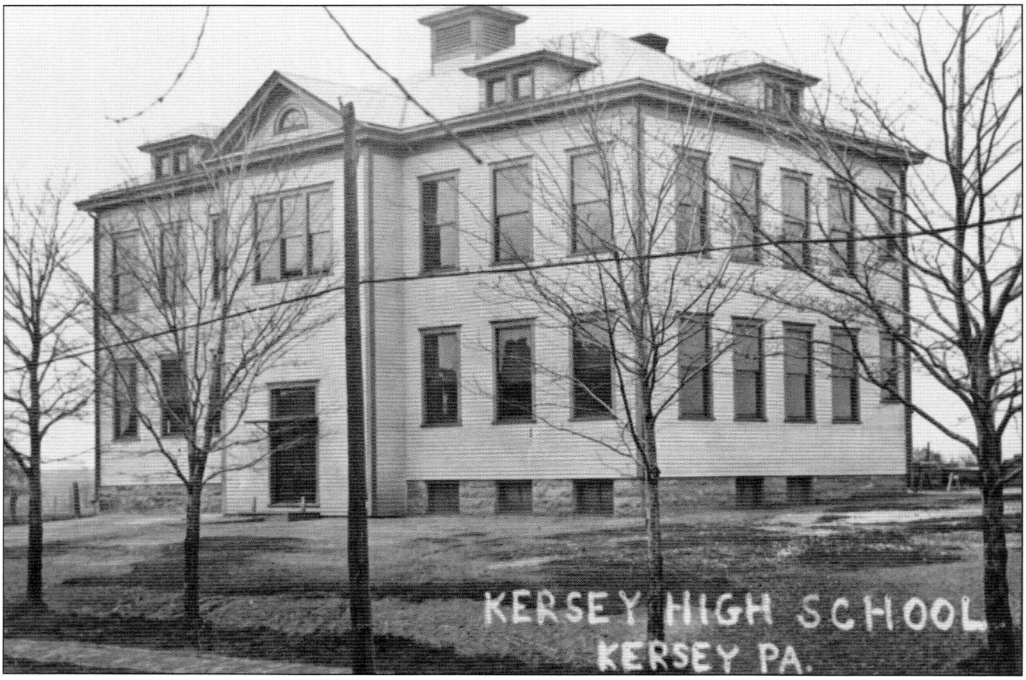

The new Kersey High School (KHS) was built in the midst of much controversy in 1913, and closed in similar fashion. It had an office and four main rooms. The Elk County School Board closed the school amid fanatical opposition in 1959, when it consolidated with St. Marys to form the current St. Marys Area School District.

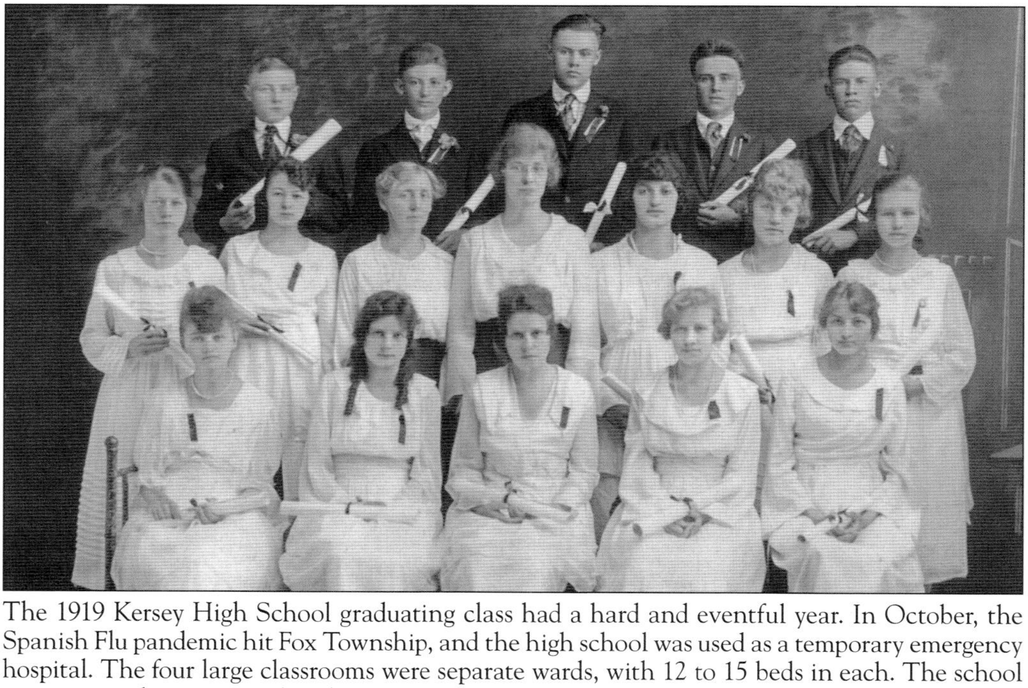
The 1919 Kersey High School graduating class had a hard and eventful year. In October, the Spanish Flu pandemic hit Fox Township, and the high school was used as a temporary emergency hospital. The four large classrooms were separate wards, with 12 to 15 beds in each. The school was reopened sometime after the New Year.

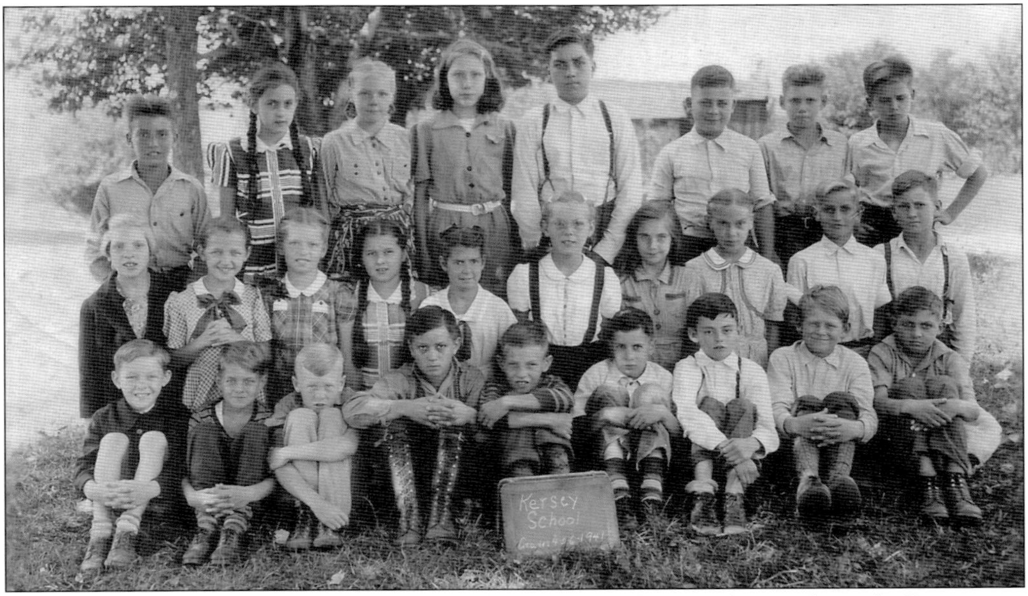

In this 1941 photograph of Kersey Elementary School's grades four, five, and six, the Depression was winding down and the United States had yet to enter World War II. Some of the surnames in this class included Meredith, McKay, Schreiber, and Weidow. Though the boys in this class missed serving in World War II, most of them served in the Korean War. (Courtesy of Ken Meredith.)

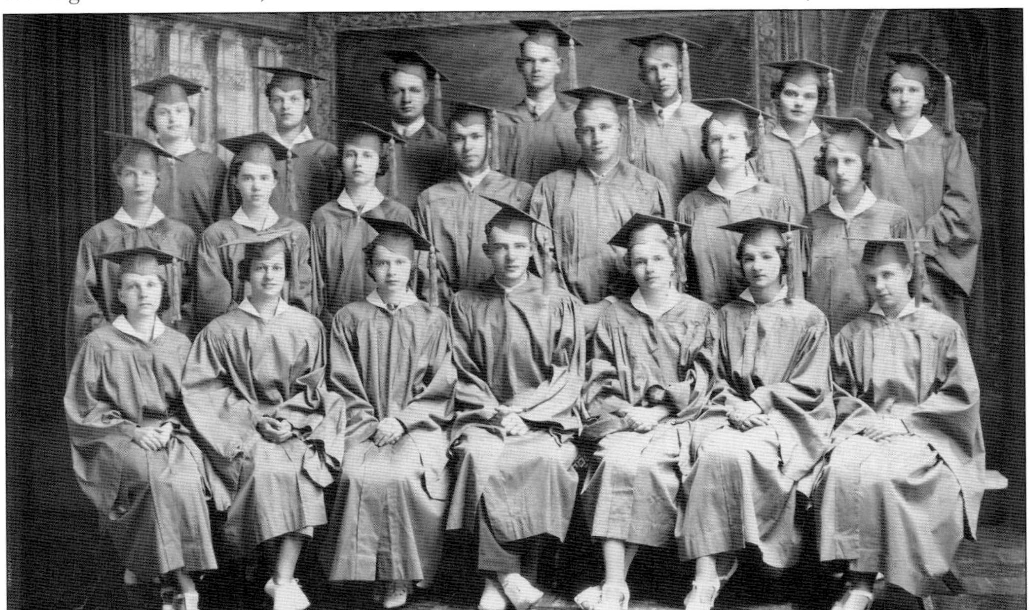

By 1936, in the midst of the Great Depression, graduating classes at KHS were growing and ceremonies became more formal, as seen by the caps and gowns. Girls still outnumbered boys—15 to 6 in this class. The students, identified only by their last names, included, from left to right, (first row) Brown, Ernst, Spuller, Sennett, Carlson Sicheri, and Green; (second row) Coppella, Sennett, Eberl, Schreiber, Hyatt, Schreiber, and Garvelli; (third row) Gradizzi, Haizer, Zani, Green, Neureiter, Lawrence, and Agosti.

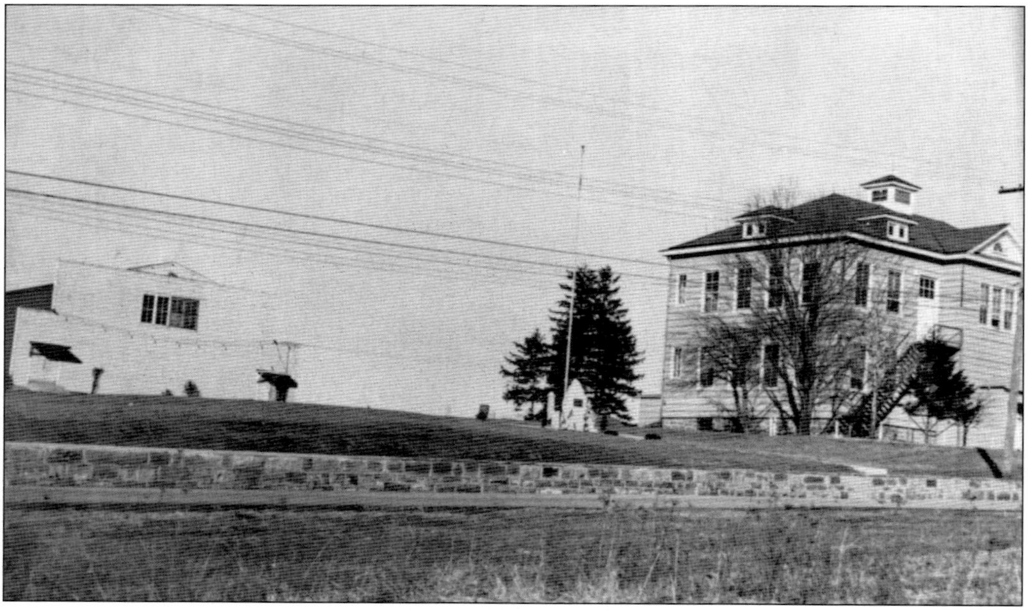

In 1951, the school board denied a request to build a gymnasium at Kersey High School. Consequently, the township residents took it upon themselves to raise the money and build a community building. Under the leadership of the school's alumni association, Tom Carpin and Fred Hippchen, with donations of labor, material, and time from throughout the township, completed the project by 1952. Since its construction, the Community Building (above, left) has been an integral part of the political and social life of Fox Township. The photograph below shows the first graduation in the building. The speaker was Professor Donavan, a respected teacher, coach, and administrator. (Both, courtesy of Kathy Dowie.)

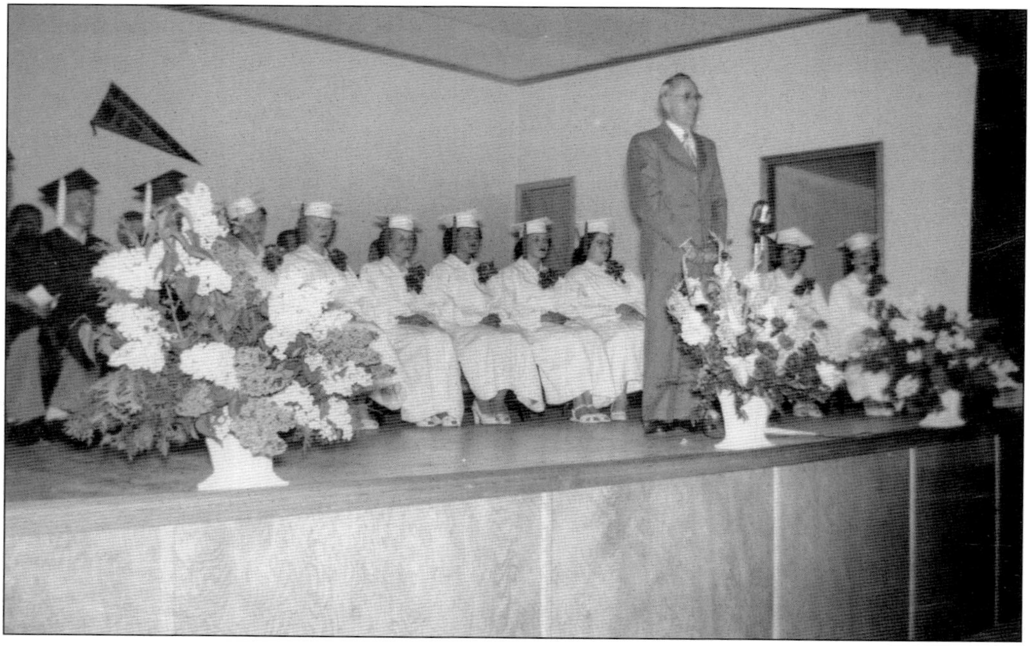

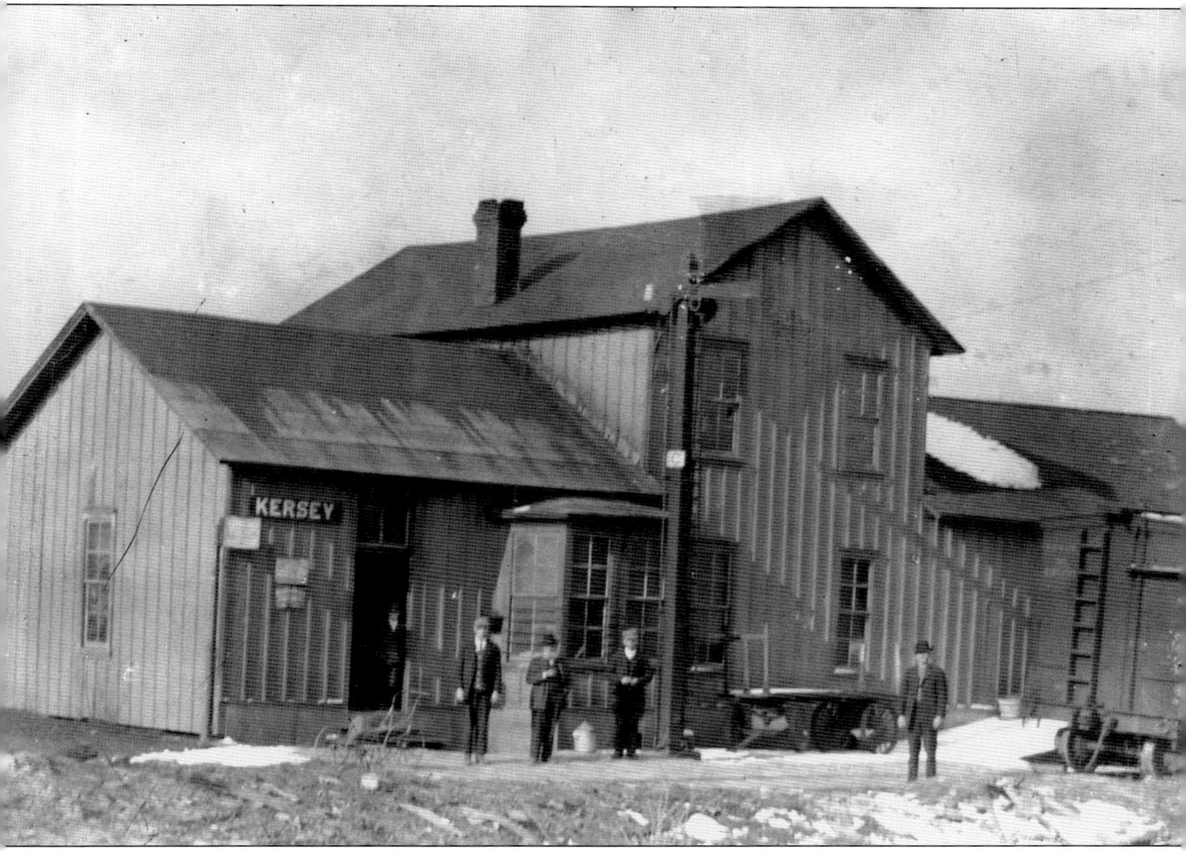

The Kersey depot was on Irishtown Road across from the current Fox Township Municipal Building. This depot served the St. Marys & Southwestern Railroad, and, later, in 1894, the Pittsburgh, Shawmut & Northern (PS&N), the third railroad to come to Fox Township. The 10-mile line to St. Marys, which used the first steam-powered shovel in the area, had numerous cuts and a 650-foot trestle. The line was built to connect Haul and Kaul's recently purchased coalfields in Elbon and Shawmut to the main line in St. Marys. Though the lines mainly hauled coal, passenger service was also available. From 1921 to 1934, the popular, small, six-cylinder, gas-powered "hoodlebug" made daily trips between Kersey, St. Marys, and Olean. It could seat 20 to 30 people and strap-hold two or three times that. The service ended after roads improved and people began driving their own cars. (Courtesy of Chris Casey.)

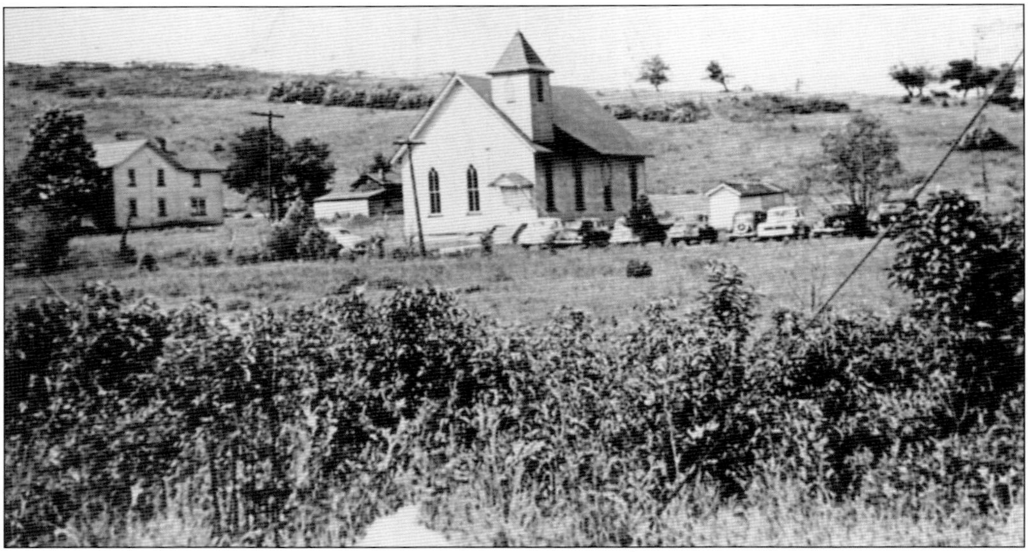

The Kersey United Methodist Church, on South Main Street on the way to Dagus Mines, was chartered in 1885. It was originally on Skyline Drive, near Taylor Street, but moved to its present location around 1900. Some early pastors included Reverends Burns, Hovis, and Ryan. (Courtesy of Joan Verbka.)

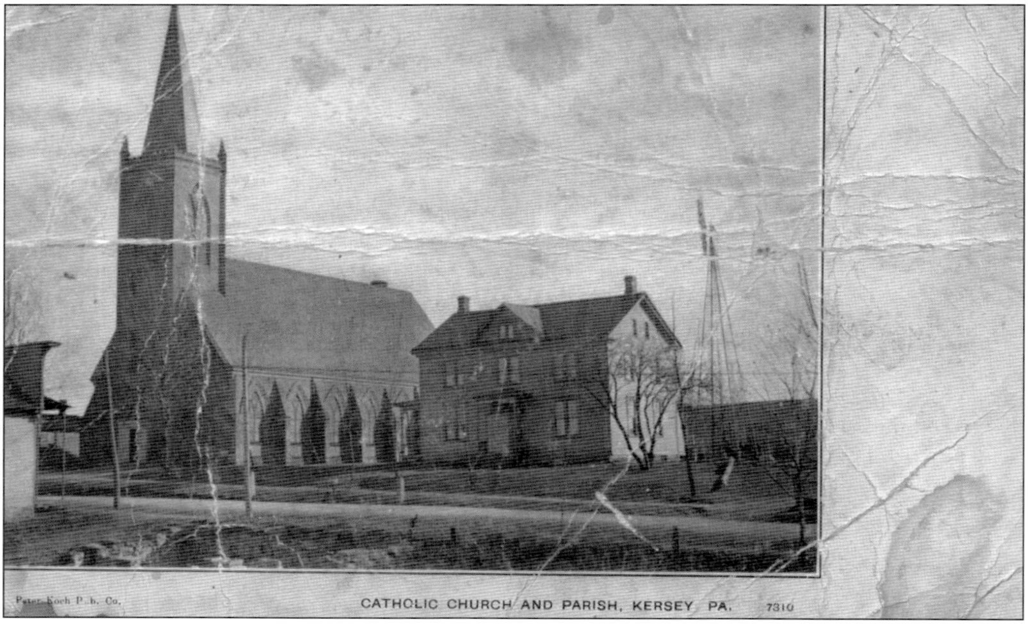

The second Catholic church in Kersey, seen here, was dedicated in 1894 during the tenure of Rev. Benjamin Raycroft. It was built under the direction of Barney Auman of St. Marys by local artisans, craftsmen, and laborers. Much of the labor and materials were donated, and it took a little over a year to build. The other structure is the rectory. (Courtesy of St. Boniface.)

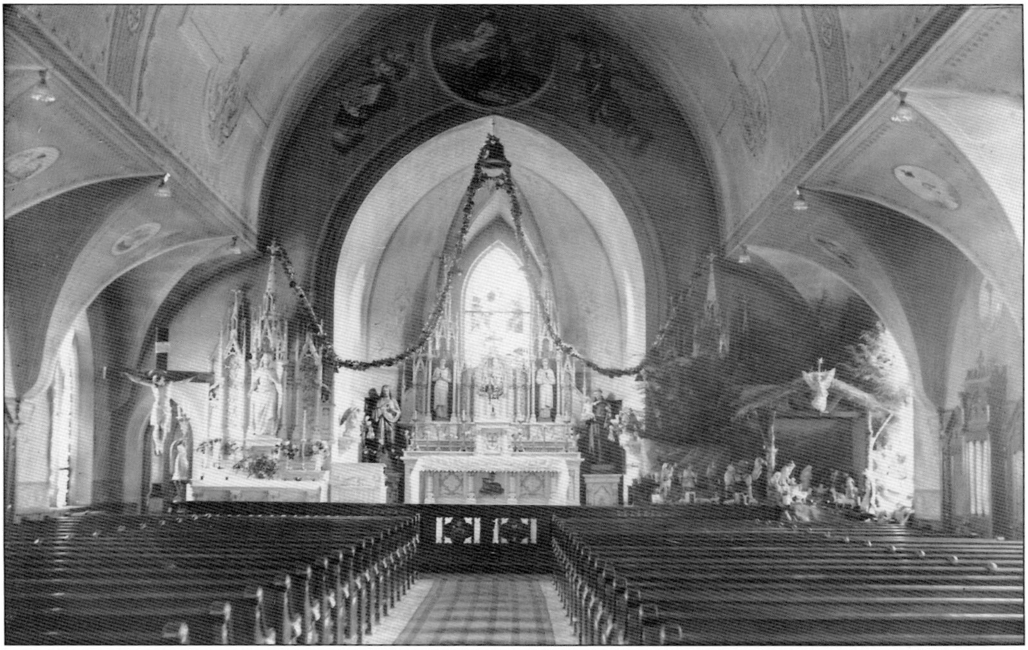

This Christmas photograph shows the original interior of St. Boniface Church. C.H. Bayer made the oak pews in St. Marys, and the walls were painted much more ornately than they are today. The pastor donated the stained-glass window, *The Resurrection*, behind the altar. The church is currently being renovated and remodeled. (Courtesy of St. Boniface.)

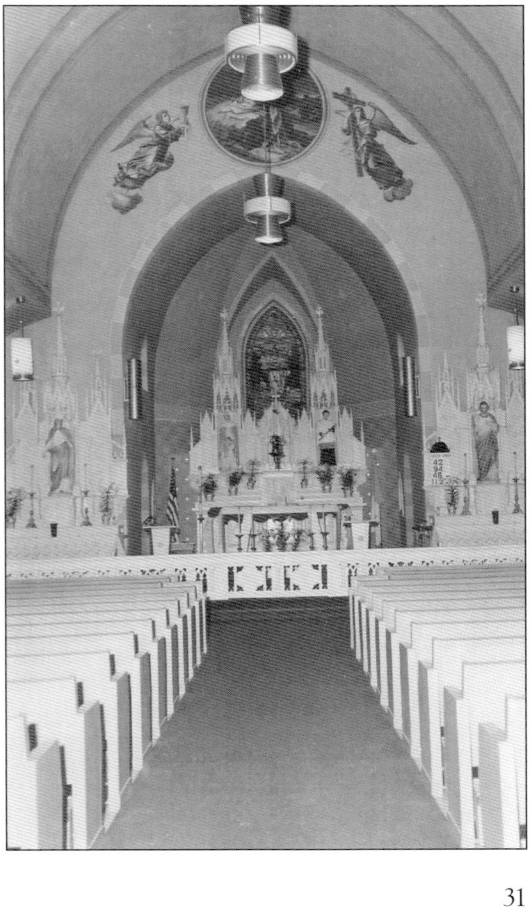

In the 1960s, under the direction of Father Frank Zacharewicz, much work was done to St. Boniface Church. This interior view shows the original altars. New lighting was installed in 1963, and new pews in 1965. Despite much controversy, to comply with directives created by the Vatican II Council, the original altars were removed and the sanctuary was remodeled in 1967. (Courtesy of St. Boniface.)

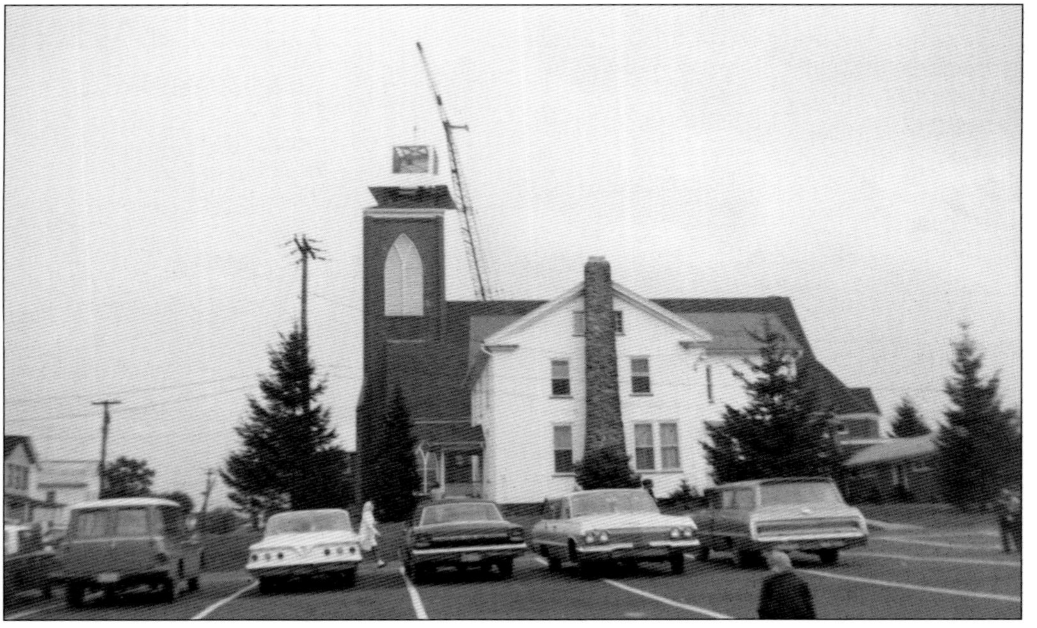

The original 1894 steeple was removed in the first half of the 1900s for safety reasons. The new steeple was assembled, piece by piece, in October 1966. It is 10 feet higher than the original, and designed to withstand 110-mile-per-hour winds. It can be seen from miles away, especially at night when it is illuminated. (Courtesy of St. Boniface.)

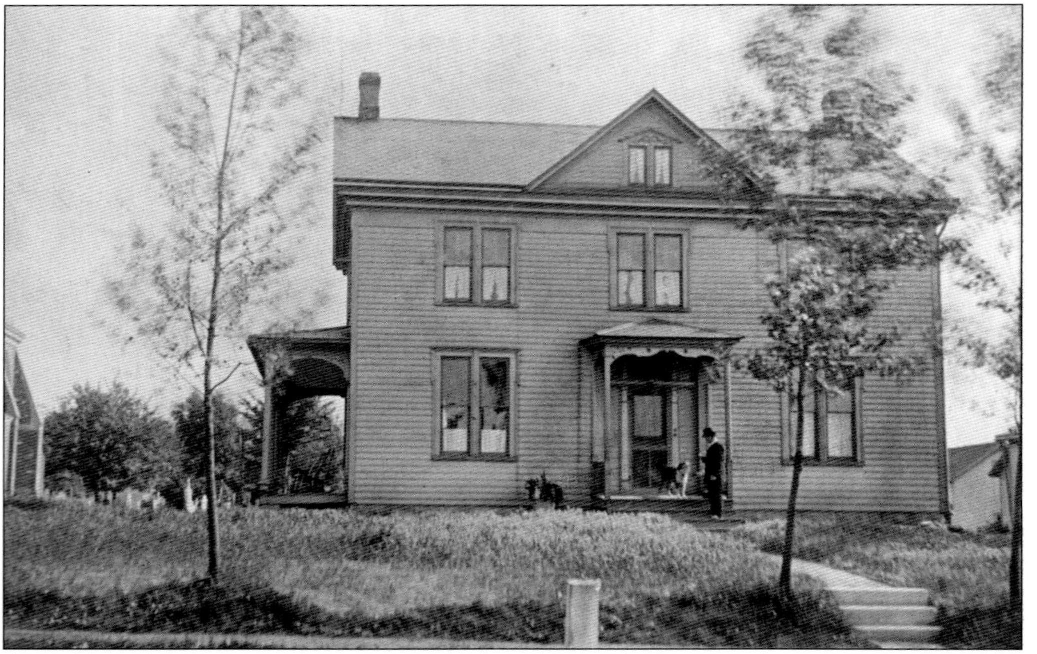

Father Frank Wagner is seen here on the porch of the 1864 rectory, located just west of the church. The rectory served as a convent for the Benedictine nuns who taught at St. Boniface School after the construction of the current school in 1956. Early on, it may have also served as a school for a time. It was demolished in 1984. (Courtesy of St. Boniface.)

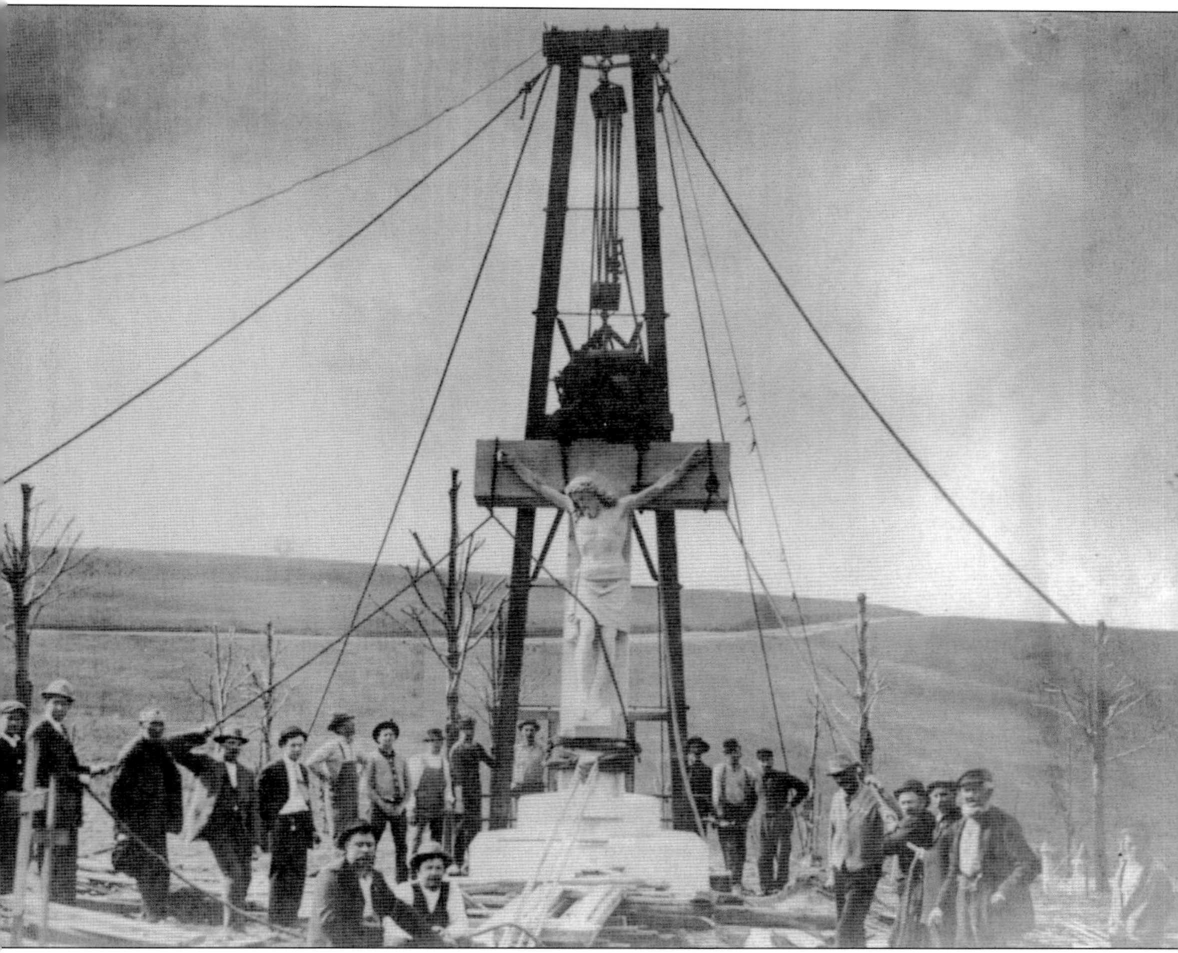

Alois Urmann, a local bottler and brewer, and his wife, Teresa, donated this crucifix. It cost $5,000 and was carved from a single piece of granite from Barre, Vermont. It weighs 20 tons, and required seven teams of horses and 20 men to move it from the Kersey depot to the site. The ingenuity needed to erect this cross without the benefit of modern machinery is a testament to the skills of the workers. Notice the large ropes and block and tackle used to raise the cross. It is 20 feet high, 10 feet wide, and almost 5 feet thick. It was dedicated on June 11, 1911. Observe the absence of trees in the background, typical of the era, and that there were no houses along Skyline Drive. Father Frank Wagner personally planted the maple trees in the cemetery just a few years before. Today, most of those trees are gone or dying, and are gradually being replaced by the parish.

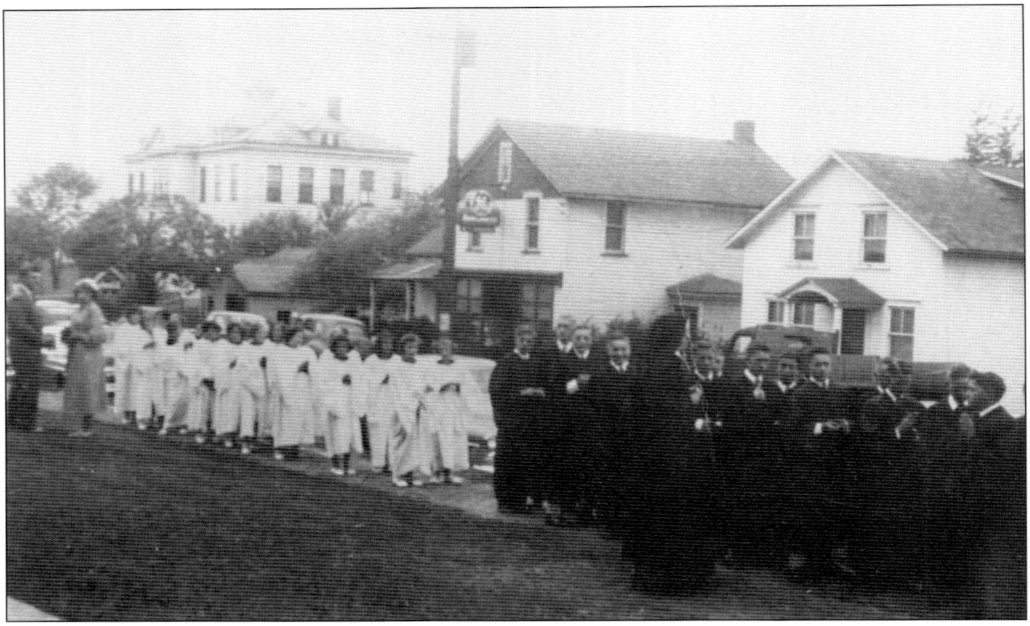

The eighth-grade graduates of St. Boniface Elementary School are seen here on their way to ceremonies in the church. In the background are Maurice Malone's General Electric Appliance store, and, farther in the distance, Kersey High School. The number of students was growing so fast, because of the Baby Boom generation, that a new elementary was built three years later. (Courtesy of St. Boniface.)

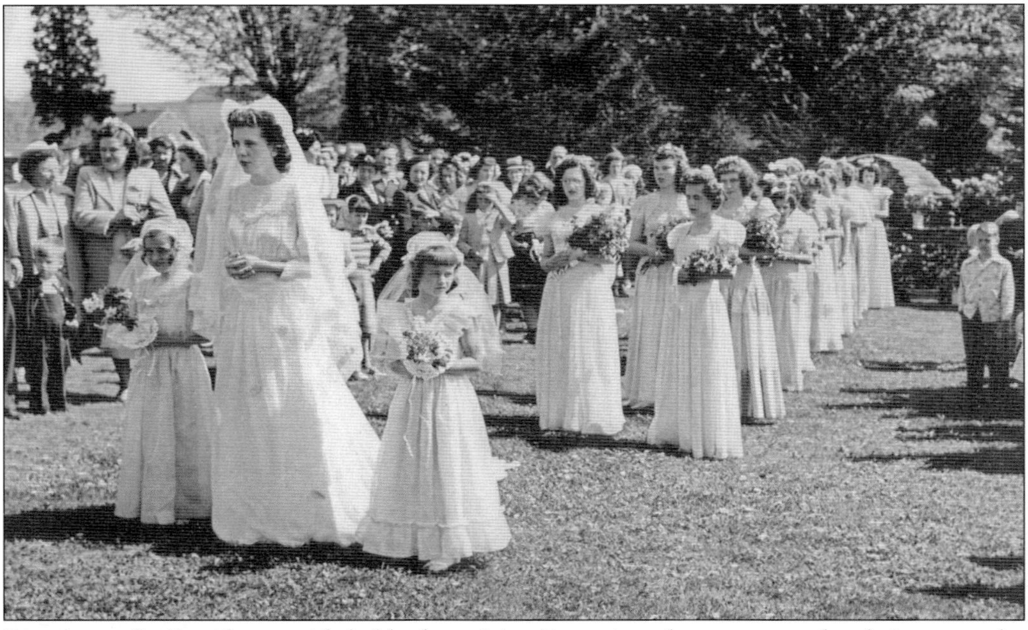

Every year, St. Boniface parish held a huge May Crowning observance at the shrine near the cemetery. This photograph shows how large and elaborate the ceremonies were. In the 1949 event seen here, the May queen was Anna Mae (Dietz) Parmigiani. Father Kleeber was the pastor. The event continues today, but on a much smaller scale. (Courtesy of St. Boniface.)

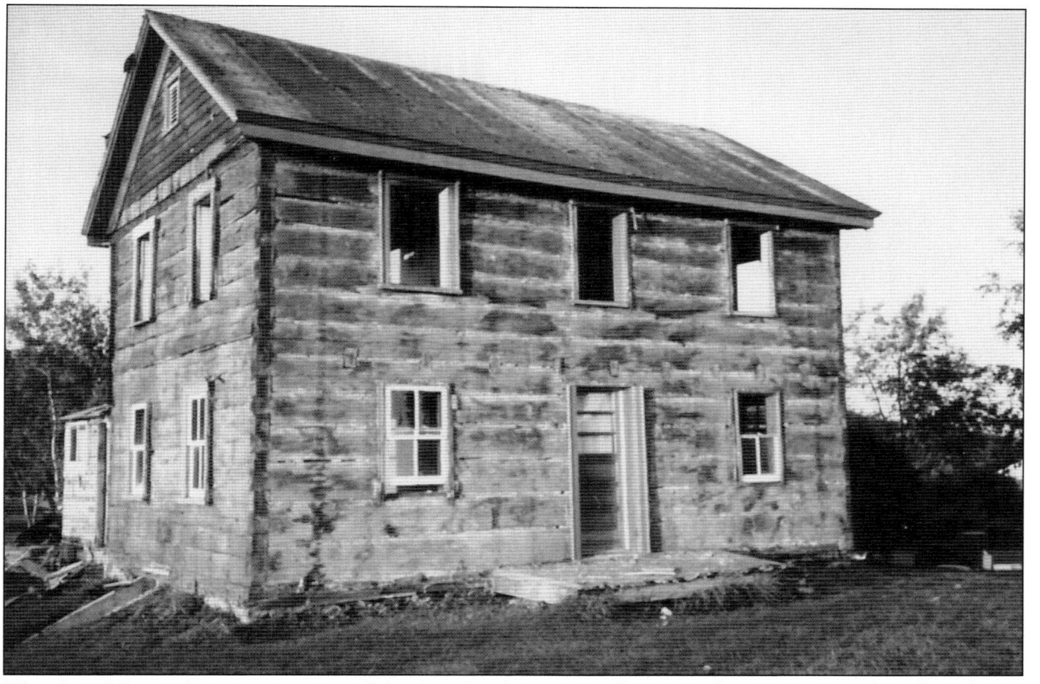

The Smithbauer house was one of the last log homes in the township. It was enclosed within a modern home, and then torn down in 1989. It was located near the intersection of the Milesburg-Smethport Turnpike and modern Route 948, about one mile east of Kersey. Note the chinking, the dovetailed corners, and the second-floor joists. This photograph was taken just prior to its demolition. (Courtesy of Harriet Moyer.)

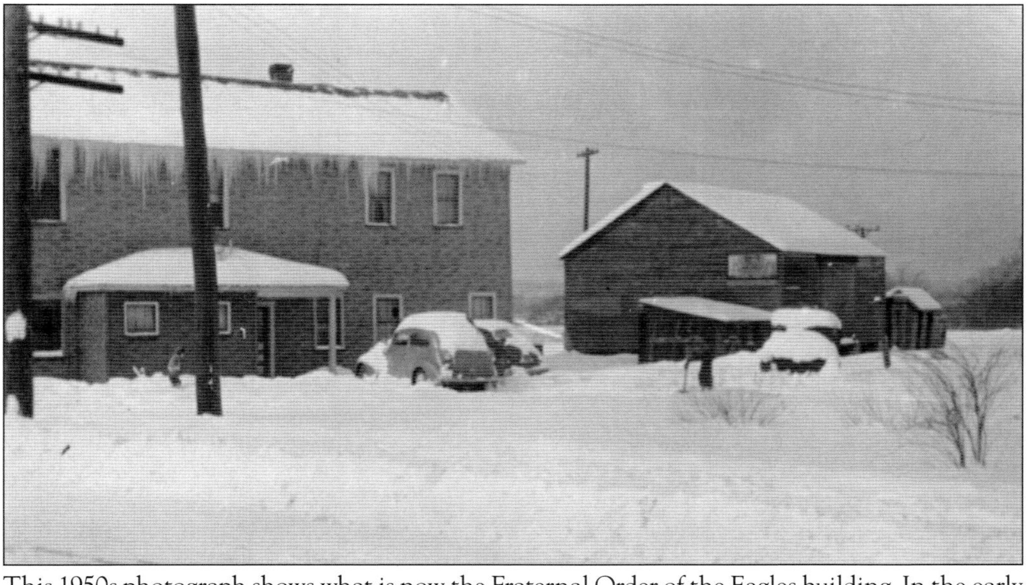

This 1950s photograph shows what is now the Fraternal Order of the Eagles building. In the early 1900s, it was known as Andersons Hall. It was the first building in Kersey with enough space for dances, meetings, and other large gatherings. Most Kersey High School graduation ceremonies were held here. When silent films began, it also served as a movie theater. (Courtesy of Joan Verbka.)

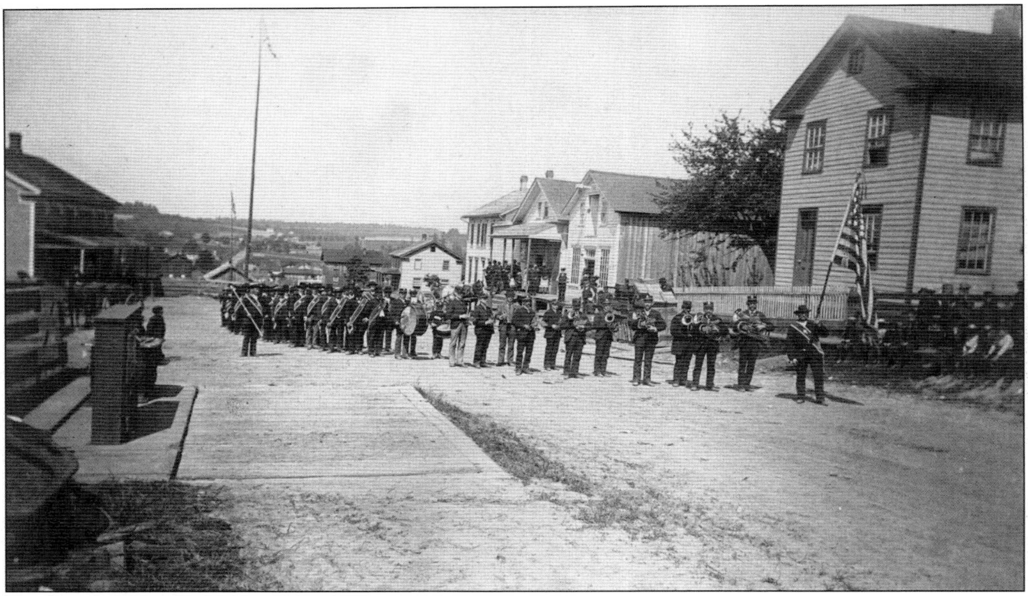

Music has always been an important part of life in Fox Township. Each community had its own band, as did some fraternal organizations, and there was much rivalry between them. They gave concerts, and played in parades and other social events. There were also dancing bands and smaller groups. Above, the band known as the First Band in Kersey parades in front of St. Boniface Church as many people watch and listen from porches and along the street. As the road was not paved and no electric or telephone poles are visible, it was probably in the early 1890s. Note the drum major on the right of the approximately 35-member band. The Centerville Cornet Band (below) was organized by Misters Eberl, Feunfinger, Hahn, Koch, and Brandenmiller in 1887.

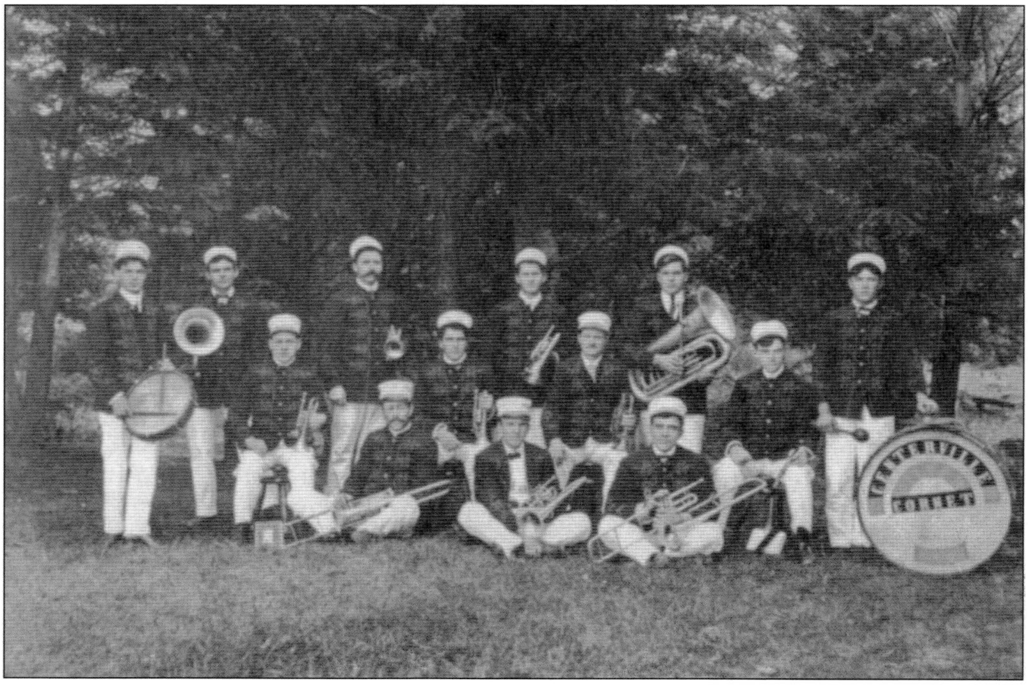

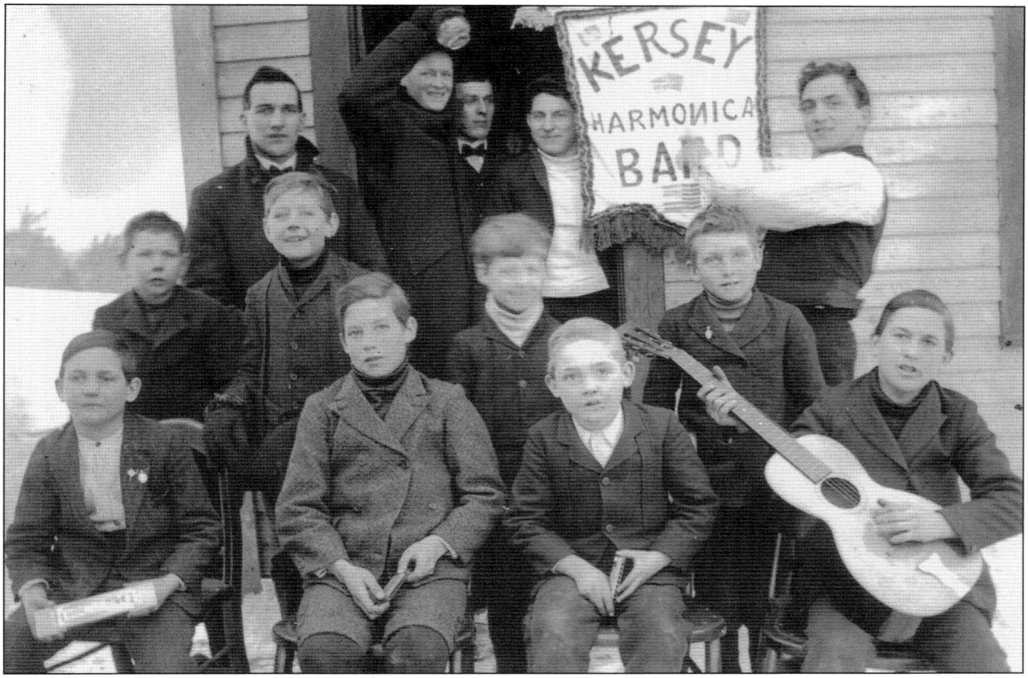

In the early 1900s, harmonica bands were a popular, cheap way to teach children music and discipline, and to provide a social outlet. Harmonica bands entertained at many school and community functions. The Kersey Harmonica Band was sponsored partly by the members of the Centerville Cornet Band. (Courtesy of Chris Casey.)

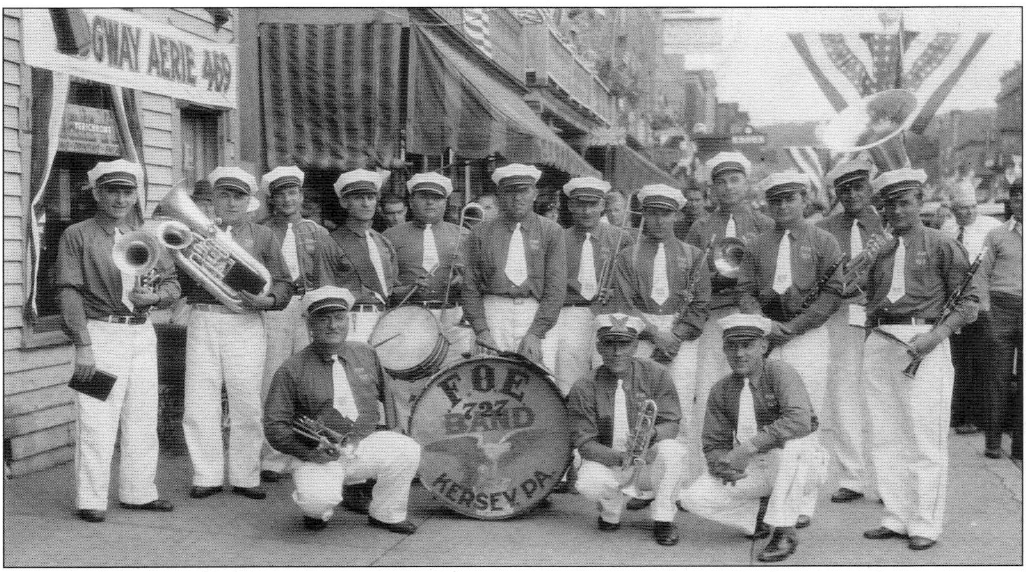

The Fraternal Order of Eagles band is seen here at a celebration in Ridgway in the summer of 1935. They are, from left to right, (kneeling) Tony Pnellie, Johnny Pnellie, and Joe Serafini; (standing) Bean Agosti, Barber Pnellie, Mario Contrini, Mario Parmigiani, Fats Argoni, Happy Oldani, Pal Contrini, Tony Orsi, Dad Moyer, Don Cameroni, Tanny Oldani, and John Falcetoni. (Courtesy of Harriet Moyer.)

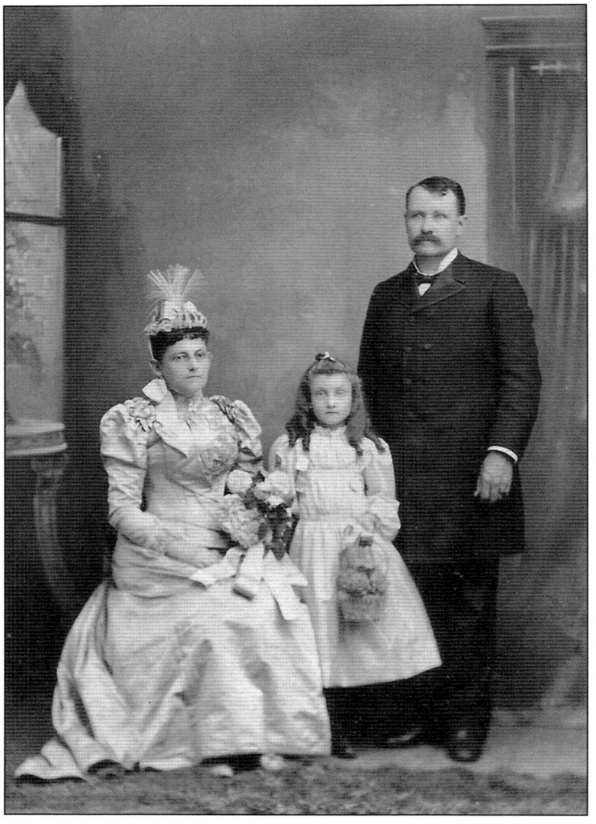

George and Mary Straessley Boyer, seen here with their daughter Susan, lived in uptown Kersey across from Beveridge's store, in a house that was formerly Hedberg's tailor shop. George, a Civil War veteran, later became postmaster and, along with his daughter Caroline, operated the post office in their home until the 1950s. Caroline Boyer Mosier operated a candy store there as well. Mary Mosier, Caroline's granddaughter, still lives in the home. (Courtesy of George Mosier.)

The Gahr family has owned and operated a farm at the end of Gahr Road for more than a century. The family is seen below around 1917. The parents, John and Mary (seated, center), were immigrants from Germany. The young boy on the left is Frances "Bucky" Gahr, who ran the farm after his parents. Today, his son Ray operates the farm. (Courtesy of Barb Lenze.)

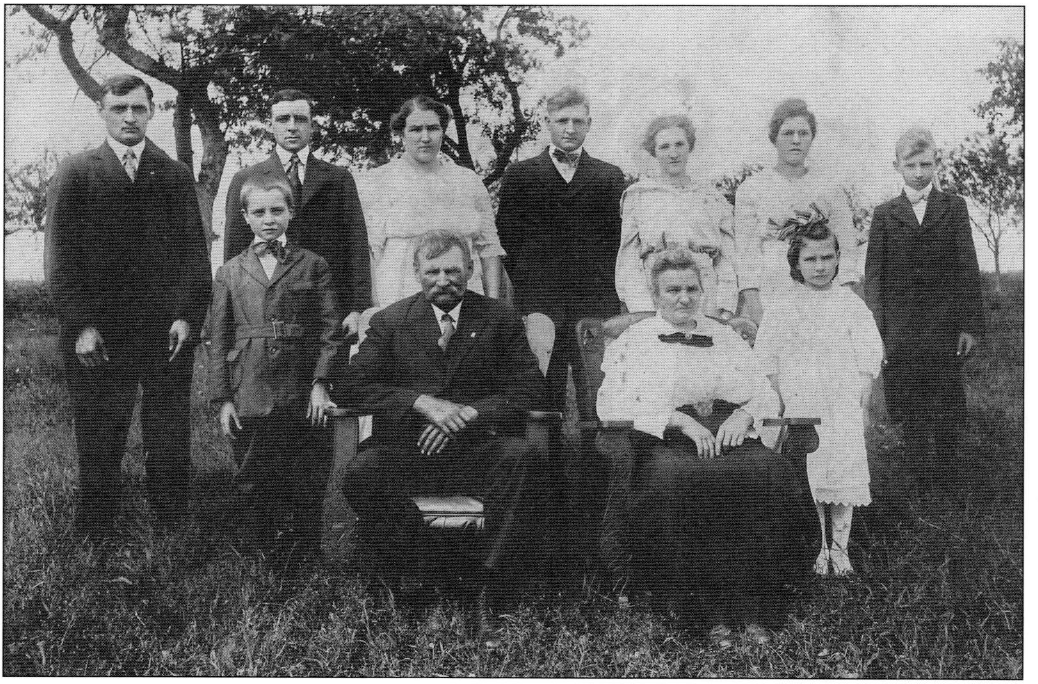

Two

Dagus Mines

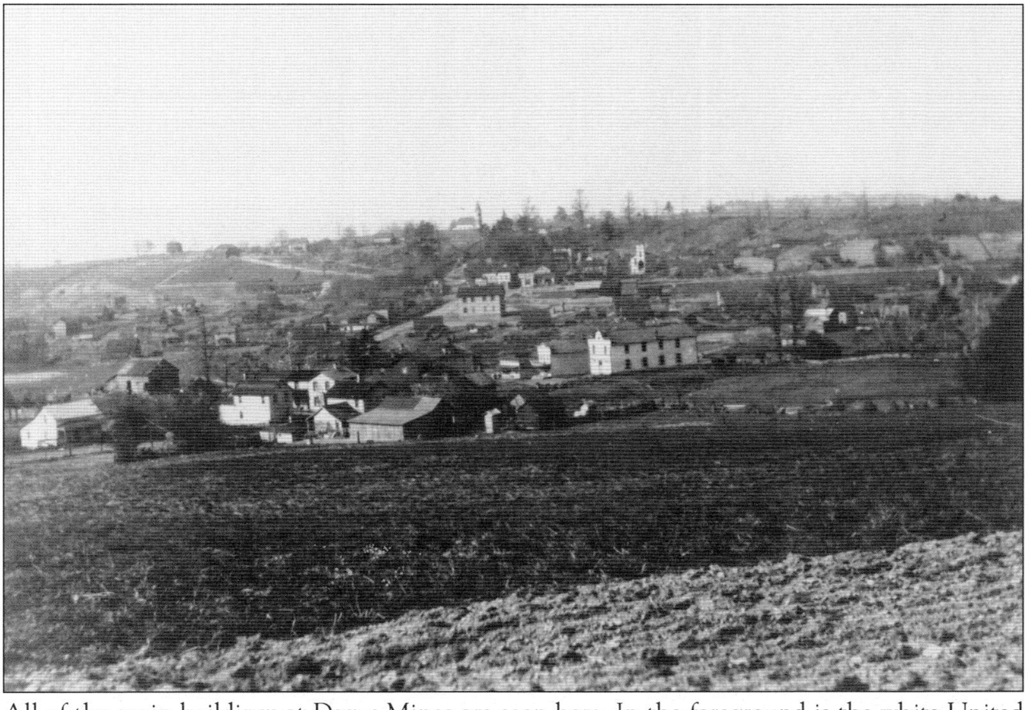

All of the main buildings at Dagus Mines are seen here. In the foreground is the white United Mine Workers (UMW) hall, beside what would become Falcettoni's Recreation Center. The school is in the background, with the company store directly behind it. To the right of the store are the drugstore, the post office, the doctor's home, and the Presbyterian Church. On top of the hill are the Maria Lutheran Church and the water towers.

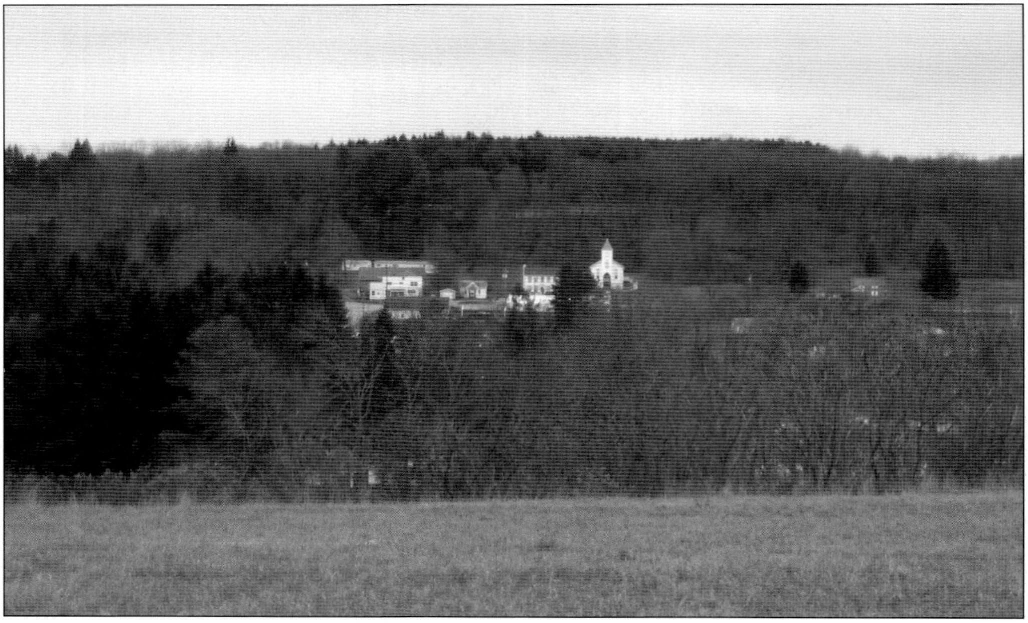

Above is a current view of Dagus Mines taken from the same location as the photograph below. Notice the growth of the trees in the last 100 years. In the distance are, from left to right, the company store, the 1884 post office, the company doctor's house, and the Presbyterian Church. In front of the store is the old schoolhouse, today the American Legion building. Below, the UMW hall is predominant, and across the road is the Eureka Hotel, which later became Hau's Hotel and is now the Last Chance.

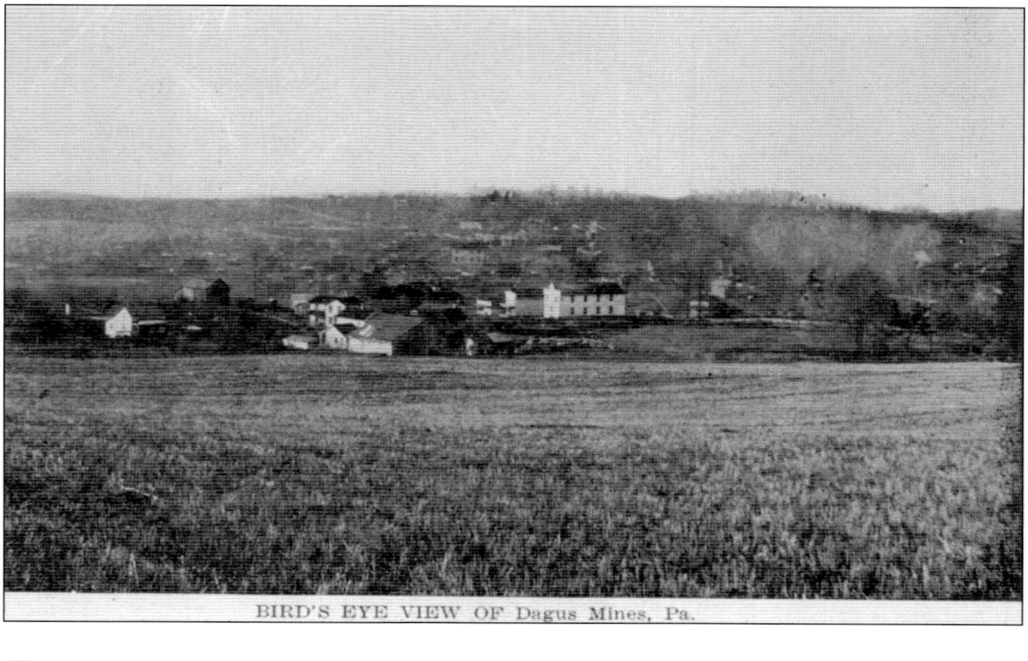

BIRD'S EYE VIEW OF Dagus Mines, Pa.

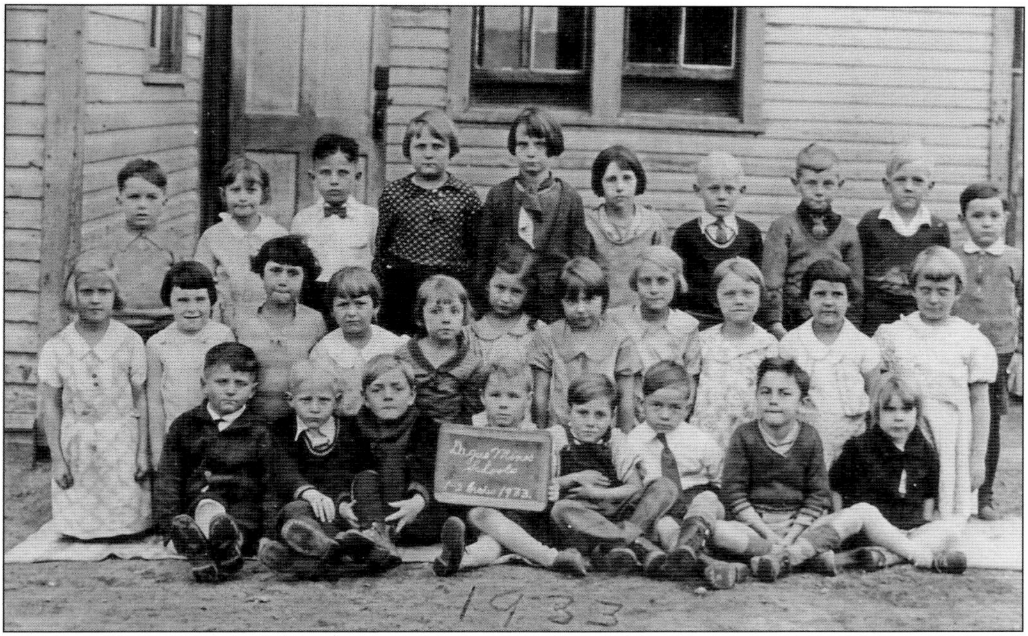

The Dagus school building is more than 130 years old. It served as a schoolhouse until 1960, when the students were bused to Kersey and the American Legion acquired the building. In 1918, students from Coal Hollow were sent here. The first and second grades in 1933 are seen here.

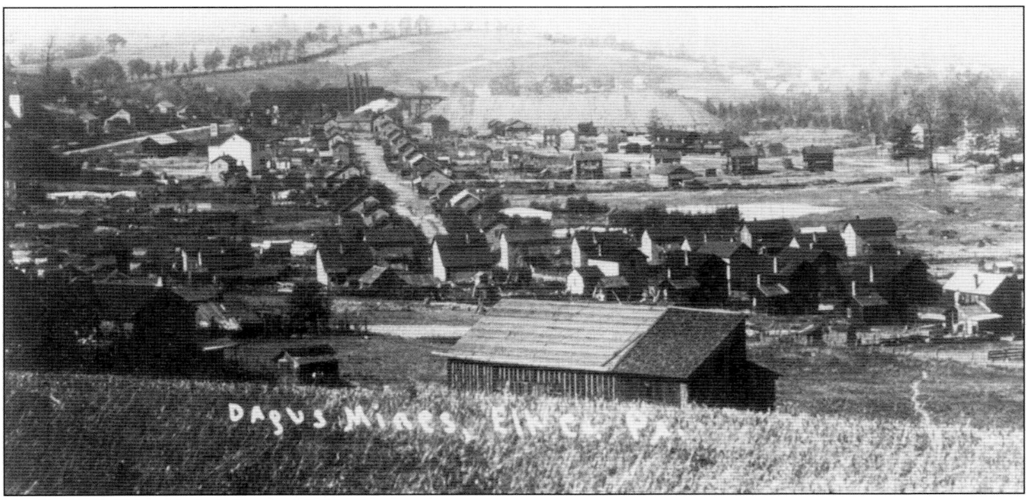

This view is from Chicken Hill. The street, Scotland Street, may have extended to the right in the direction of the current Armstrong home and connected there to Meredith Road. In the distance is a tipple, a powerhouse, and rock dumps. The rock dumps were removed in the 1980s thanks to federal environmental laws passed during the Nixon administration. The bare area in the center right is a baseball field. (Courtesy of Ken Anderson.)

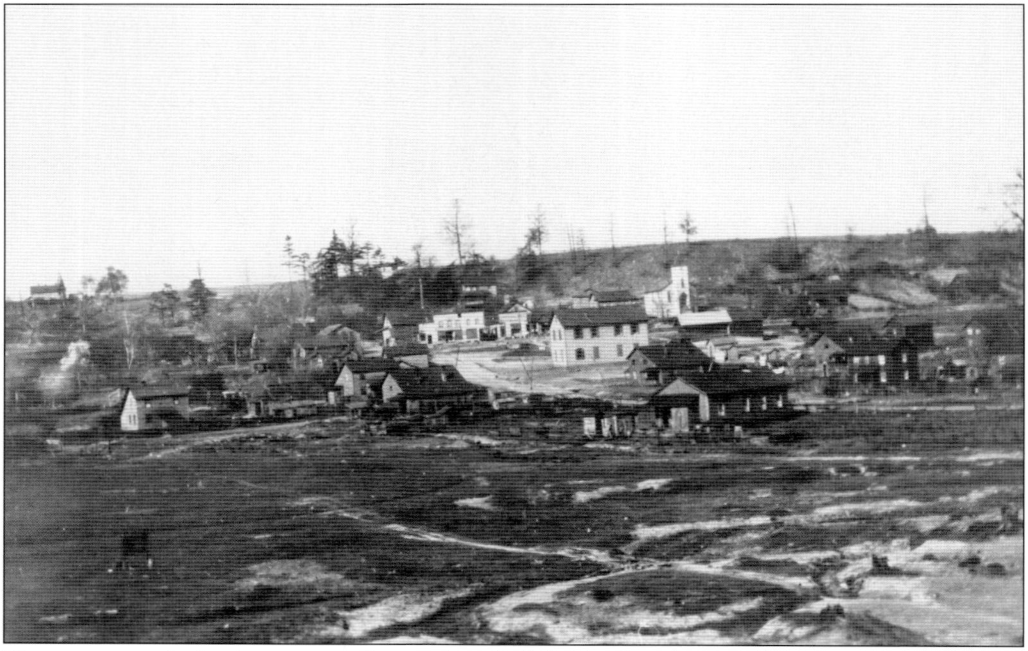

This view overlooks the current Legion baseball field. The photograph may have been taken from another set of rock dumps that extended from a nearby hillside. The vacant land in the foreground has never been developed, and has usually been a ball field. There was a mine entrance near the field.

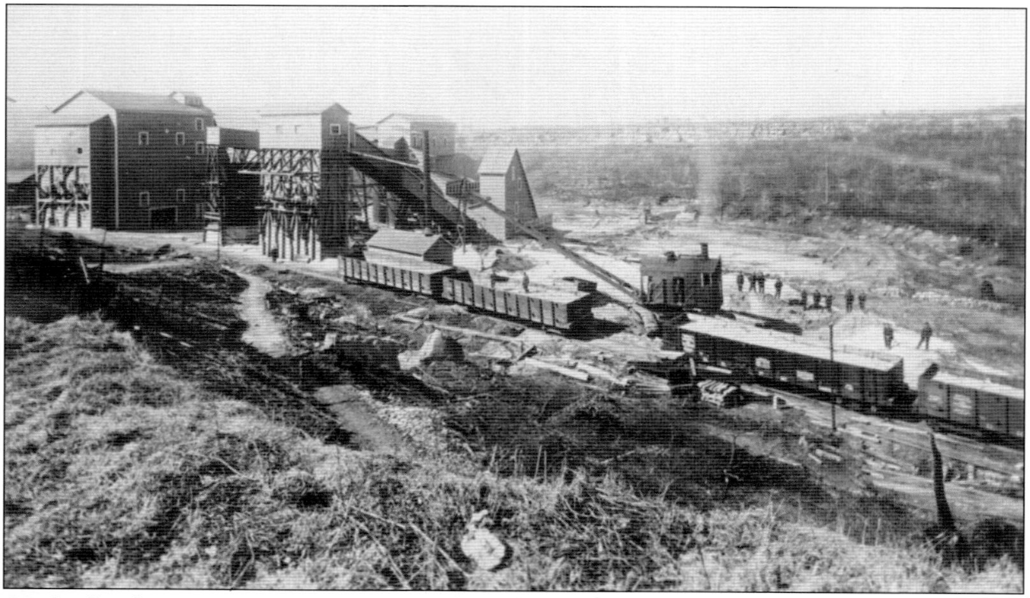

On the flats located along Meredith Road was the Eureka mine. It was the first major mine opened, and one of the first closed. Dr. C.R. Early was the most important entrepreneur in developing mining and railroads in Fox Township, and was a major stockholder in both the Erie Railroad and the Northwest Mining and Exchange. This view was photographed from Chicken Hill. (Courtesy of William and Janice Haller.)

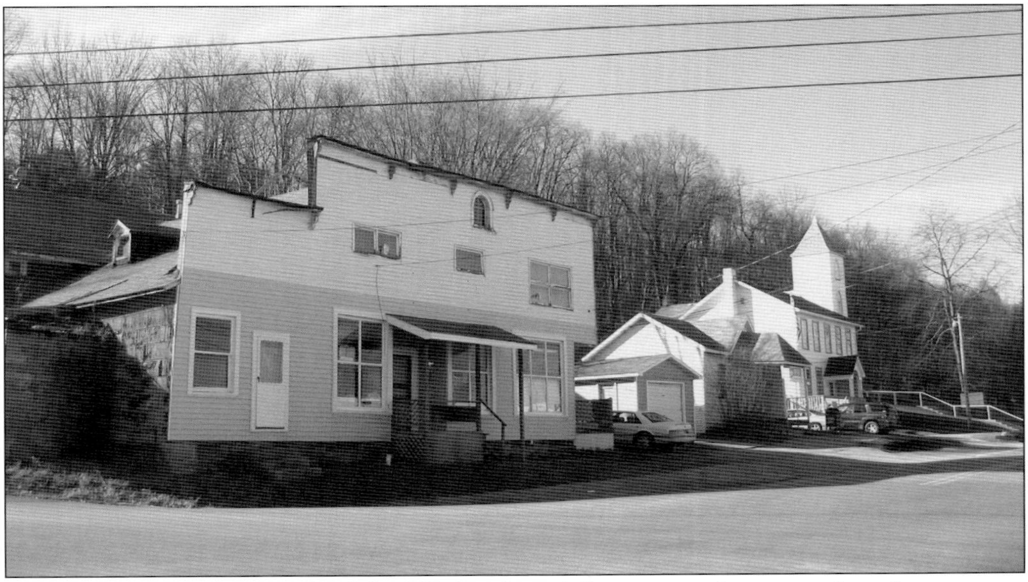

This is a modern photograph of the J.H. Steele and Co. store and meat market, the company store for the Northwest Mining and Exchange. All the miners had to buy their mining equipment and supplies here. The miners could buy almost all their family needs there as well. Credit was extended to the families, with payment taken out of the miners' next paycheck.

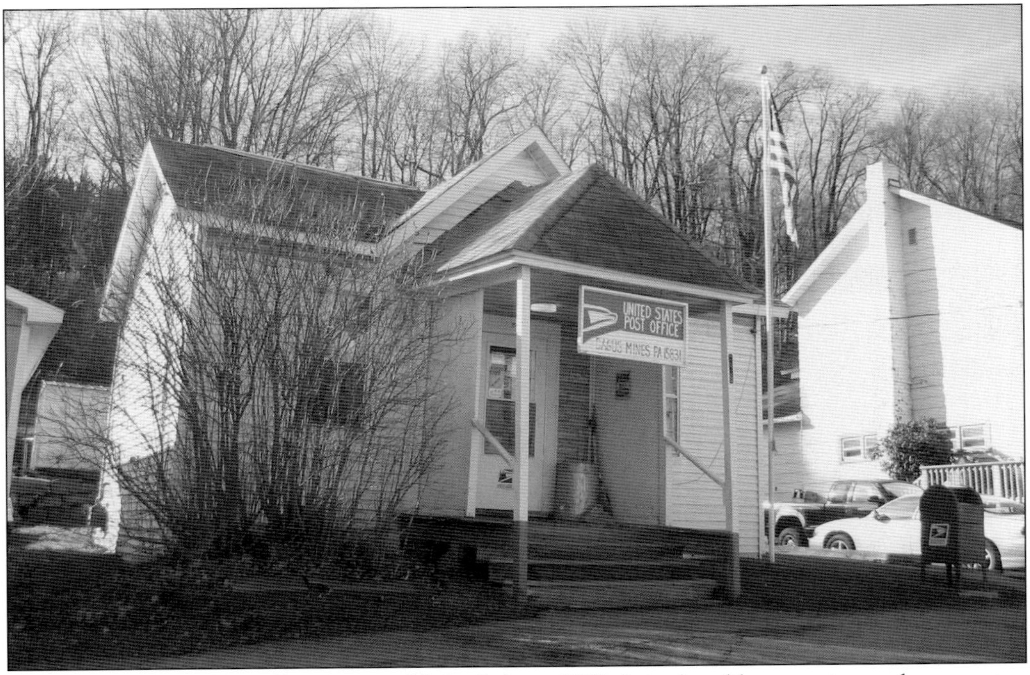

The Dagus Mines post office was established about 1880. It is the oldest continuously operating post office building in Pennsylvania, as it is still in its original structure. The first postmaster was J.R. Beadle, and the postmaster in 2013 is Mark Primerino. Due to its age, small size, and volume, the post office has been considered for closure, with the mail possibly being delivered through the Kersey post office in the future.

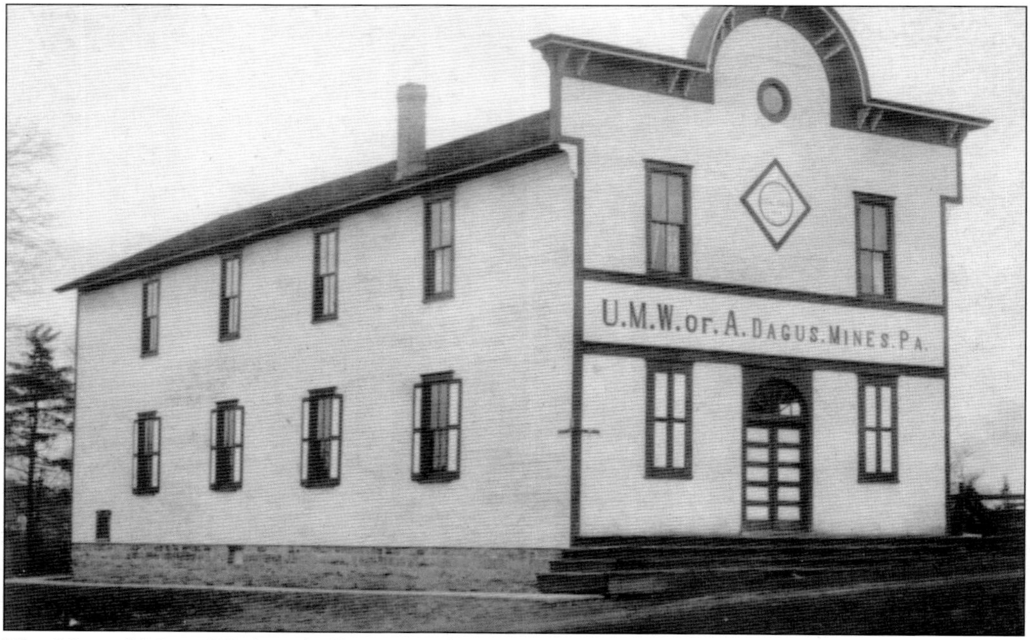

The United Mine Workers hall was on the site of the current Fox Township Medical Center. The building held union meetings and served as a community center. Plays, graduations, church socials, medicine shows, and more were held here prior to the construction of the Community Building in Kersey. The low ceiling gave the home basketball team an advantage, as it was in play and could be used for bounce passes.

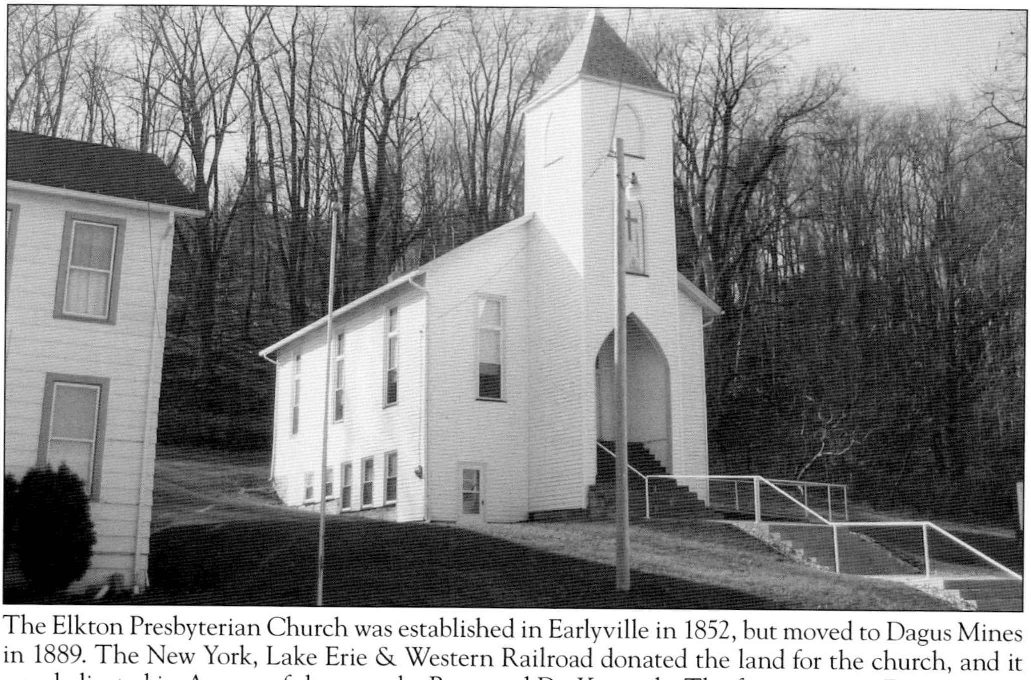

The Elkton Presbyterian Church was established in Earlyville in 1852, but moved to Dagus Mines in 1889. The New York, Lake Erie & Western Railroad donated the land for the church, and it was dedicated in August of that year by Reverend Dr. Kennedy. The first pastor in Dagus Mines was Rev. James Dickson.

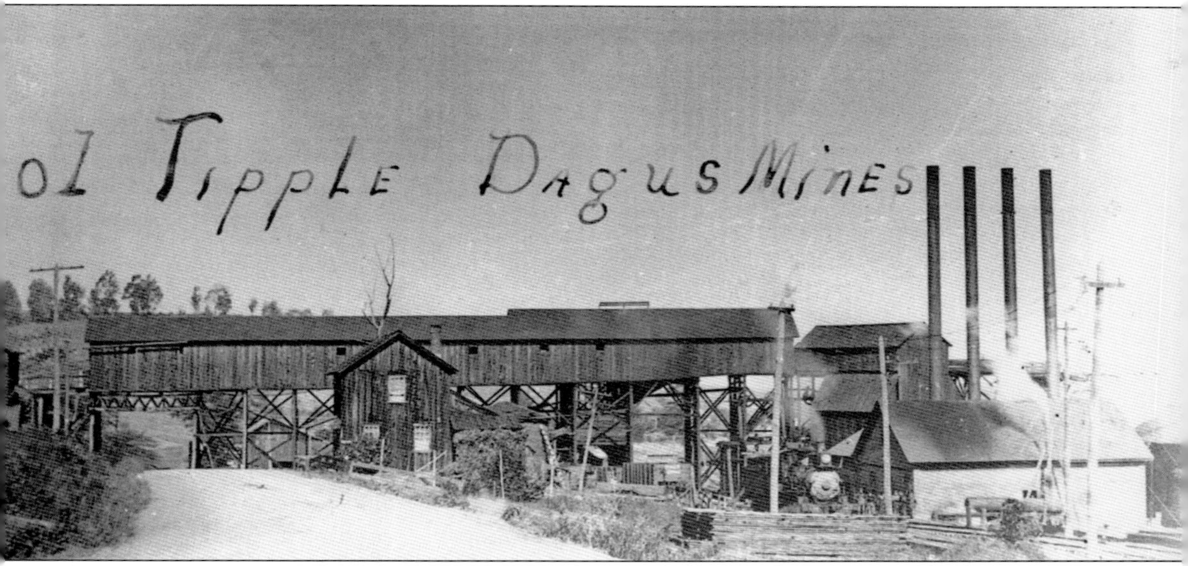

This photograph, from as early as 1906, shows the coal tipple along the railroad grade between Kersey and Dagus. The building with the four smokestacks is the power station, which produced electricity for the electrified mine cars and for the lights in the mines. Coal was brought out of the mine and then tipped into the waiting railroad cars below, thus the name tipple. Waste products like rocks and shale were dumped on nearby piles called rock dumps. The dirt road seen here is now Dagus Mines Road. The engine under the tipple is not pulling any cars, but may be moving up the valley to another tipple. This is the first tipple along the Erie tracks. Coal was taken from Dagus to Daguscahonda and the main line, and then often to New York via the Kinzua Bridge Viaduct, for use as boiler coal in steamships. (Courtesy of Joan Verbka.)

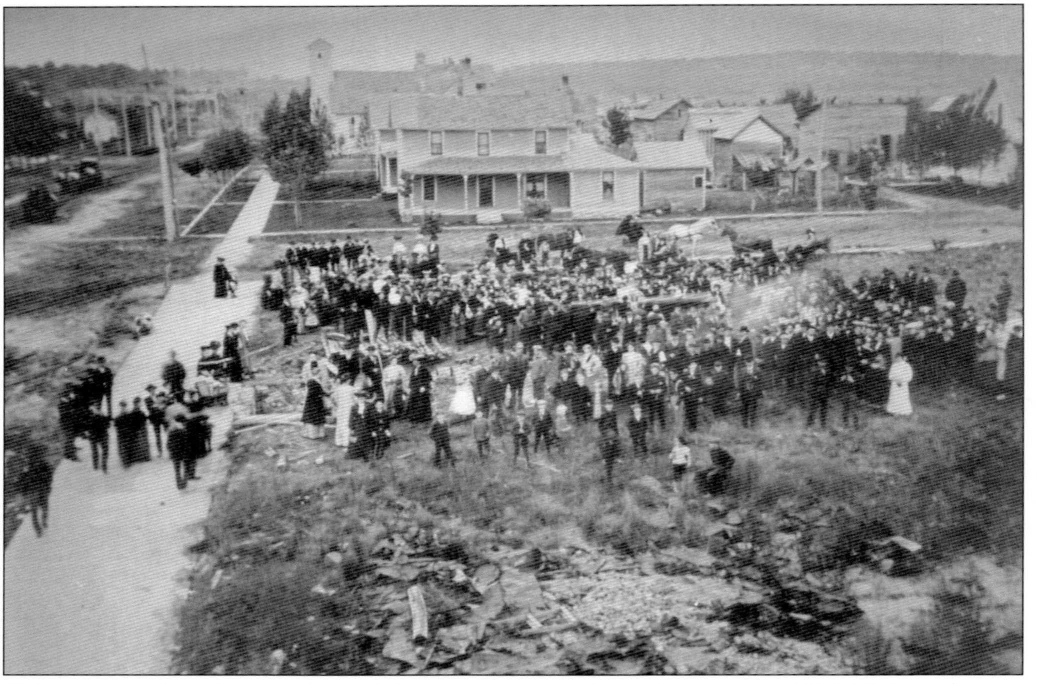

This photograph looks along South Main Street toward Dagus Mines around 1900. It is not known what the gathering was for, although the photographer is likely standing on a tipple or rock dump near what is now the Jireh Lanes bowling alley. The white dresses and the leaves on the trees indicate a summer activity, perhaps the Fourth of July. (Courtesy of Chris Casey.)

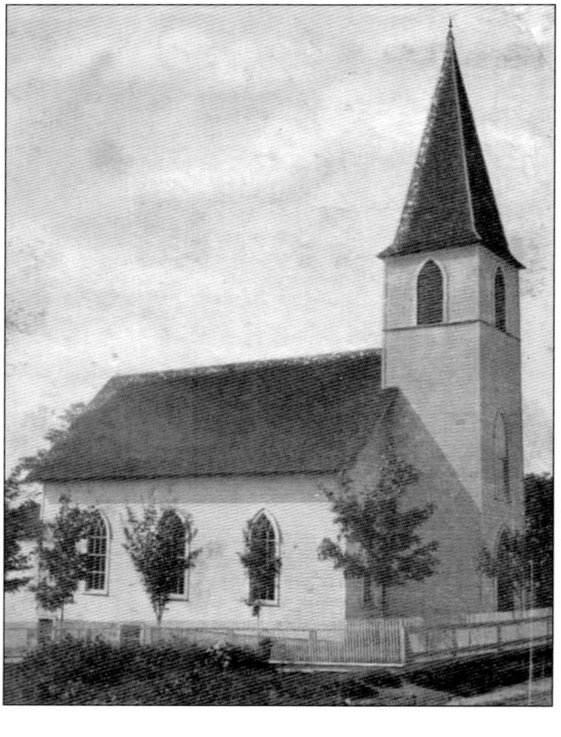

The Maria Lutheran Church, locally known as the Swede Church, was dedicated in 1891 on land donated by the mining company and the mine superintendent, Mr. Robertson. The site was chosen because of its central location between Toby, Coal Hollow, and Dagus Mines. There were 25 founding families in 1890, with surnames still familiar to the area, such as Anderson, Benson, Carlson, and Johnson.

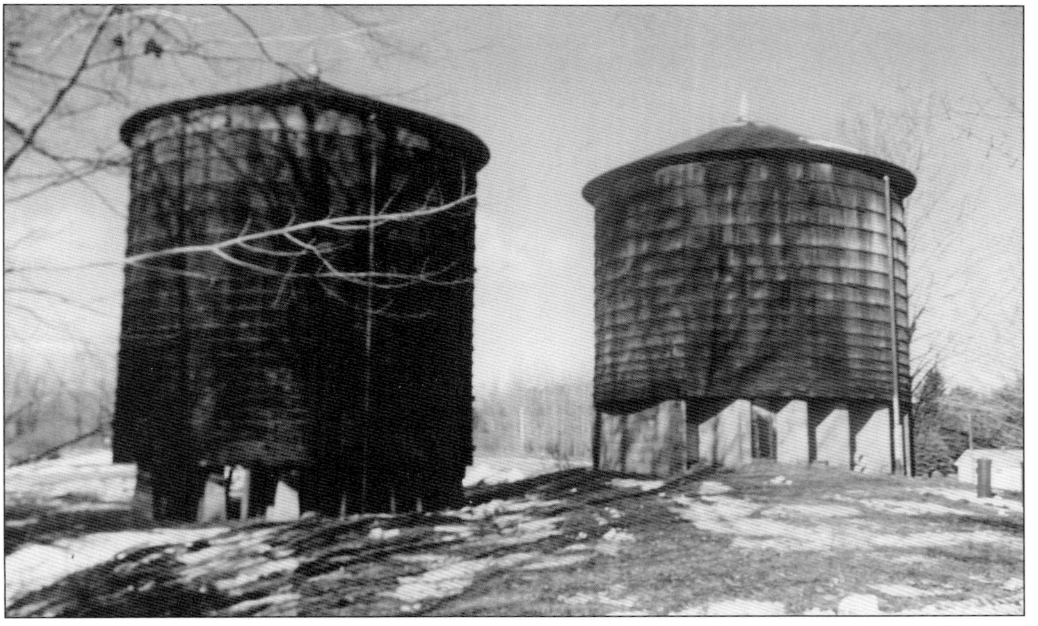

Due to pollution from the mines, water was pumped from Jackson Springs, near Byrnes Run, in a three-mile-long, hand-dug line. These water tanks above Dagus Mines held more than 4,500 gallons of water, for gravity flow to more than 180 homes. During World War II, they were guarded around the clock. The system served the community from 1914 to 1995. (Courtesy of Ed Huff.)

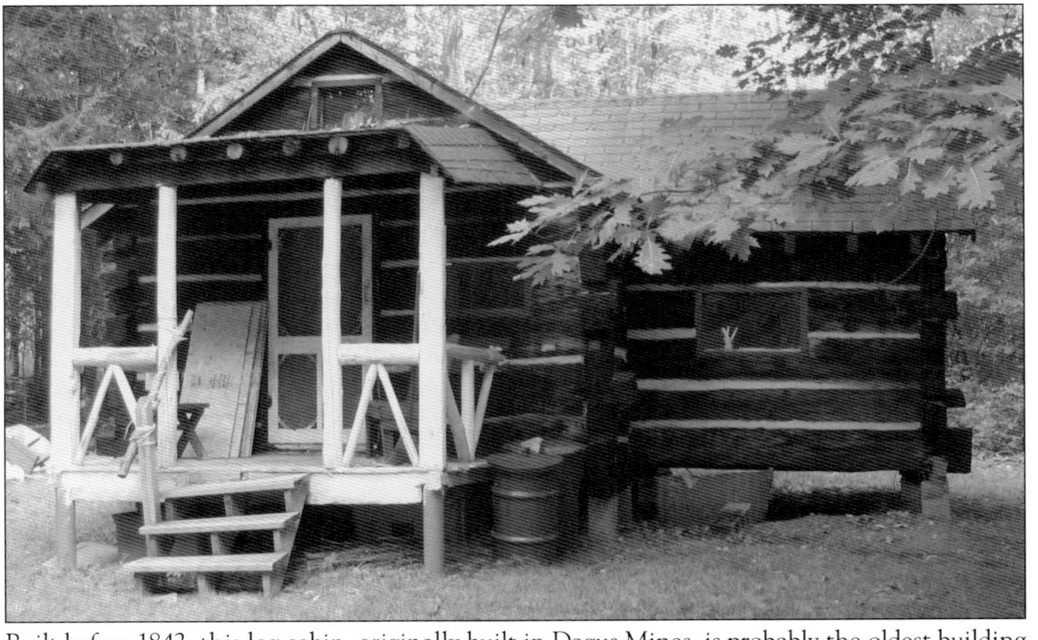

Built before 1842, this log cabin, originally built in Dagus Mines, is probably the oldest building in the township. The logs were numbered and the cabin disassembled in the 1940s, before being reassembled by Elmer Johnson in Toby, where it still stands. The hand-hewn logs are more than 18 inches thick and are dovetailed at the corners and connected with augured, and then hammered, wooden dowels.

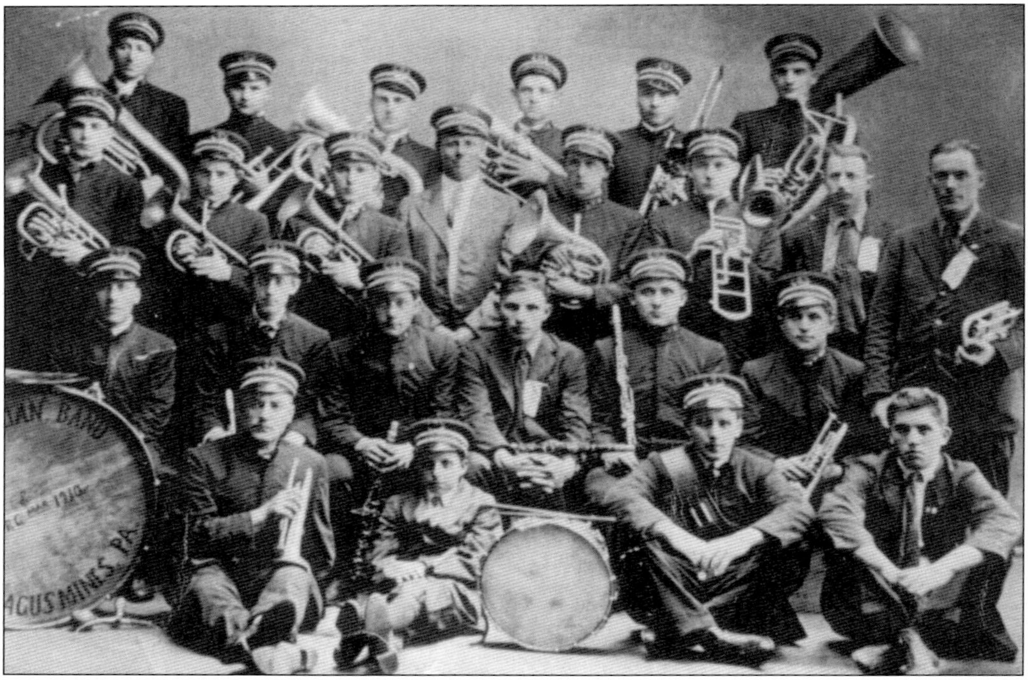

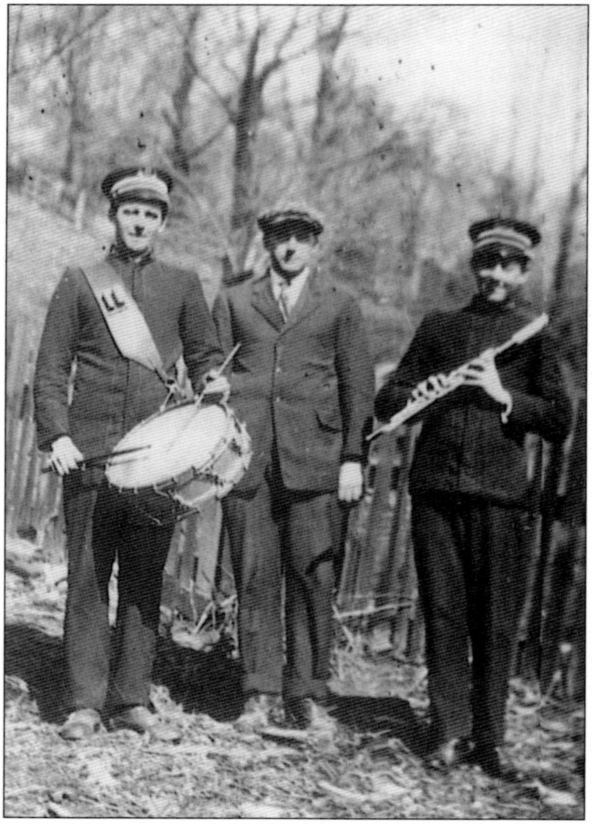

The 1918 photograph above shows the Dagus Italian Band before two of its members, Ernest Oldani and Santo Cesa, left for the service. The Dagus Orchestra and the Northwest Band also performed around that time. Seen here are, from left to right, (first row) Tony Pnelli and three unidentified; (second row) Harry Caimi, Dave Oldani, Louis Agosti, Dave Angelo, Ed Agosti, Santo Cesa, and John Pnelli; (third row, excluding man in center with no instrument) Frank Monti, Carl Pearson, Charlie Angelo, Ernest Oldani, and Mario Tirabaski; (fourth row) Steve Gornati, Jim Meloni, Barber Pnelli, Hugo Agosti, Nick Monti, and Tanny Oldani. At left, from left to right, John A. Pearson (drums), Carl B. Pearson (flute), and an unidentified bandmate pose for a photograph in their Dagus Italian Band uniforms in 1910. (Above, courtesy of Pat Catalone; left, courtesy of Joan Verbka.)

Three

Toby Valley and Coal Hollow

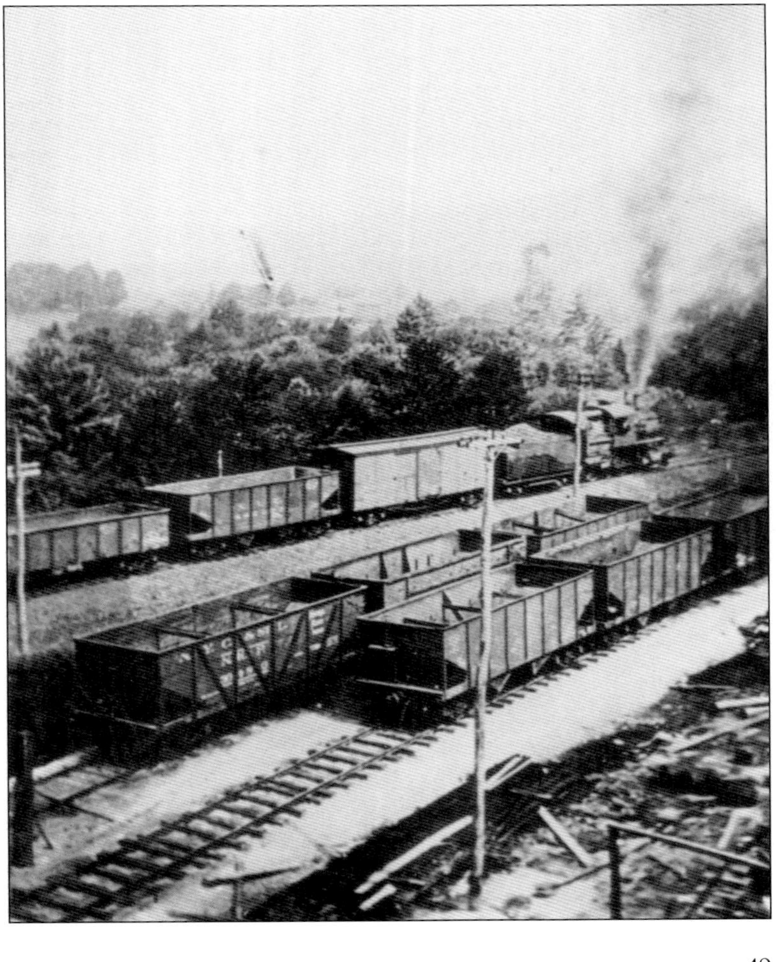

The history of the Toby Valley and Coal Hollow is entwined with coal mining. Here, gondola cars wait empty at the railroad site in Limestone Hollow, between the two valleys. Coal came here via underground passageways from a number of miles away, from the Limestone mine and other area mines, and was then tipped into the waiting cars. (Courtesy of Harriet Moyer.)

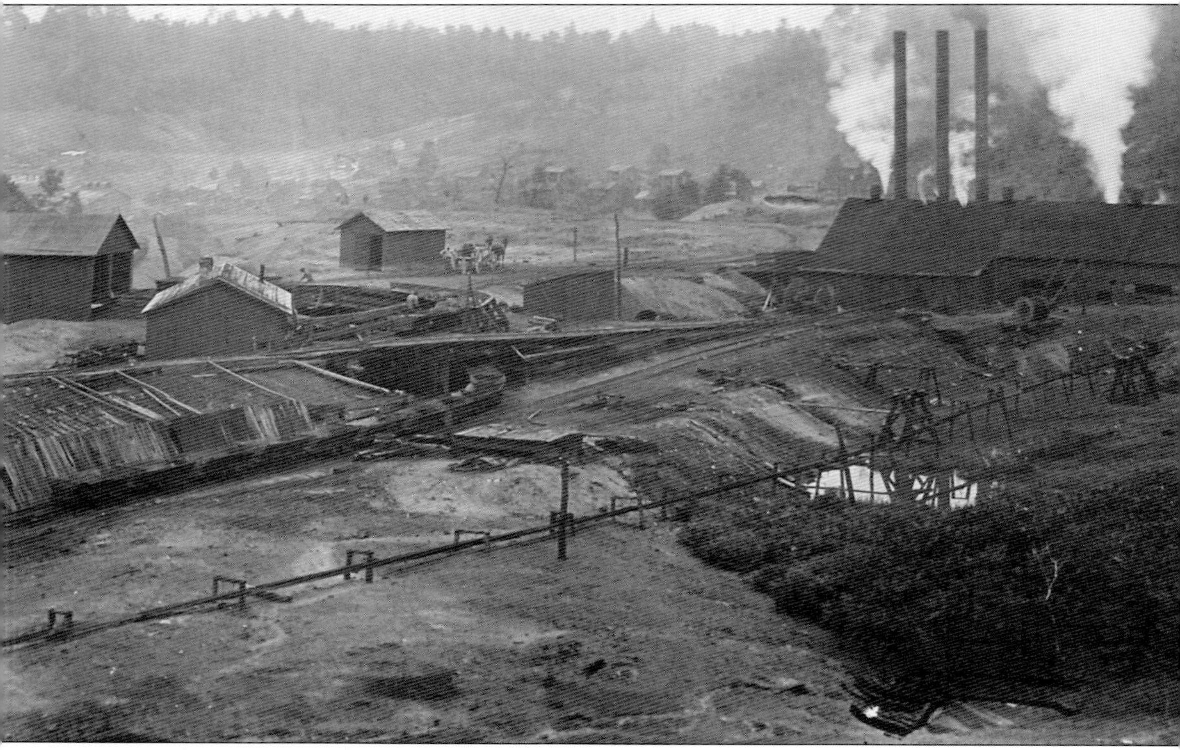

In an era without mining or environmental regulations, the landscape of Toby and Coal Hollow during the mining period often resembled a moonscape. The hillsides were stripped bare of trees and the ground was exposed to rapid water runoff during storms, often causing floods and erosion. Toby Creek turned red with sulfur and acid mine drainage. Rock dumps and boney piles were scattered throughout the valleys. It took federal regulations in the 1970s and 1980s to require cleanup, and decades of work by volunteer groups to reforest Toby and Coal Hollow and make Toby Creek run clear again. Though harder to find than it used to be, evidence of the mines is still visible if one looks for it. In this 1920 photograph of the Coal Hollow mine works, the power plant is visible on the right as coal cars exit the mine. A wagon with two mules and various workers is also seen, and houses are barely noticeable in the distance. (Courtesy of Jim Catalone and Joan Verbka.)

These photographs show some of the bridges and trestles in Coal Hollow. They both appear recently built, and may have replaced previous trestles. Nearly identical company houses can be seen in each image. Families could rent these homes as long as a member worked in the mines of the Northwest Mining and Exchange. There was also a company store. Swedes were the first to inhabit Coal Hollow, but in the late 1800s, many Italian immigrants settled there. Some of the earliest Italian families came from the Milan area. They included families such as the Cameronis, Gornatis, and Oldanis. At first, some others were prejudiced against the Italians, partly based on fears that the newcomers were taking away jobs and driving down wages. (Both, courtesy of Joan Verbka.)

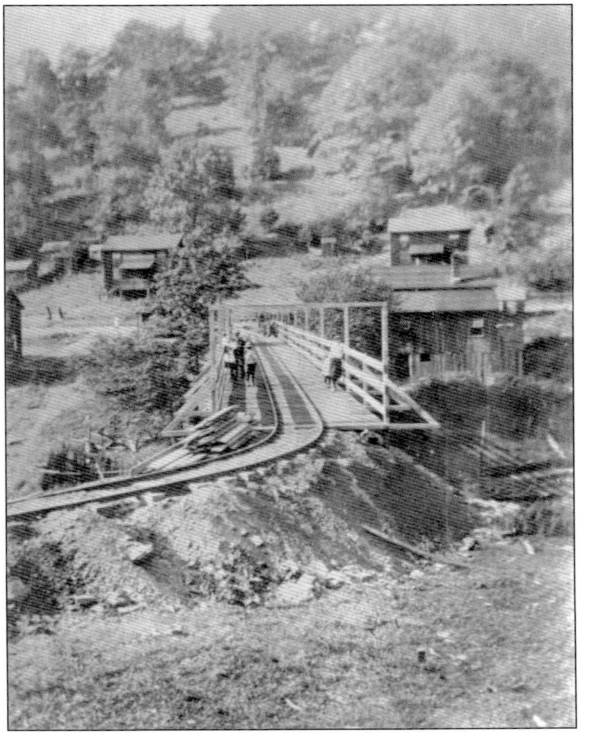

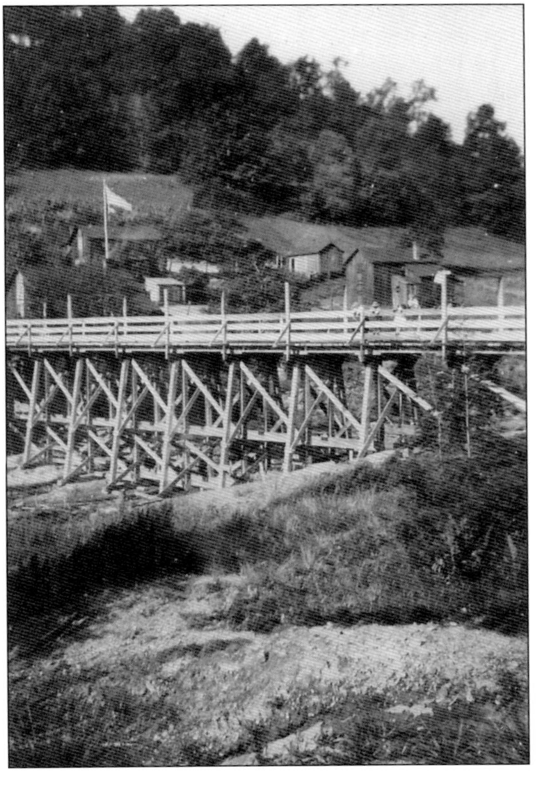

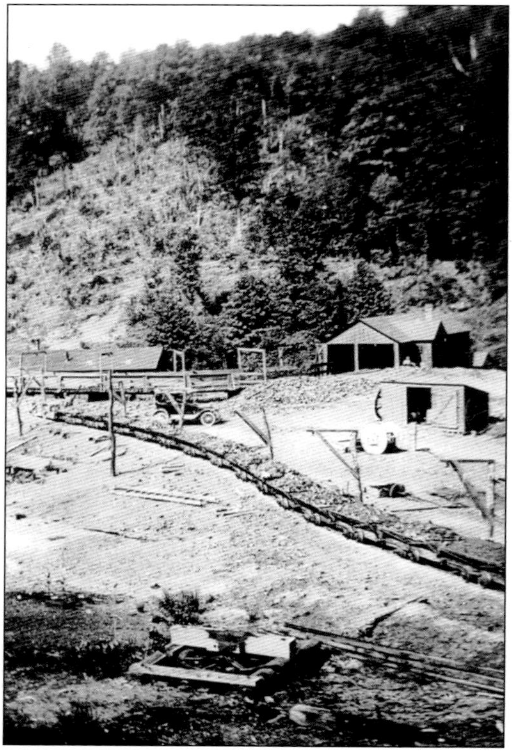

A long line of full, low-slung, underground electric coal cars passes in front of Ward Frantz's Ford Model T and the blacksmith's sheds and shop in Coal Hollow in 1923. Blacksmiths were important for repairing tools and sharpening or making bits. Electric cars replaced mules outside the mines around 1900. (Courtesy of Joan Verbka.)

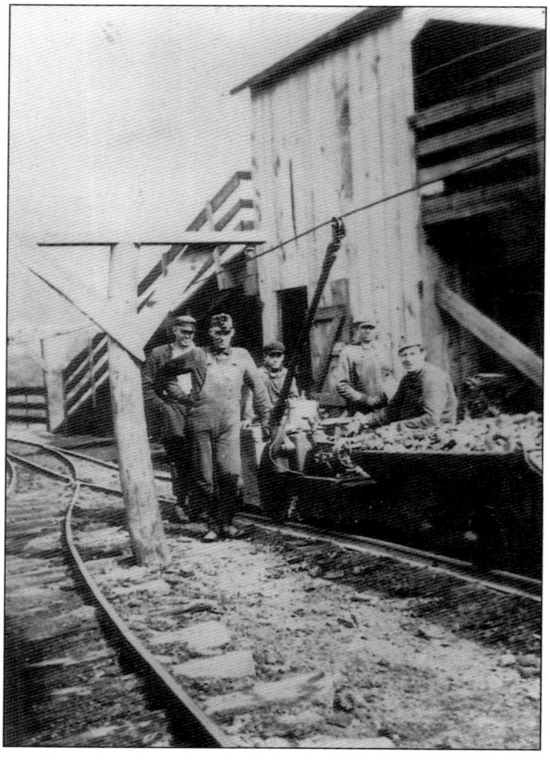

The electric cars in this 1920 photograph each hold four tons of coal. John Pearson is seated on the far right. Note the young boy in the background. Boys began working in the mines at age 13 or 14, though sometimes earlier. The cars are traveling to a tipple for loading into waiting Pittsburgh, Shawmut & Northern Railroad (PS&N) cars, for delivery to Brockway and points beyond. (Courtesy of Joan Verbka.)

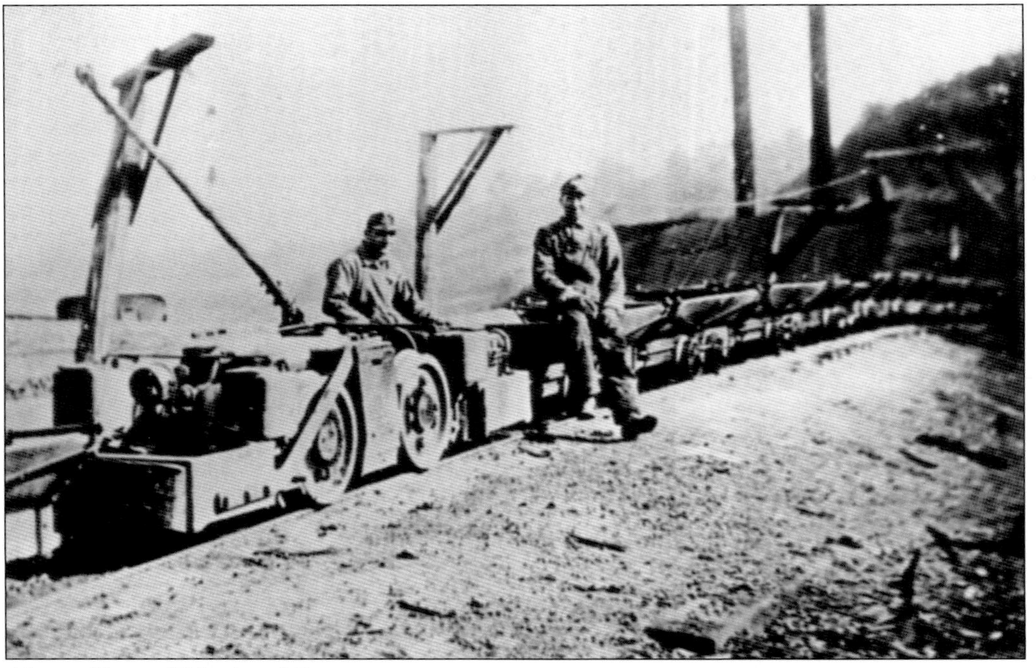

Above, Tanny Oldani and Steve Gornati are aboard an electric motor car, or "mule," used to haul coal cars out of the mine. In the background are the stacks of the engine house, which used coal to generate the electricity for the mines. Most of the Northwest mines were electrified in 1914. This photograph is from the 1930s. (Courtesy of Joan Verbka.)

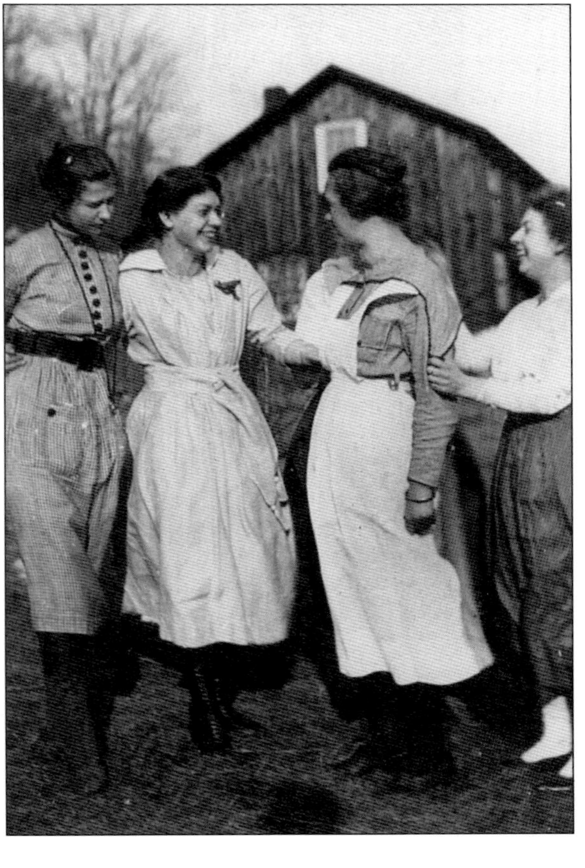

These Coal Hollow ladies in the typical garb of the mining years seem to be having fun in this early 1920s photograph. Skirts started getting shorter after World War I, making work much more comfortable for women. The second girl from the left had the surname of Holtzhauser, and she is the only one who is identified. Notice the unpainted company house in the background. (Courtesy of LeRoy Wolfe.)

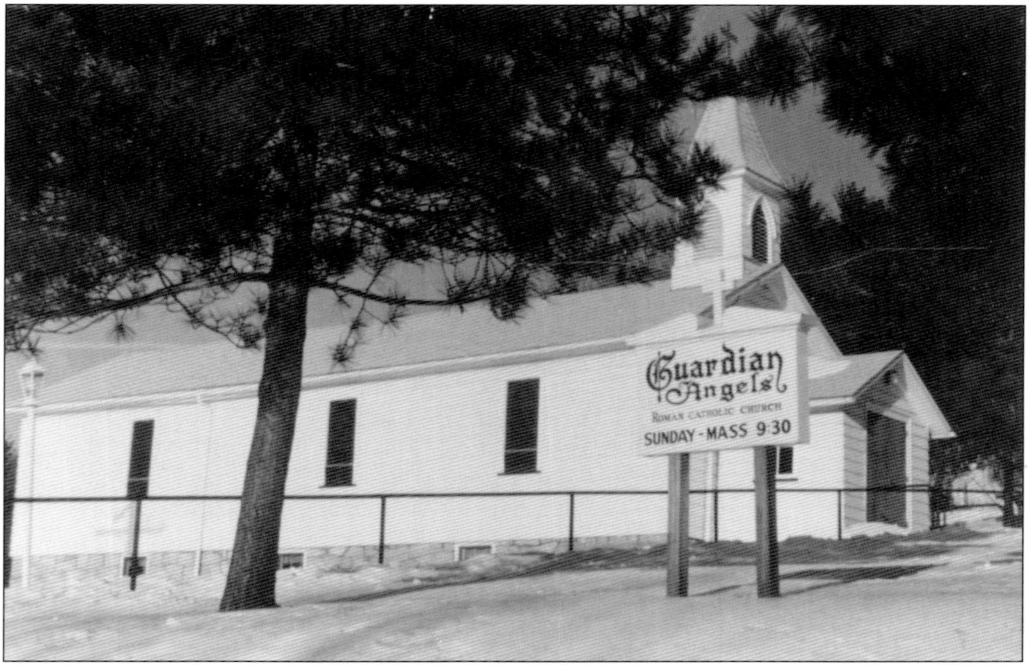

Guardian Angels Church was built under the direction of Rev. George Winkler, beginning in 1910. The old Cross Roads school from Toby was added to the new construction and used as a Catholic school for two years before being rented to the Fox Township School Board for use as a public school. The church closed in the 1980s; today, the building is used by the Guardian Angels Center, a charitable organization.

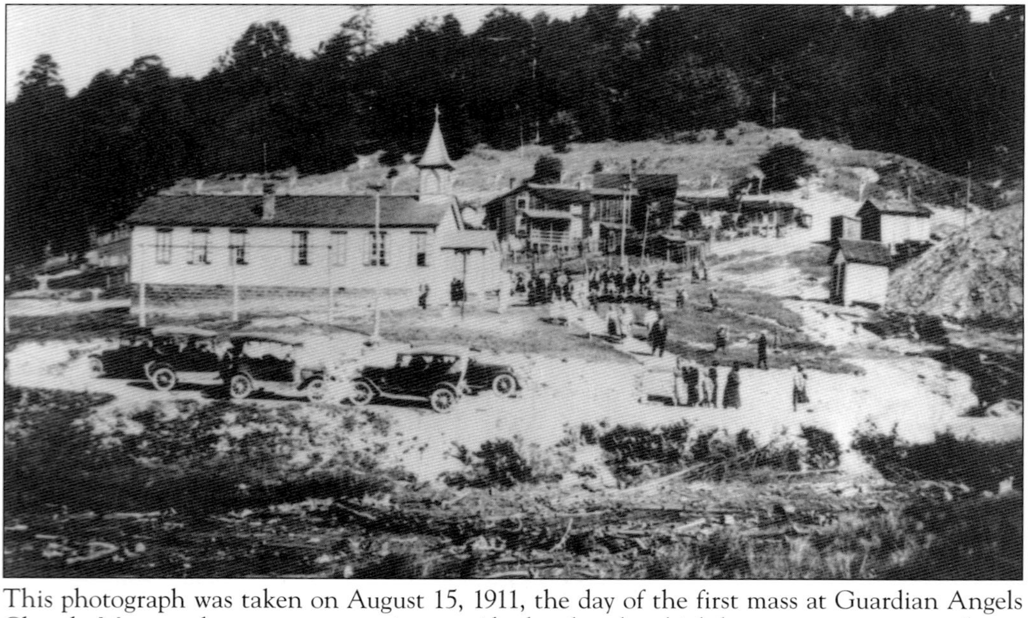

This photograph was taken on August 15, 1911, the day of the first mass at Guardian Angels Church. Men can be seen congregating outside the church, which became a common tradition both before and after services. The church, a mission of St. Boniface, was closed by the Erie Diocese. Today, Coal Hollow Catholics attend mass in Kersey.

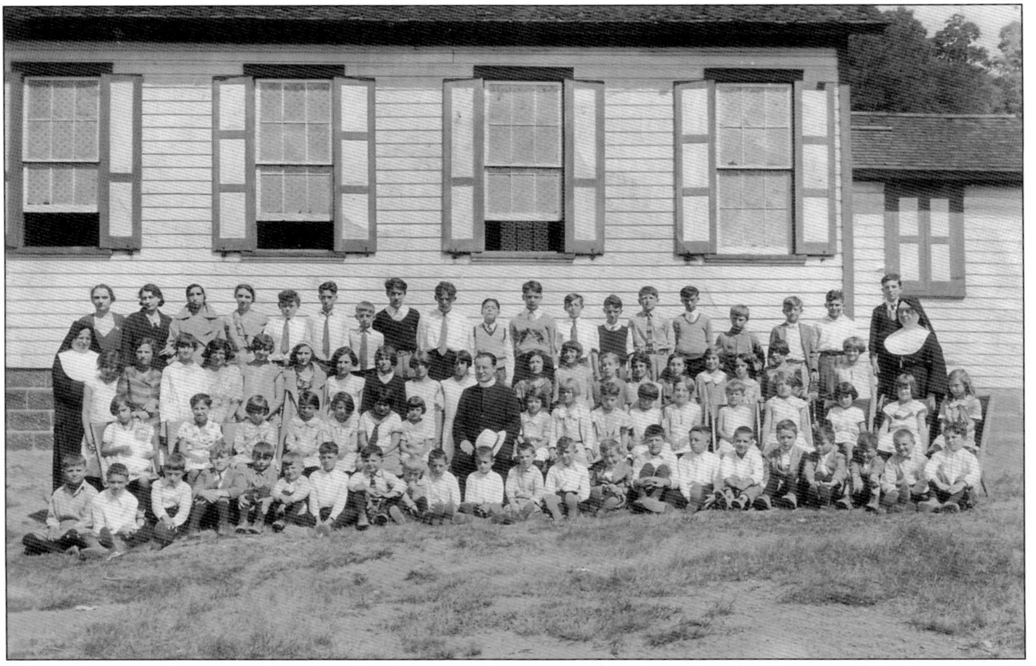

This photograph was taken beside the Guardian Angels Church, which served for a time as a school as well. It was between 1912 and 1914, as the public school system took over in 1915. The priest is Father Winkler (center), and one of the nuns is Sister Madeline OSB. The photograph was taken before the installation of the stained-glass windows.

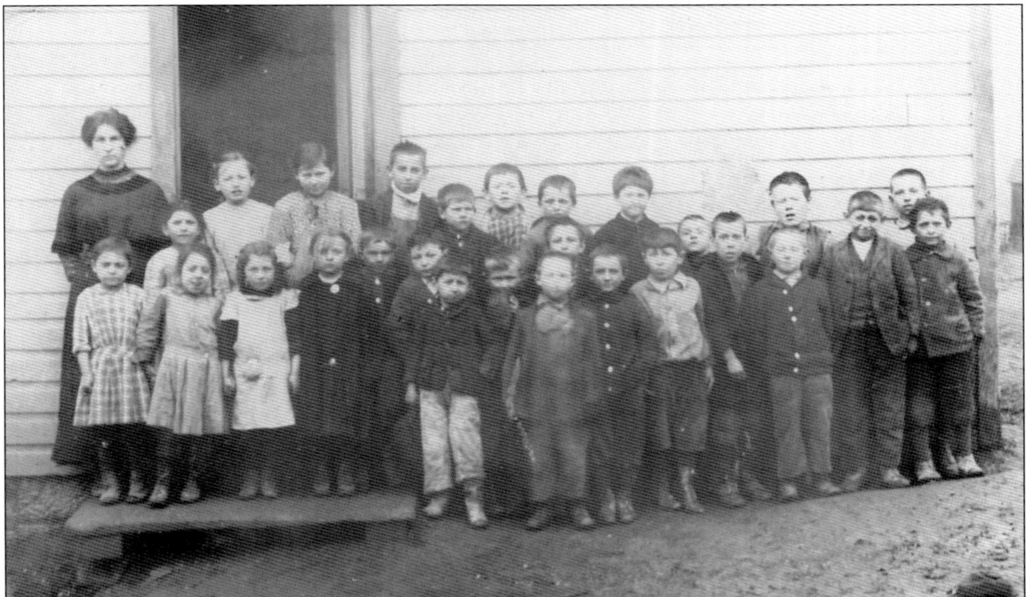

Between 1915 and 1917, the public school board operated the Coal Hollow school. The teacher was Josephine Schreiber, fresh out of Slippery Rock Teachers School, who is seen here with one of the classes. Schreiber and many of the children moved to the Dagus Mines school in 1917. From this point forward, Guardian Angels served just as a church.

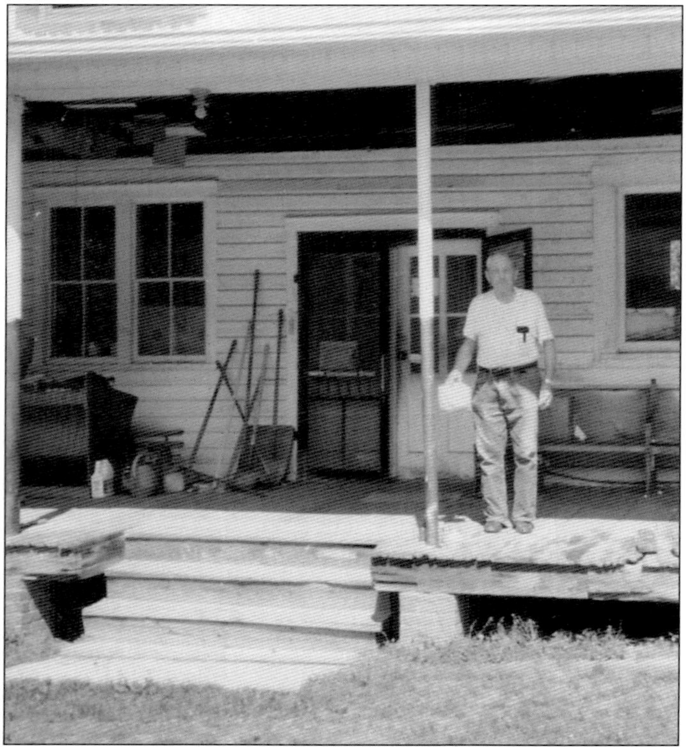

Guildo Lavella stands on the porch of the former company store, which he bought in 1979 and operated until it closed in 1990. The general store served the people of the valley for most of their common needs, as the nearest store was in Kersey and the nearest large store was in St. Marys, 15 miles away. (Courtesy of Hazel Luchini.)

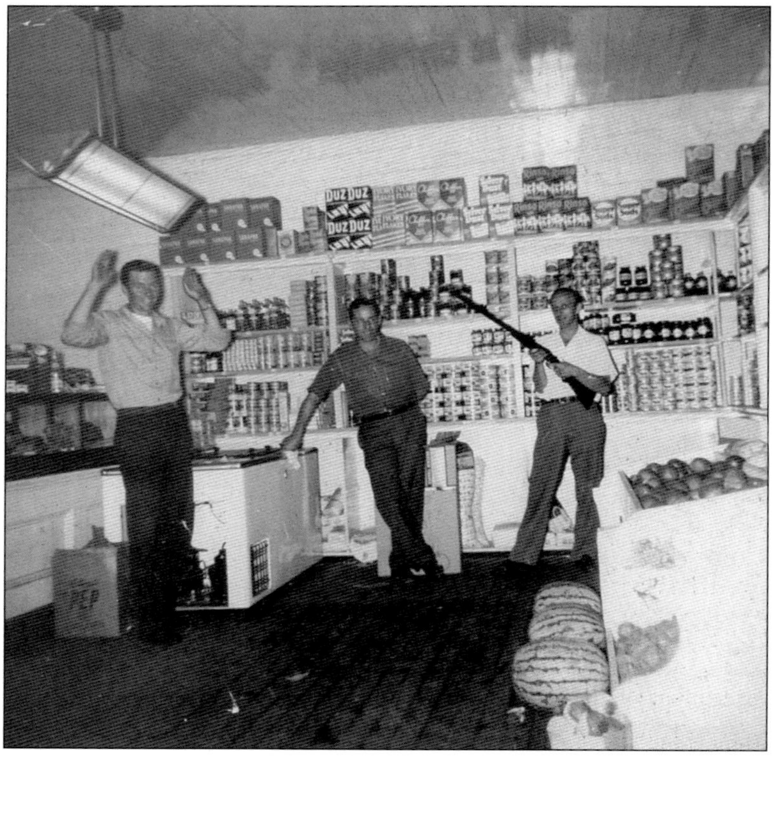

Feigning a robbery inside Lavella's store are, from left to right, John Caimi, proprietor Guildo Lavella, and A. Sicheri, with the gun. The shelves show the kind of products general stores generally carried. From the watermelons on the floor to the Duz, Rinso, and Super Suds on the top shelf, the store tried to provide basic products to Coal Hollow and Toby. Many of the brand names no longer exist. (Courtesy of Hazel Luchini.)

Beginning in 1937, Coal Hollow had an annual homecoming celebration on Labor Day weekend. Seen here is the aerial act of Bernice Weese performing the "spectacular feats of daring" that were a fixture in the celebrations. Music, sports, and games of chance such as balla puda, bocce, and morra were part of the activities. The celebration is no longer held.

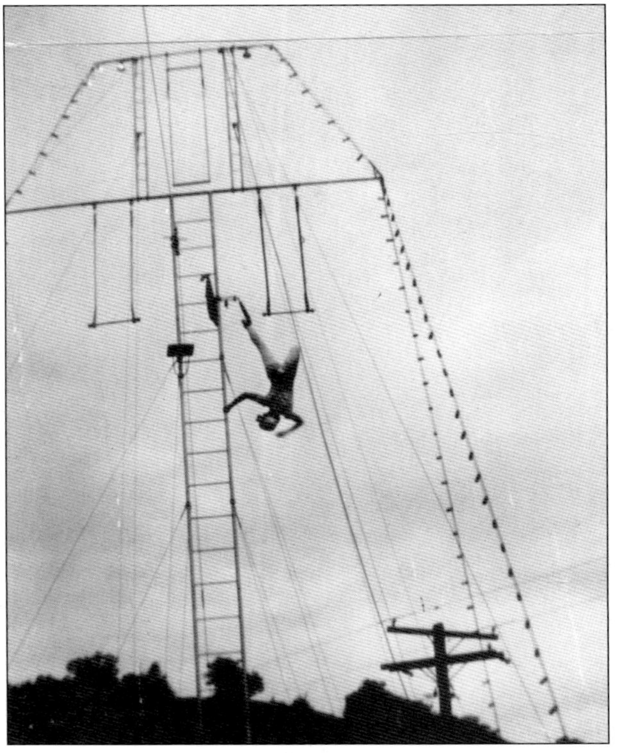

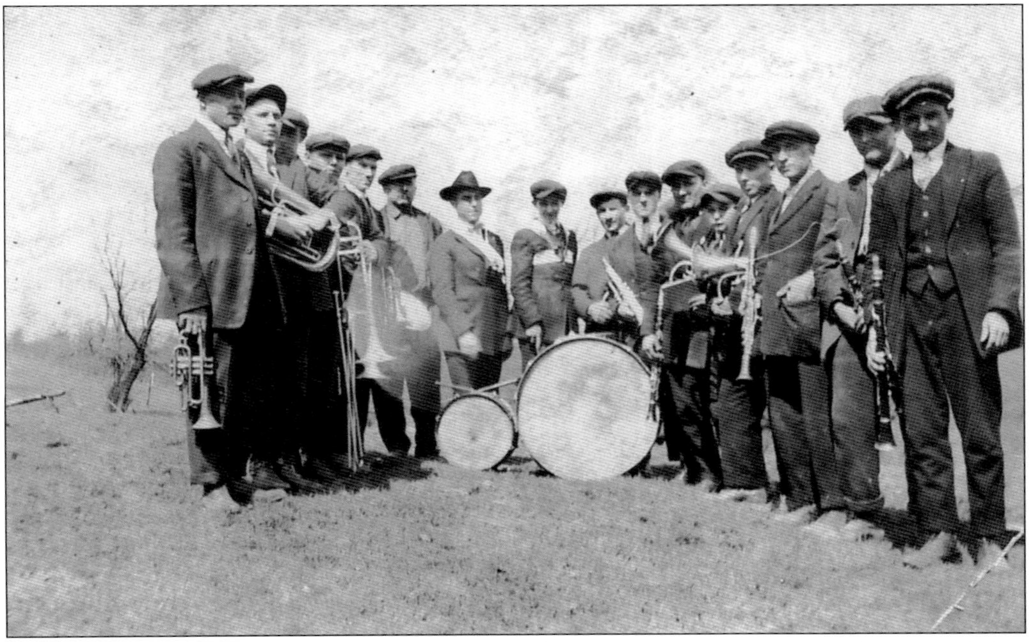

Not to be outdone by Kersey and Dagus Mines, Coal Hollow also had a marching band that entertained for decades. The band was formed in 1909 and played in a band hall on a side hill near South Kersey until the 1930s. This photograph was probably taken early in the band's existence, as they did not yet have uniforms.

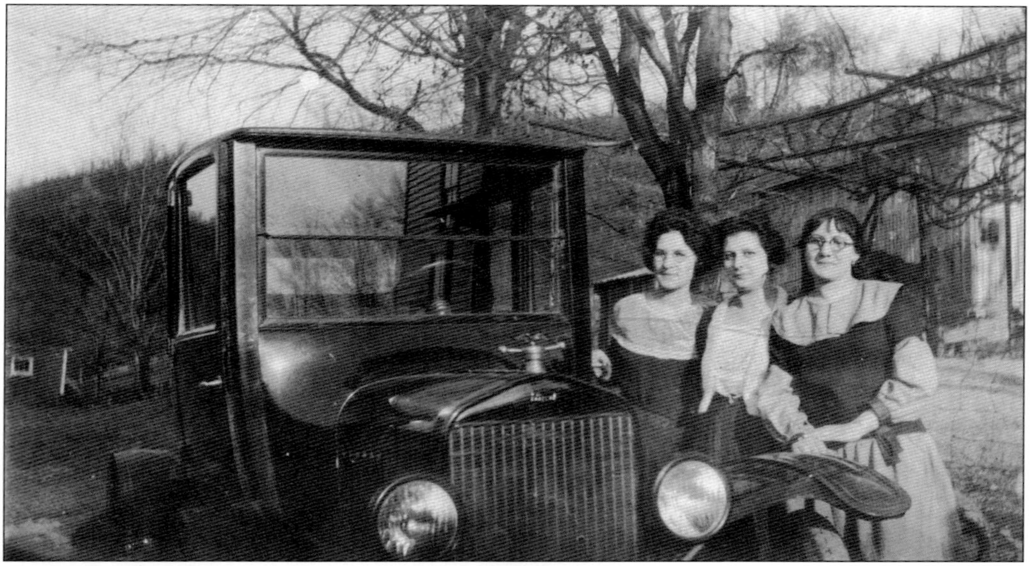

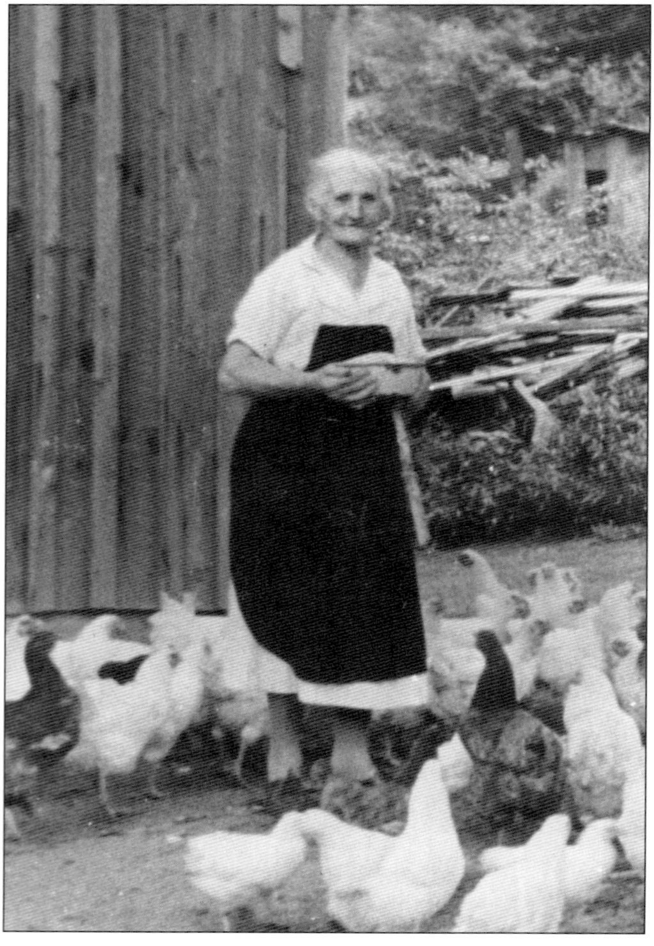

Above, three Coal Hollow girls pose beside a Ford Model T in the 1920s. They are, from left to right, Lena Lavella, Edith Angelo Lavella, and Elvira "Babe" Lavella Glance. Lena was a graduate of Fordham University, a remarkable accomplishment for a woman at the time. The daughter of Italian immigrants, she could speak five languages and served as the hospital and court interpreter. She was the judicial secretary and court reporter for both the 25th and 59th judicial circuits, as well as a leader of numerous boards and organizations. At left, feeding the chickens at her Coal Hollow home is Lena's mother, Esther Carrera Lavella, who emigrated from Bergamo, Italy, as a young girl. She and her husband had nine children: Tressa, Elvira "Babe," Mary, Tom, Lena, Victor, Peter, Rudolph, and Guildo. Two others died in infancy. (Both, courtesy of Hazel Luchini.)

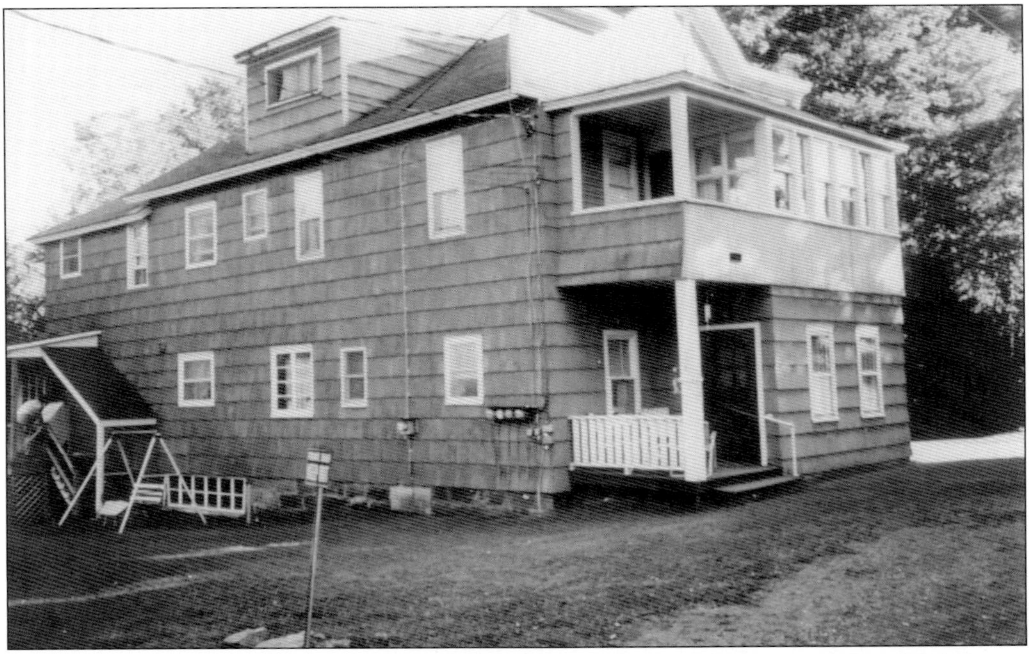

Built in 1895 by Nels and Charles Strandberg, the building above served as the premier store in Toby for many years. It had some of the first telephones, one for local calls and another for long distance. It also had the first gas pump in the valley. The upstairs was used for many community social events. It is seen above after it was renovated into a private residence. At right, a group of young men clown for the camera on the steps of the store in the early 1900s. From left to right they are (first row) Oscar Johnson, Frances G., and Joe Strandberg; (second row) Pearl Moyer and Victor Johnson; (third row) Billy Frantz and Albert Rickard. (Both, courtesy of Ken Anderson.)

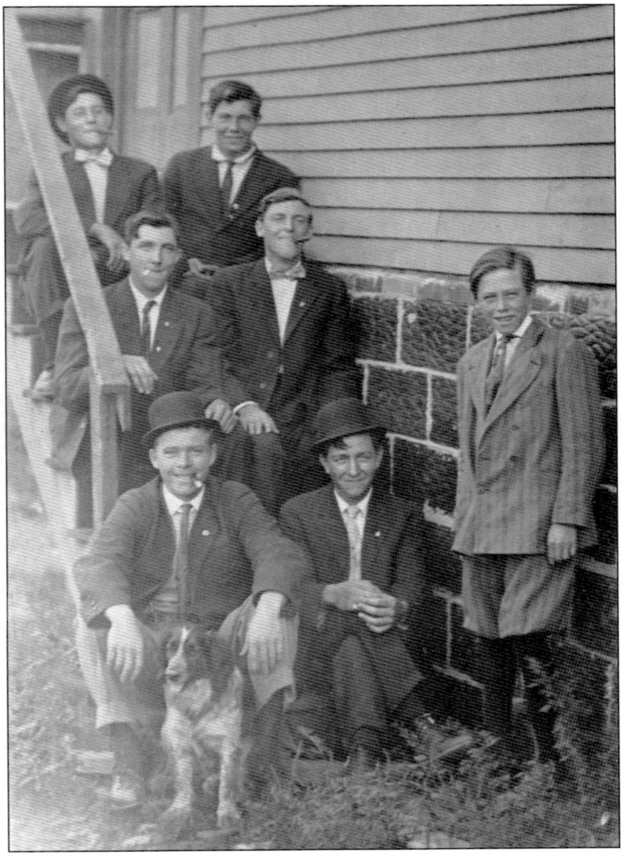

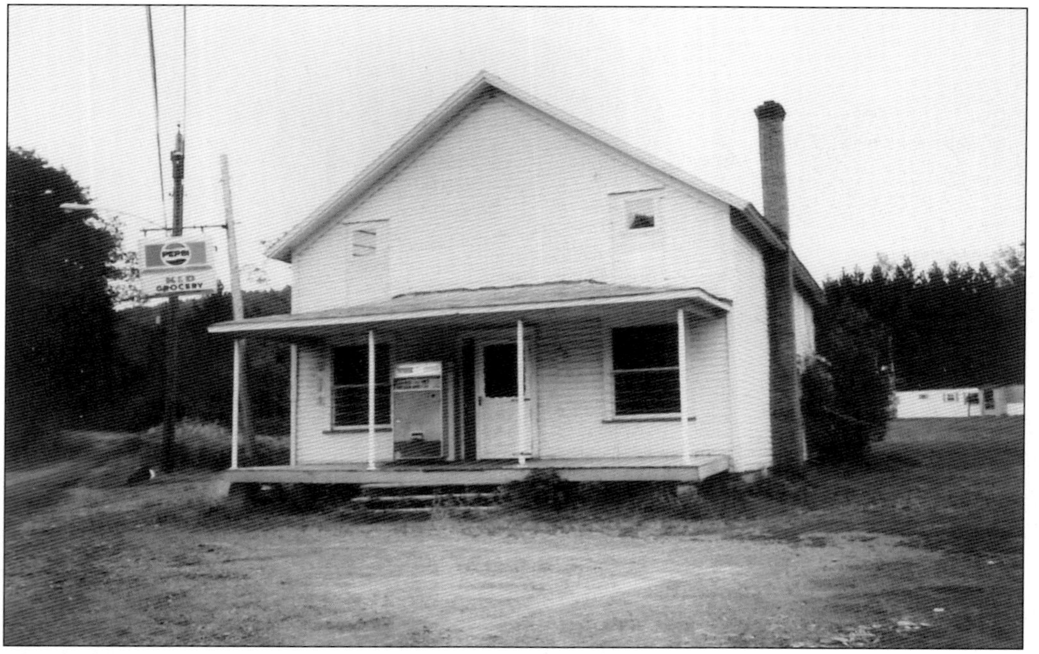

This building was originally constructed in 1890 as the Soderstrom schoolhouse. In 1914, it was purchased by Frank Sicheri for use as a home and a general merchandise store, which he opened in 1920. Prior to refrigeration, Sicheri had an icehouse to keep perishables. His son Gilio sold the business to Denny Guido in 1976, and the store closed in 1989. (Courtesy of Esther Sicheri.)

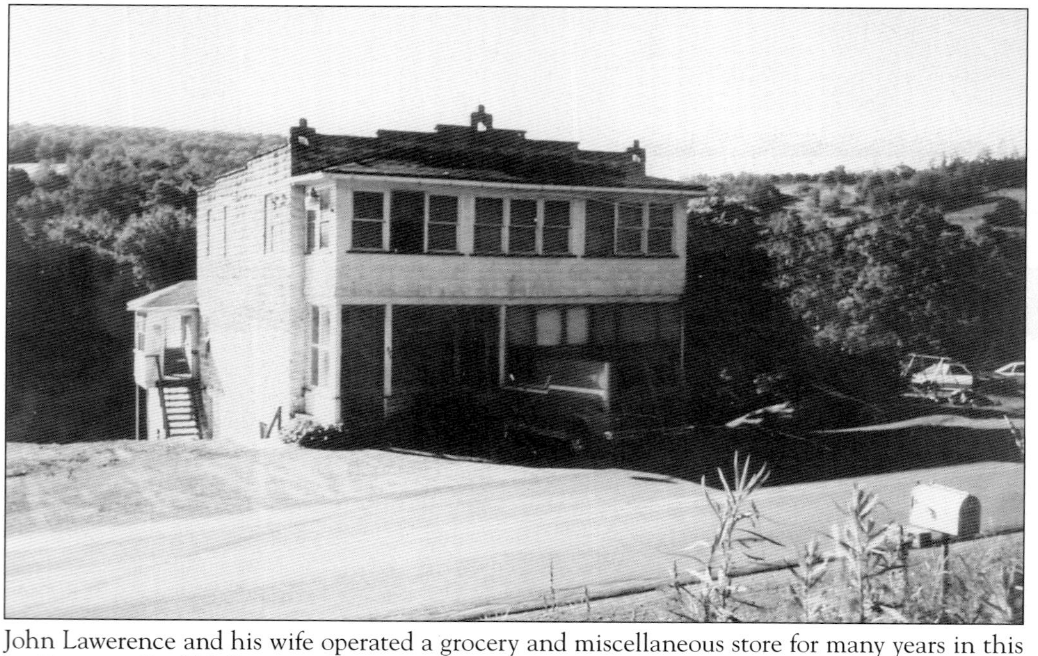

John Lawerence and his wife operated a grocery and miscellaneous store for many years in this building, on Coal Hollow Road in Upper Toby. Later, he sold it to Mr. and Mrs. Salvatore Dasaro, who ran the business for several years before converting it into an apartment building. (Courtesy of Ken Anderson.)

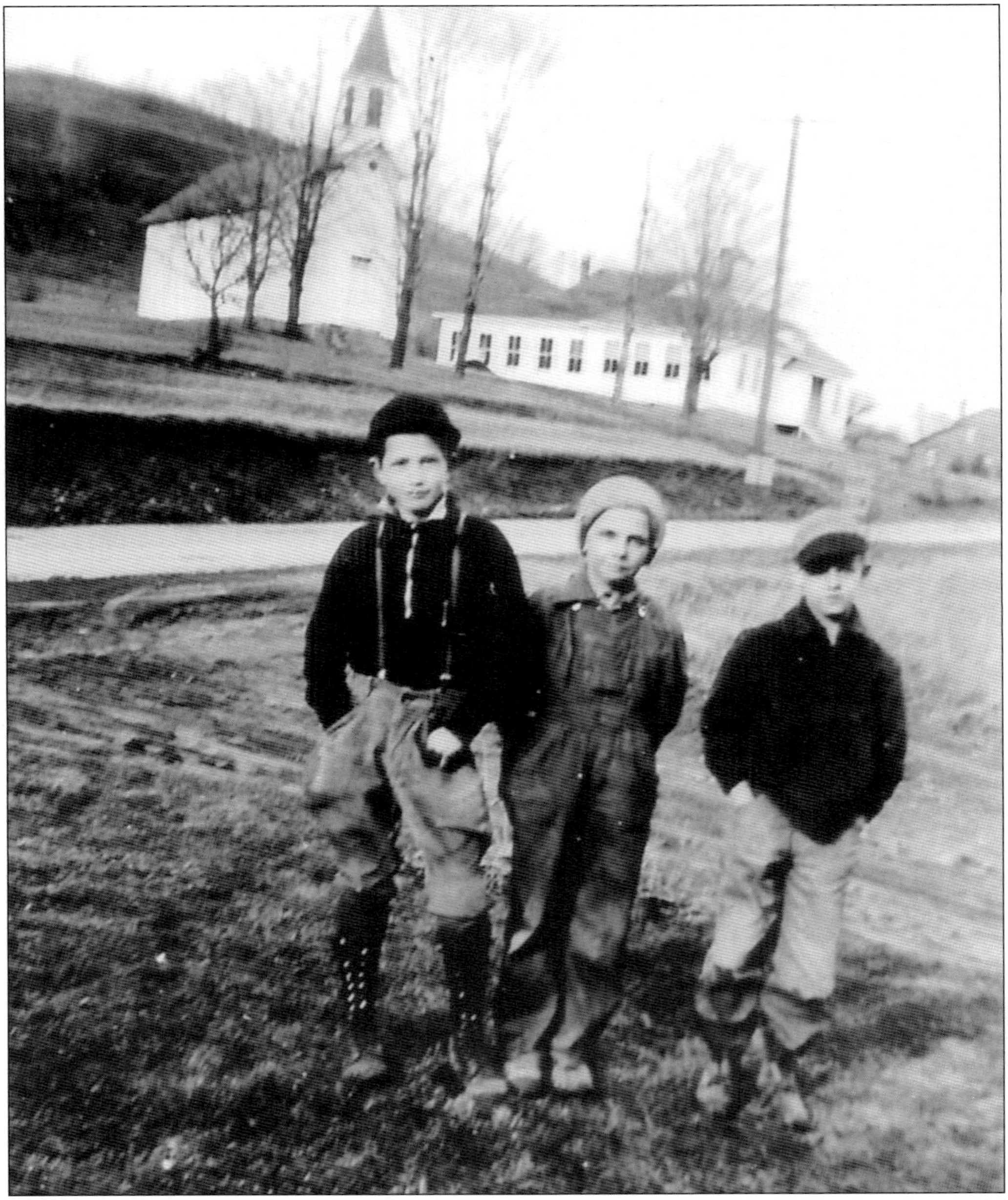

The Toby Methodist Church was dedicated in 1877 and was served by circuit riders from 1846 to 1875. It is the oldest Methodist church in the district. The pastor in 2013 is Joni K. Williams. It has an active outreach program, and both adult's and children's Sunday schools. The four-room Toby School is in the background. It opened around 1914 and was used until 1959, serving grades one through ten. In 1959, students were bused to Kersey and used the high school building until the current Fox Township Elementary School was completed. Teachers at the Toby school included Alberta James, Ellen Hallgren, Elizabeth Iddings, Elizabeth Downs, Bessie Rickard, and Irma Hanson. The school still stands, although it is now hidden behind brush and trees and is in disrepair. From left to right, Leo Bilodeau, Jack Smith, and Jack Moyer are in the foreground of this March 1942 photograph, taken on Moyer's eighth birthday. (Courtesy of Harriet Moyer.)

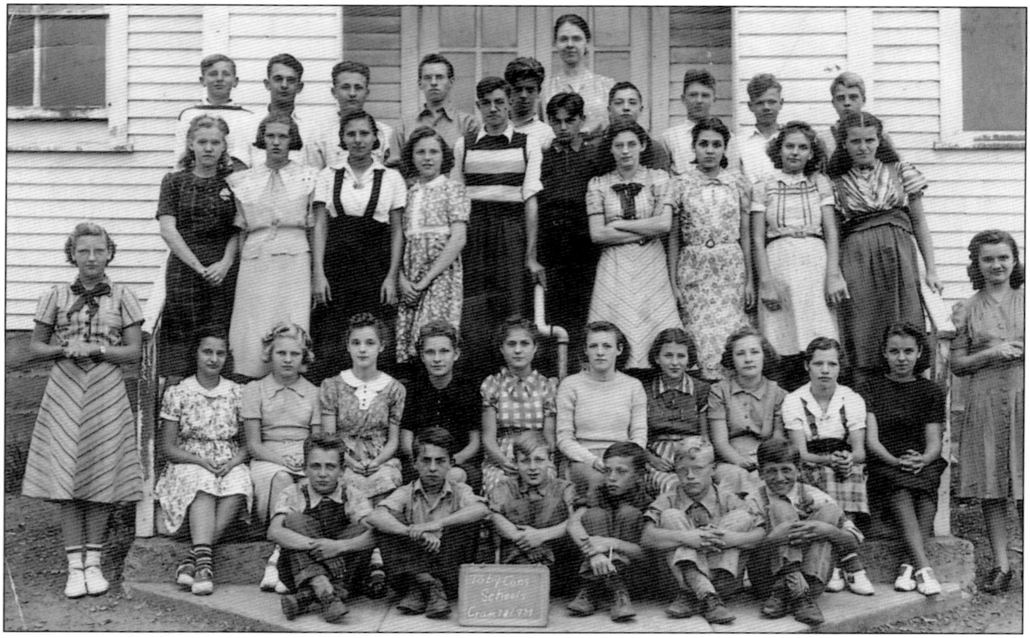

Everyone is in their best clothes for this 1939 school photograph of grades seven and eight. Some of the children are, in no particular order, Bernice Johnson, Gen Quagliani, Annabelle Swanson, Shirley Blick, Evelyn Govenelli, Bruna Christini, Helen Kline, Mae Lindenmuth, Vera Cominotti, Grace Biladeau (Keech), Doris Tamburlin, Adelia Bona, Mary Frederickson, Mae Zuccolotto, and Alice Evans. (Courtesy of Ken Anderson.)

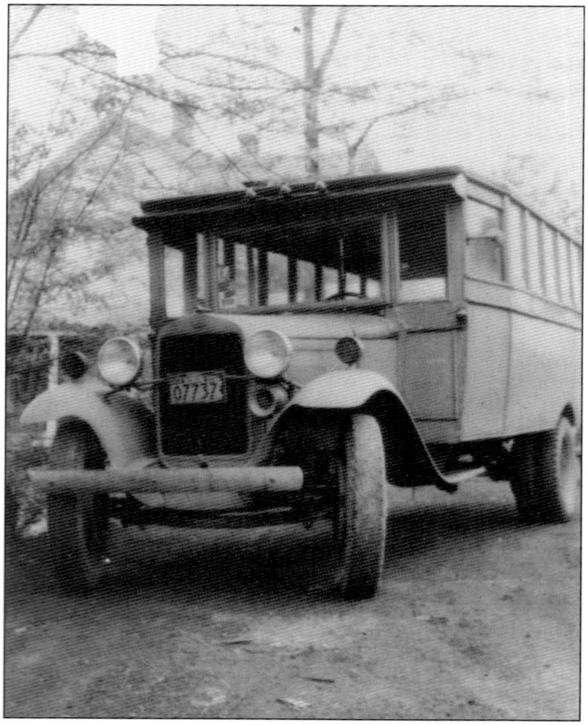

This first school bus in Fox Township was owned and operated by George Swanson and his uncle Charlie. Bus service to Kersey High began in the fall of 1933. Before this, students had to find their own way. Most walked, while others stayed with friends or family who lived closer to the school. This bus also transported miners to their workplace. Swanson family members continue to drive the school bus today. (Courtesy of Anne Swanson.)

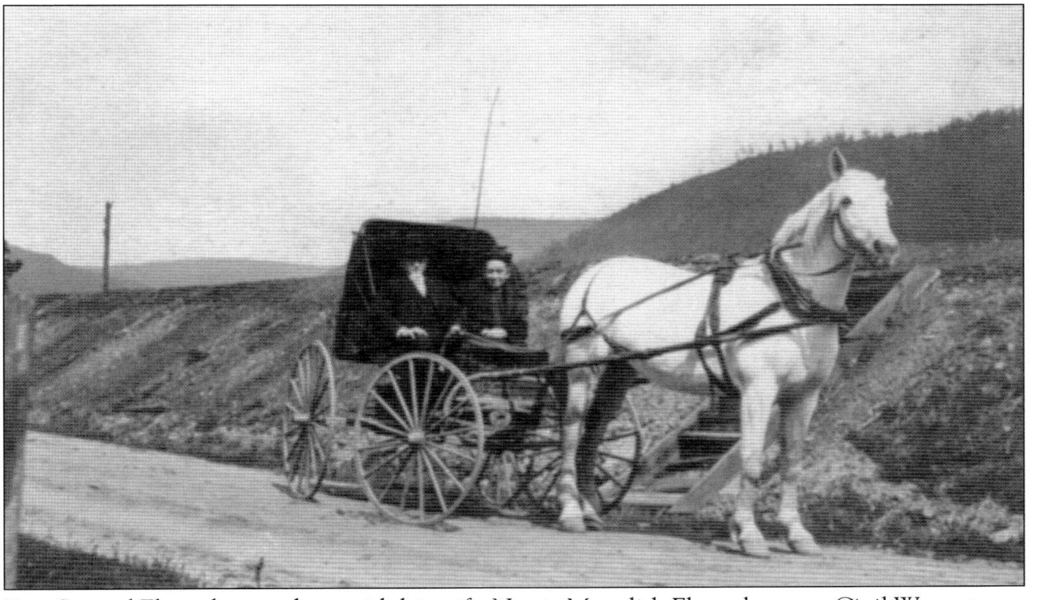

Rev. Samuel Ebersole, seen here with his wife, Nettie Meredith Ebersole, was a Civil War veteran who fought at Gettysburg and a circuit preacher for the Toby Messiah, or Advent Church, located near the current Grange building. This conservative, evangelical branch of the Seventh-Day Adventists practiced full-immersion baptism in Toby Creek. The church closed in 1918, three years after this photograph was taken. (Courtesy of Barb Pistner.)

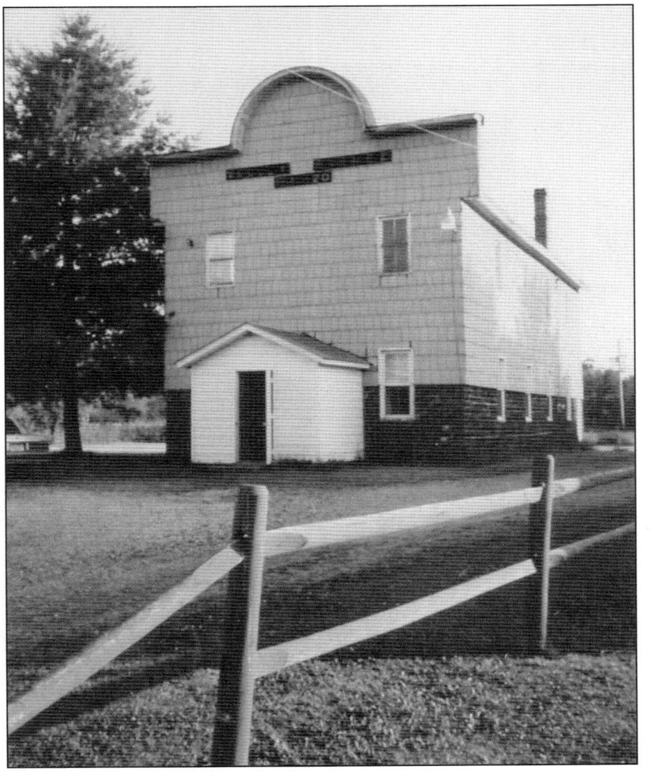

The Toby Grange was chartered in 1909 and was active until the end of the 20th century. Throughout its existence, it provided many services to the community, including raising money to plant 100,000 trees in Toby Valley. Scouts, Little League, the Junior Conservation Club, and many other community-wide organizations used the building. Halloween parties, dances, and a host of other activities took place there over the years.

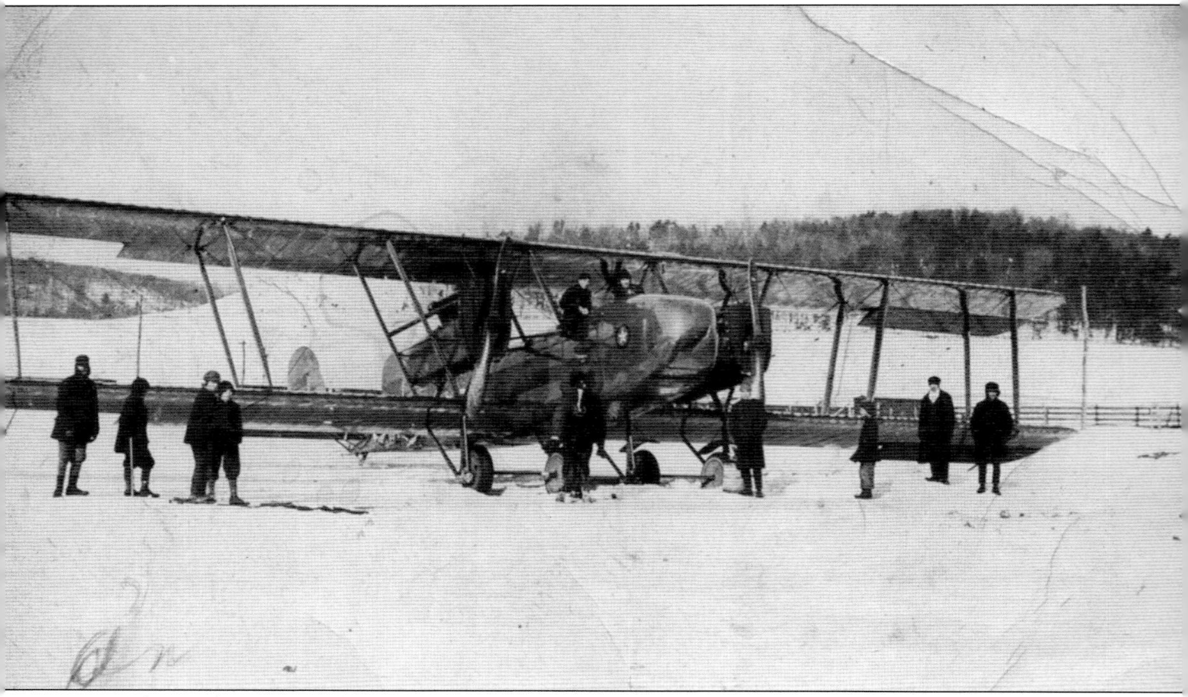

Toby residents were thrilled when this Martin bomber made an emergency landing in the winter of 1919–1920. It was designed for World War I, but entered service too late, and was probably one of the six converted bombers bought by the US Postal Service for some of the first airmail flights over the Appalachian Mountains between New York and Chicago. The bulbous nose was adapted to carry the mail. During that winter, rough weather claimed four of the planes, and the air service stopped using the remainder of them, so they were only in operation for one year. Airmail pilots knew this area as "the graveyard of the Alleghenies" because of the difficult flying conditions. Numerous crashes occurred, and lives were lost. The undulations of the hills and valleys caused unpredictable up-and-down drafts that left the pilots of the low-flying biplanes little time to react. (Courtesy of Esther Sicheri.)

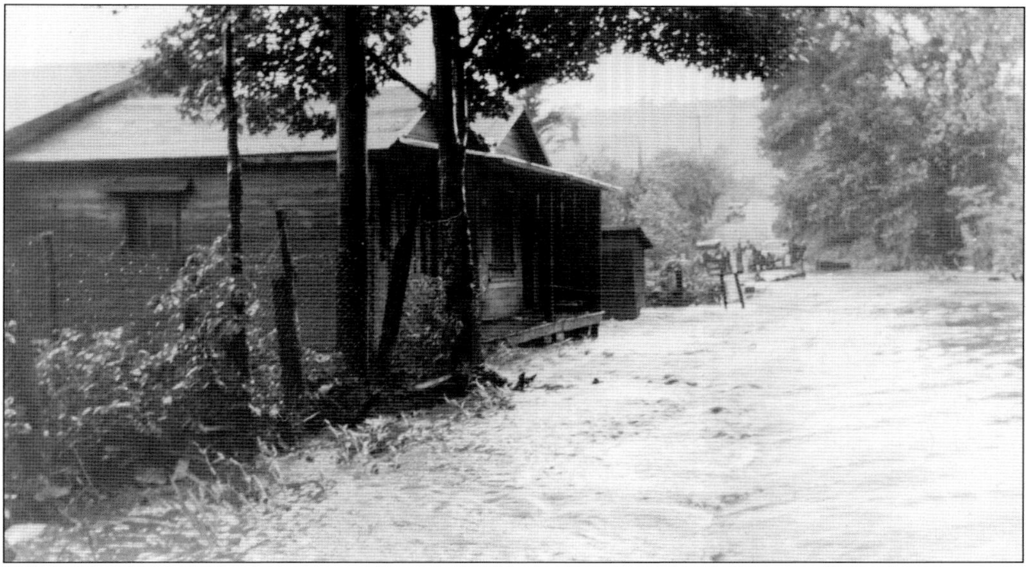

Because the hillsides were denuded of trees, almost any major storm could bring about a flood. These photographs show the Upper Toby area of Coal Hollow Road, below Limestone Hollow, after one of those storms on August 10, 1937, when the Little Toby Creek overflowed its banks. The Grange helped pay for trees to replant the hillsides, which had been left bare by strip-mining. In the 1960s and 1970s, Boy Scout Troop 94 and the Junior Conservation Club helped plant them. However, due to re-strip-mining, there was another flood in 1989; otherwise, flooding has been rare. (Both, courtesy of Esther Sicheri.)

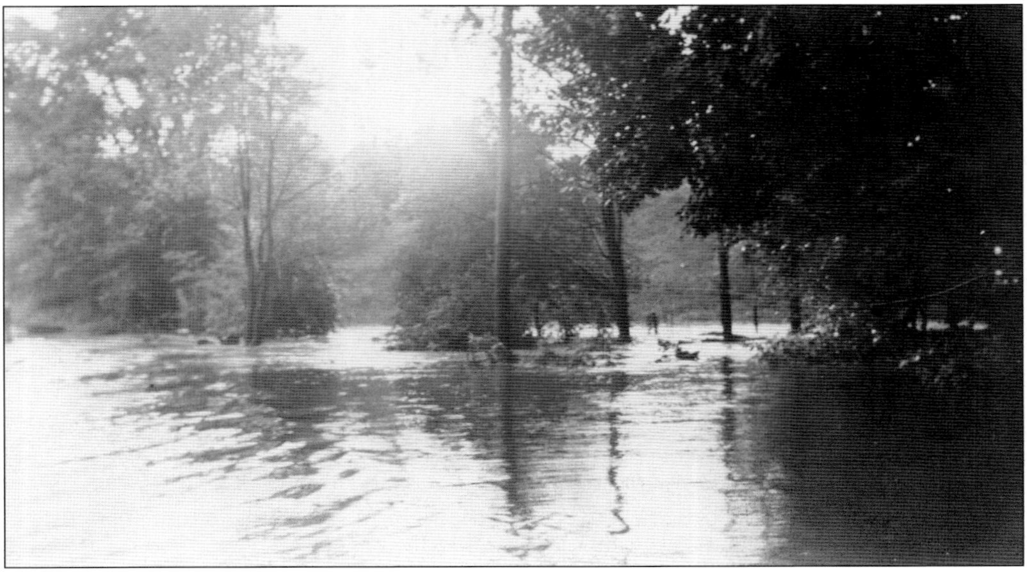

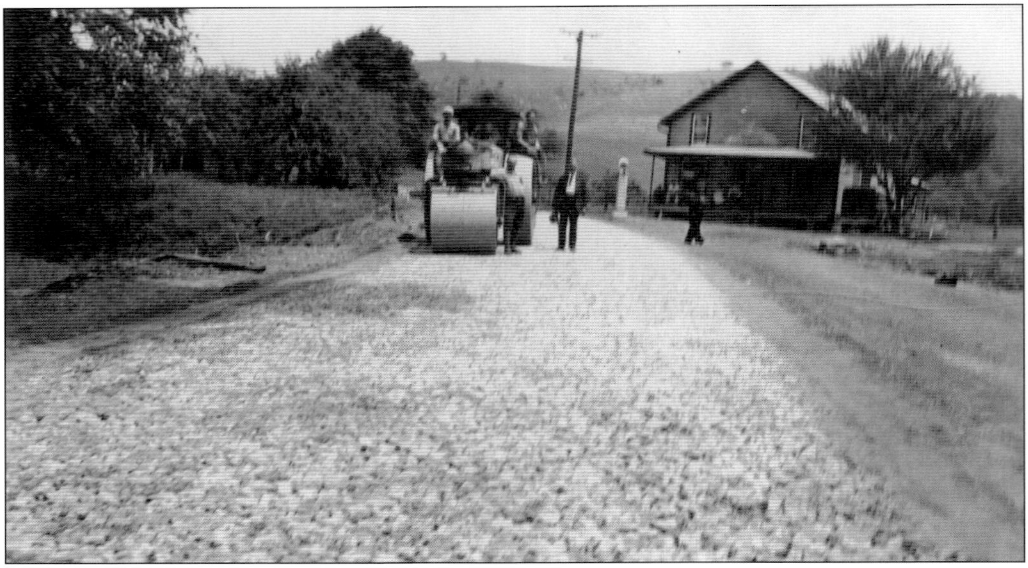

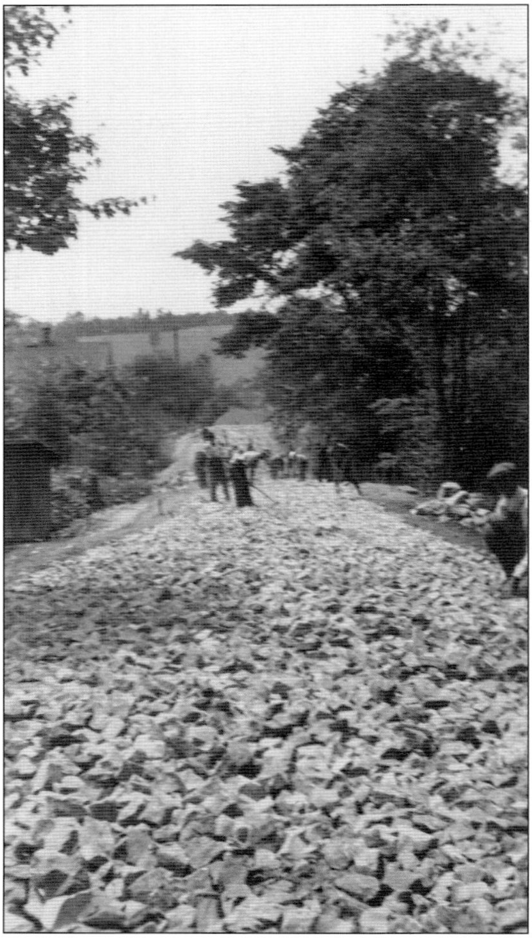

In the 1930s, Gov. Gifford Pinchot wanted "to get the farmers out of the mud." This led to the building of rural roads throughout the state. The photograph above shows the paving of Toby and Coal Hollow Roads in 1938. Most of the work was done manually and with local labor, as an effort to create jobs during the Depression. It was backbreaking work, as seen at left with men breaking the gravel with sledgehammers and hand tamping. A total of 7.6 miles of road in the Toby Valley were built in this fashion, at a cost of $36,800. Sicheri's store is in the background above, with its gas pump visible. (Both, courtesy of Esther Sicheri.)

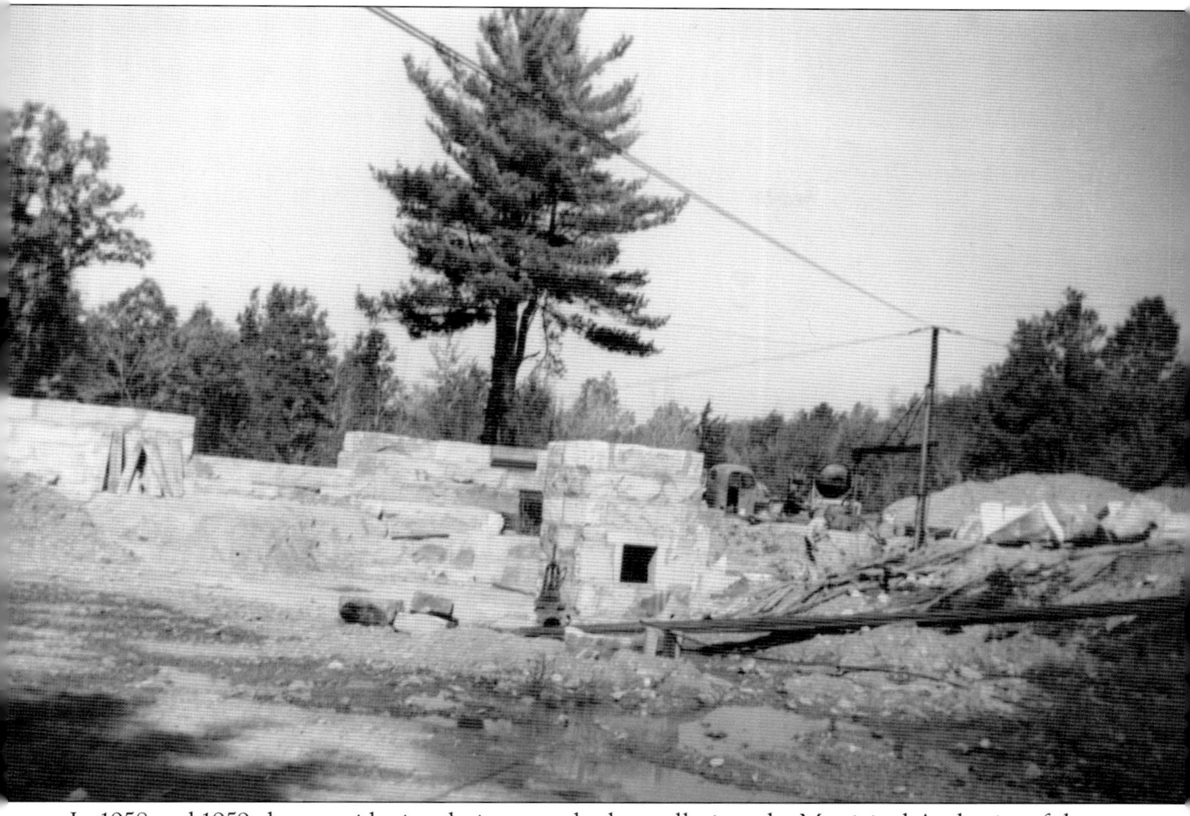

In 1958 and 1959, due to acid mine drainage and other pollution, the Municipal Authority of the Township of Fox built the Toby Valley water system, which included a dam and pipelines on 200 acres of Lost and Sawmill Runs. Each able-bodied man was asked to donate 50 hours of labor to the project. The residents of the valley owned the authority. There was some doubt that the community could do it, but $35,000 was raised by selling bonds and a $1,000 grant was donated by the Sears, Roebuck Foundation. The dam has been enlarged twice, and the gravity-flow system is still in operation. It was one of the first water systems to incorporate plastic pipe in the underground lines. The Fox Township supervisors took over billing in 2009, when the flat fee was dropped and bills became based on gallons of water used. (Courtesy of Harriet Moyer.)

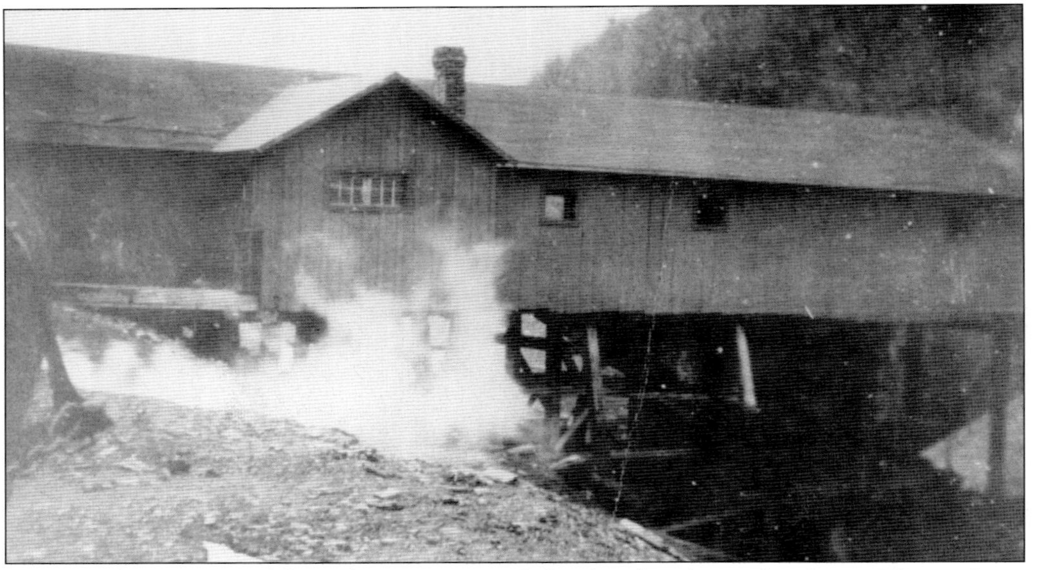

When coal was removed from the mine, it needed to be placed in railroad cars. The coal was originally hauled from the mines using mules, but starting in the early 1900s, electric cars hauled it out. The mines used tipples to load the railroad cars, with the coal tipped into the cars waiting underneath. This tipple closed in the mid-1940s. (Courtesy of Harriet Moyer.)

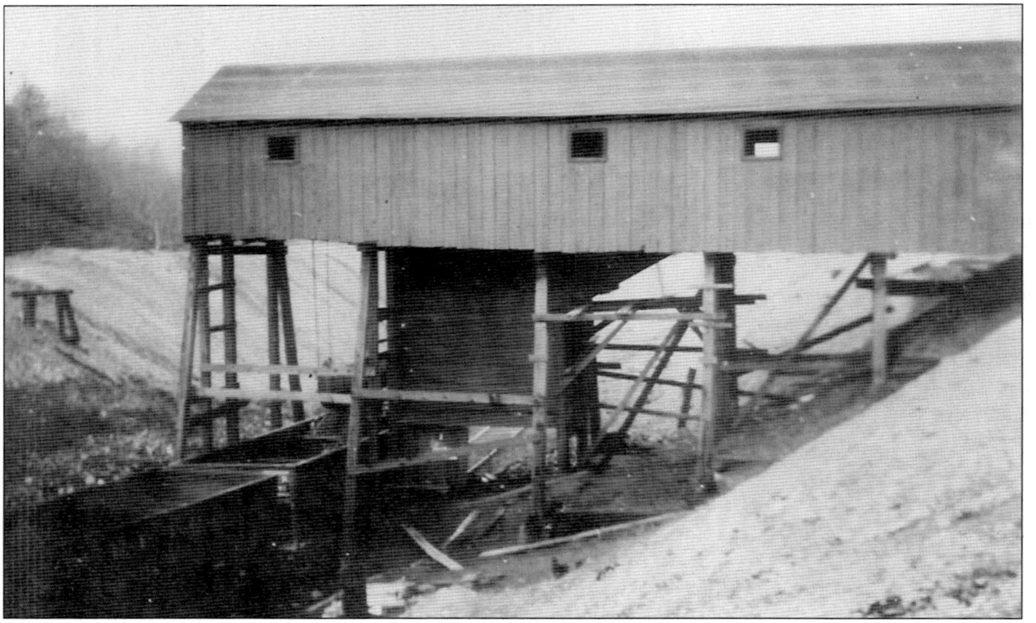

Tipples and headings were numbered in order from one to nine. Many of the mines in Fox Township were drift mines, which followed a seam of coal on a hillside. Each had its own heading. The seams were often discovered as outcroppings. This is the last load of coal taken out of the No. 3 heading, on October 31, 1924. The deep mines of Toby and Coal Hollow gradually "played out" or became less profitable. After World War I, as demand and prices fell, Northwest started closing mines and moving operations to their other, more efficient locations. In 1949, the last mine ceased operation, ending an era. (Courtesy of Harriet Moyer.)

Limestone Hollow was named for a six-foot outcropping of limestone. In fact, coal may have been accidently discovered there by Judge Kyler while he was quarrying limestone to use for burning in hive ovens to make lime for farmers' fields. Coal is still mined in that hollow, using open-pit methods, nearly 200 years later. (Courtesy of Harriet Moyer.)

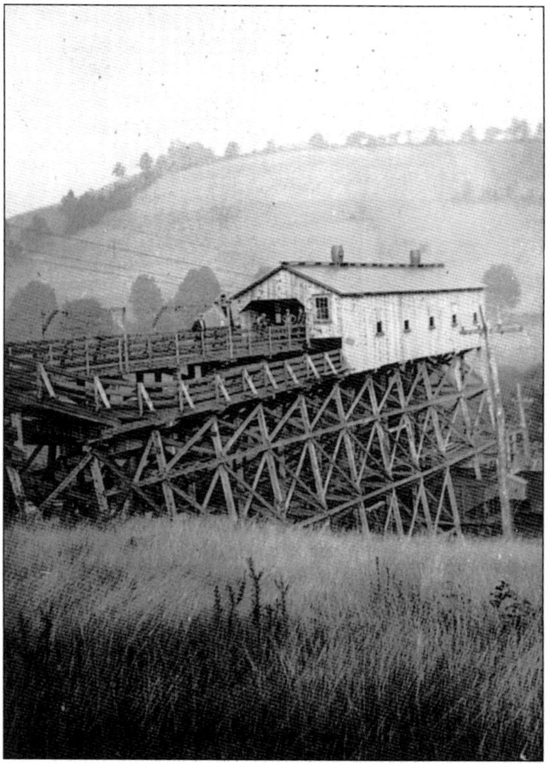

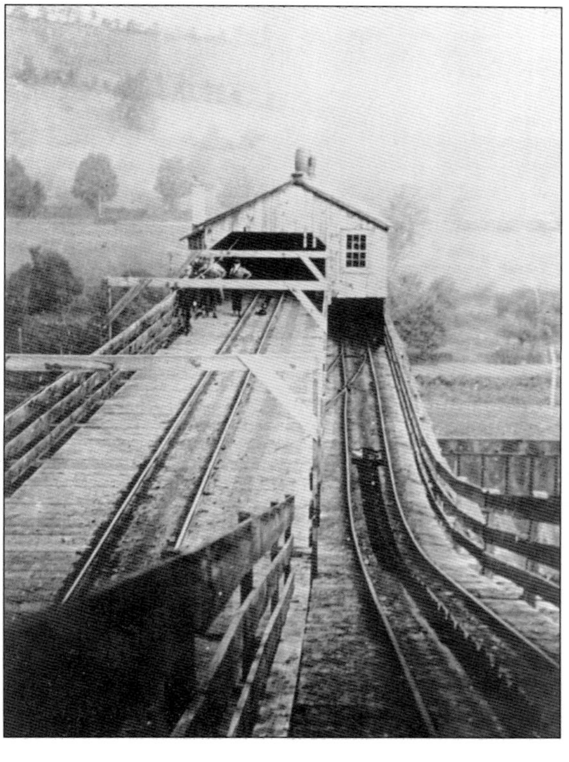

Looking down the incline of the Limestone tipple, this 1920s photograph shows weigh man Harry Caimi on the right. Weigh men were very important, as a large portion of a miner's pay depended on how much coal they mined and loaded. Each miner put a metal tag that had his number on the loaded car, and was then credited tonnage by the weigh man. (Courtesy of Harriet Moyer.)

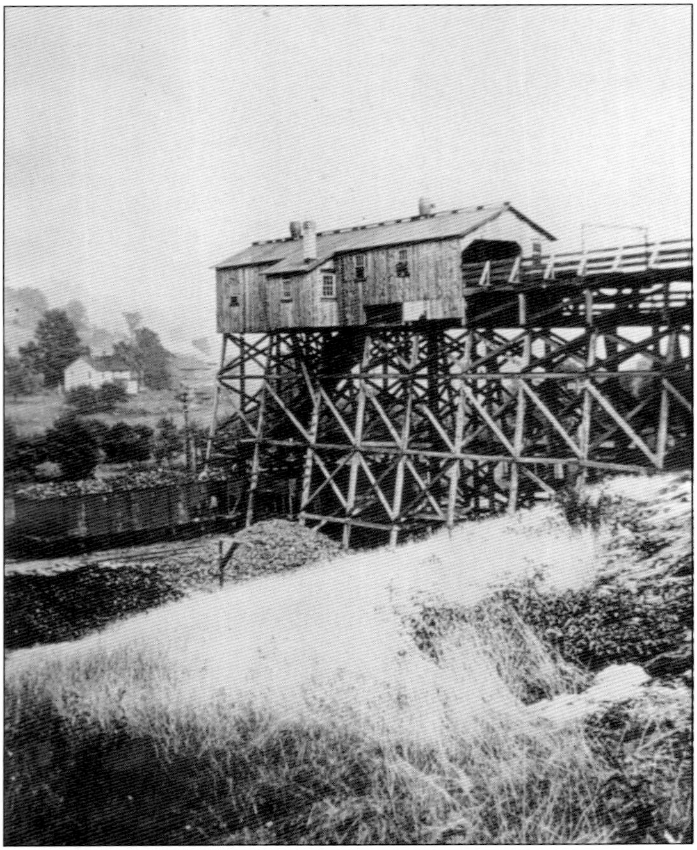

Another view of the Limestone tipple, probably taken after the mine closed, this photograph shows the size and extent of the construction that needed to be done at each of the headings and tipples. Coal from Coal Hollow traveled underground to get to this tipple. Toby Valley is in the background, as well as a nice home. (Courtesy of LeRoy Wolfe.)

The cable suspension bridge below ran from the mouth of the Limestone mine to the tipple. All the coal coming from the mine crossed it using motorized, and later, electric, coal cars. This bridge became a site for Sunday afternoon excursions that amazed the adults and delighted the children, who would climb and swing on it. (Courtesy of LeRoy Wolfe.)

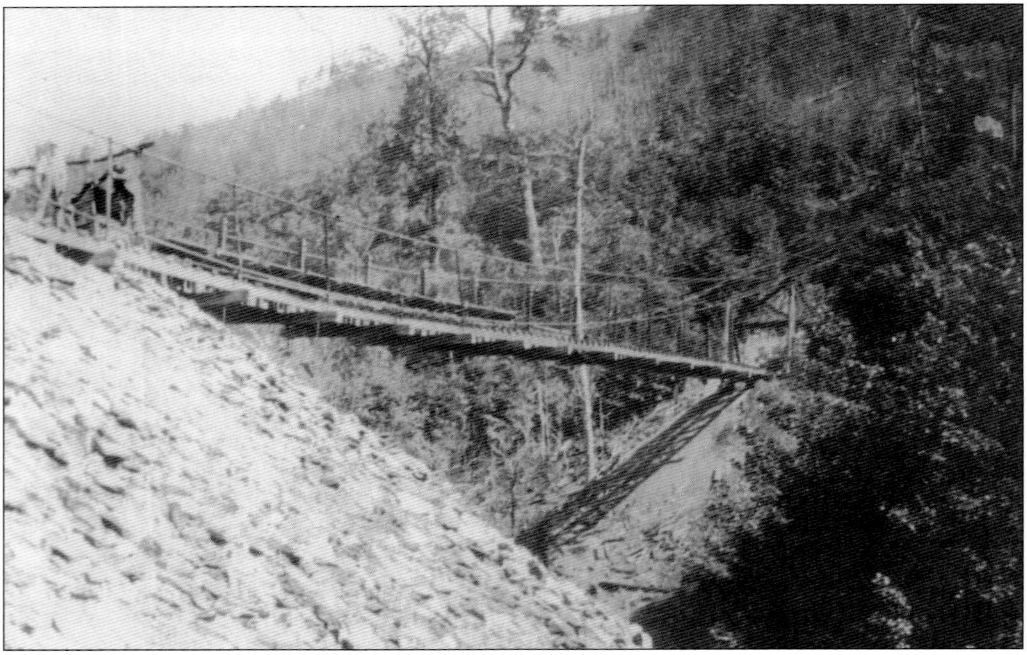

A load of coal cars emerges from the suspension bridge on its way to the Limestone tipple around 1938. Notice the operator on the front of the cars. At their peak, between 1910 and 1920, the Toby and Coal Hollow mines averaged about 1.1 million tons of coal annually. (Courtesy of Harriet Moyer.)

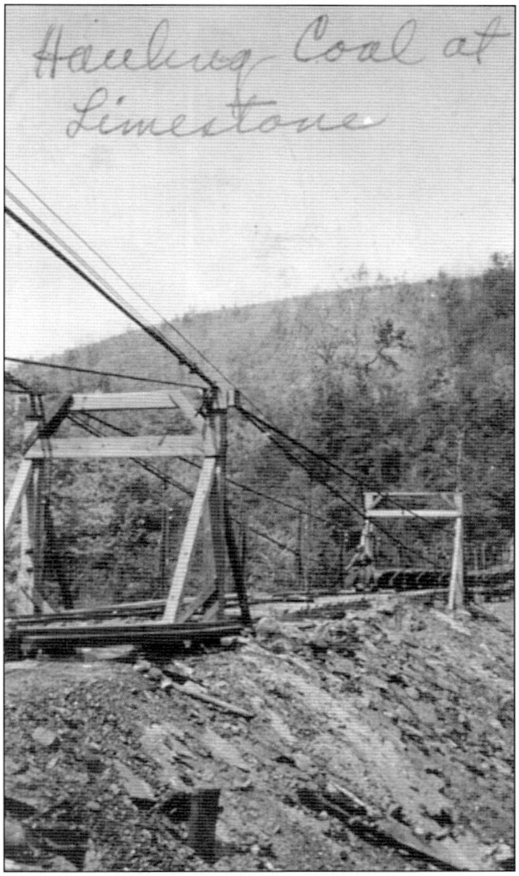

The building below provided electrical power for the mines in the Coal Hollow/Toby Valley area. Currently, that same area includes a mine-acid treatment plant, which attempts to reduce the acid content of Limestone Run and Little Toby Creek and return the streams to a pristine state. The public-private partnership has been very successful, and much of the Little Toby is again supporting aquatic life. (Courtesy of Esther Sicheri.)

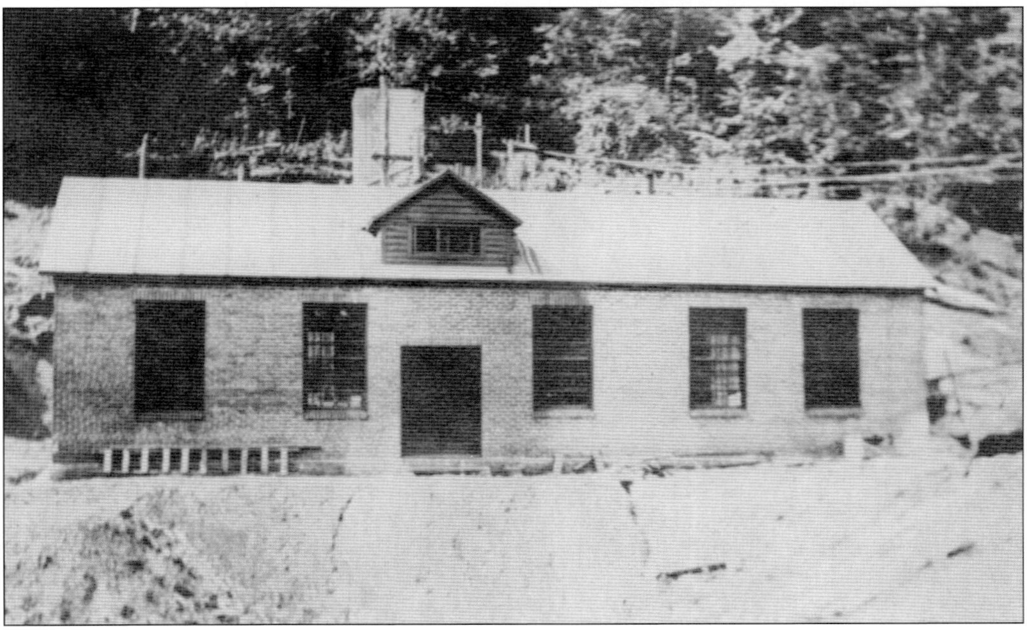

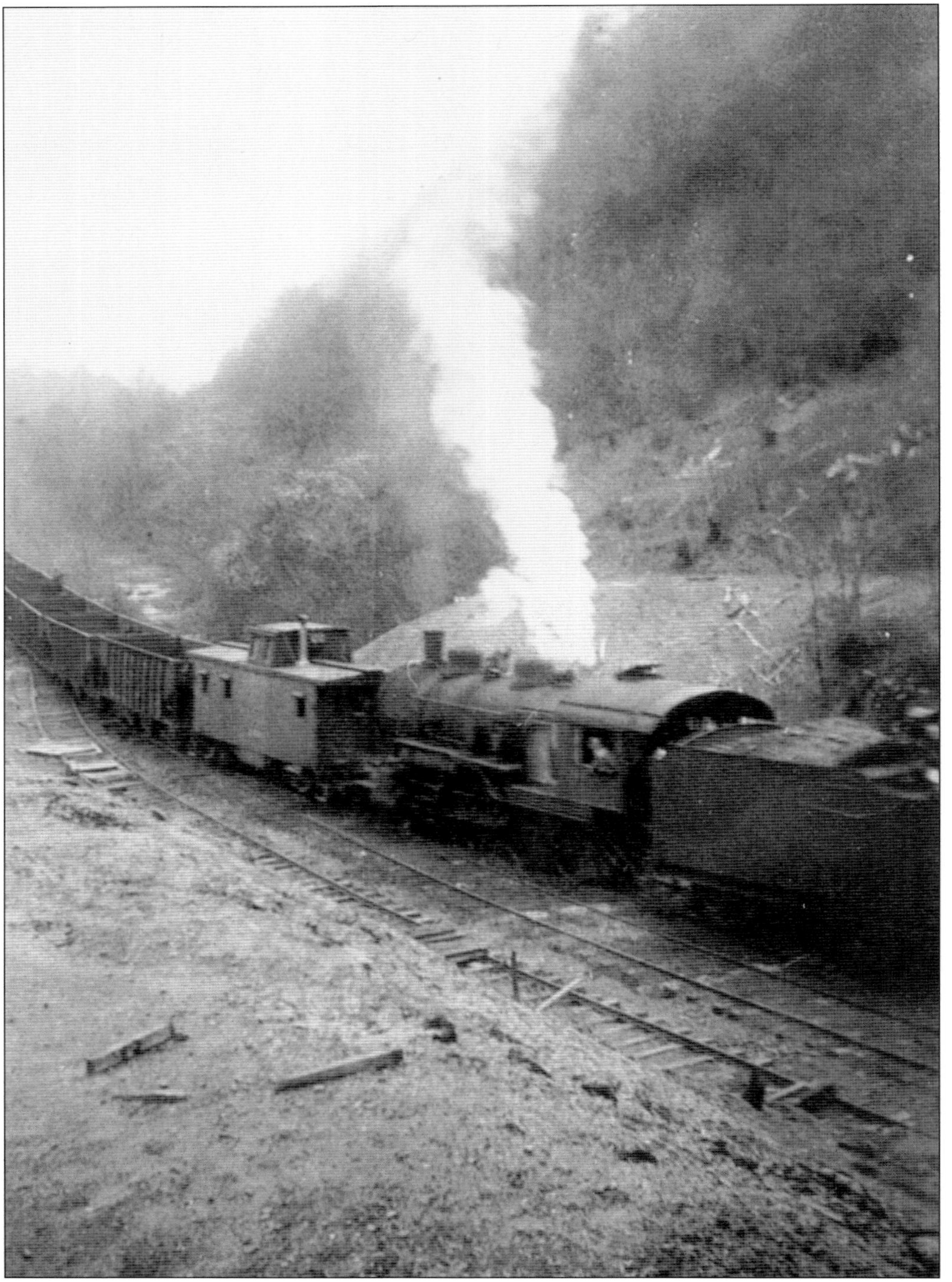

A train of Shawmut "empties" returns to Toby Valley from Brockwayville. In 1900, three trains a day made the 11.4-mile trip to the main line in a little more than an hour. In September 1887, a total of 3,500 loads of coal had made the trip. The line was abandoned in the 1970s. (Courtesy of Joan Verbka.)

Four

Other Areas of Fox Township

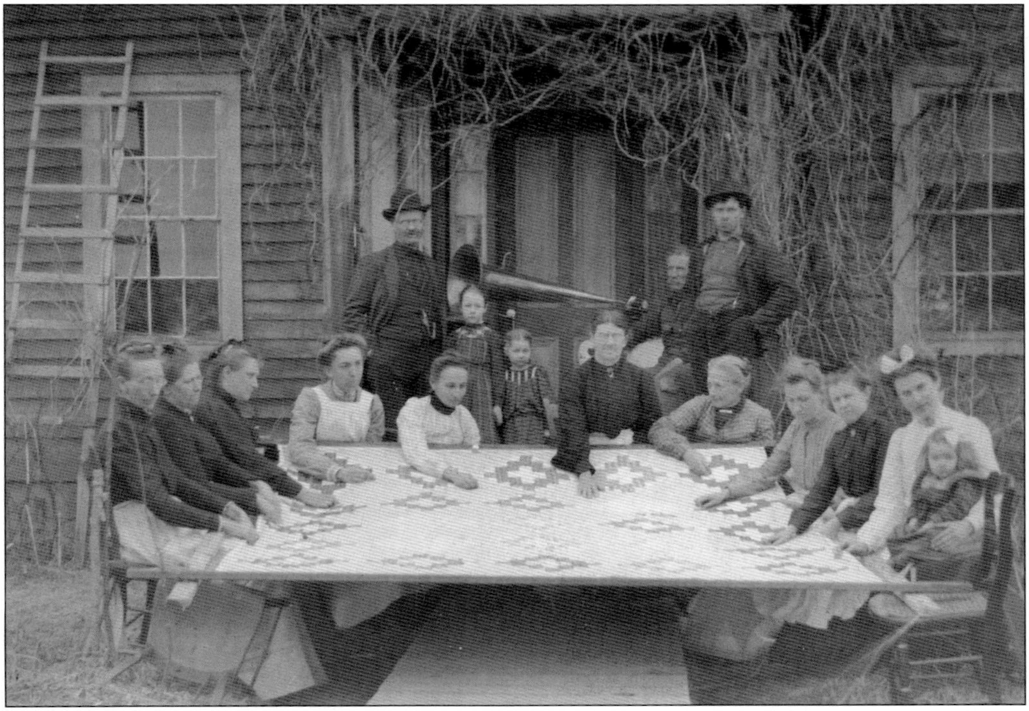

South Kersey was the location of some of the first and most prosperous farms in Fox Township. This photograph shows a quilting bee on one of the Meredith family's farms in South Kersey around 1900. The Merediths are the descendants of Elijah Meredith, the patriarch of one of the township's first families. Socializing often revolved around work. Here, there is a gramophone in the background providing music for the ladies. (Courtesy of Ken Meredith.)

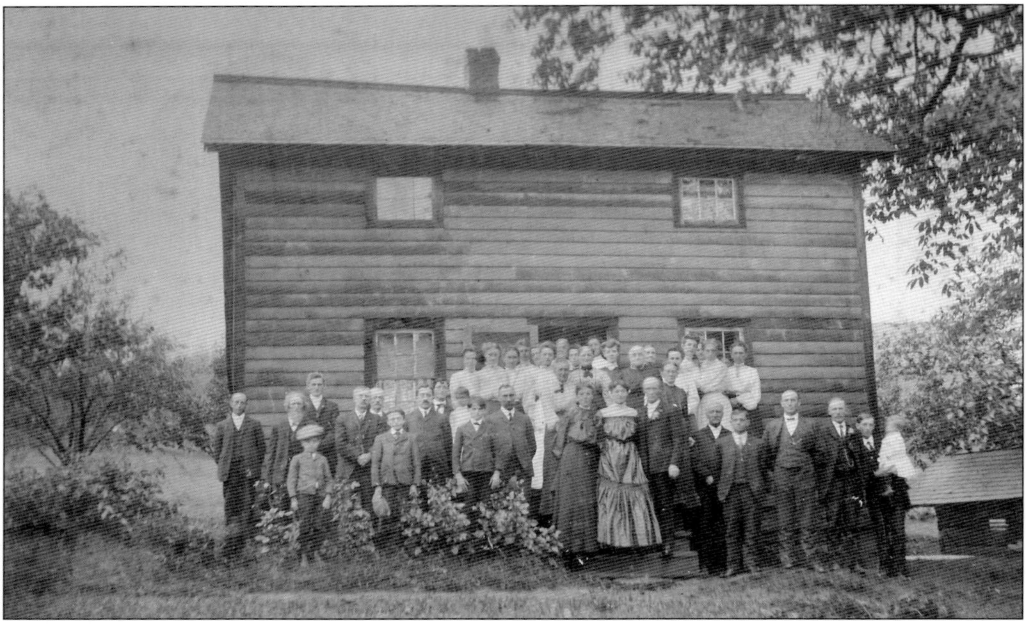

The wedding of Harry Meredith and Mable Case was at Case's grandparents' home, between Greens and South Kersey Roads, in 1903. The home no longer exists, but it is typical of log homes that were later clad with wooden siding. Today, Charlene Armstrong, a descendant of these newlyweds, and her husband, Bob, live in Mable Case's parents' home, on the corner of Meredith and Chicken Hill Roads. (Courtesy of Charlene Armstrong.)

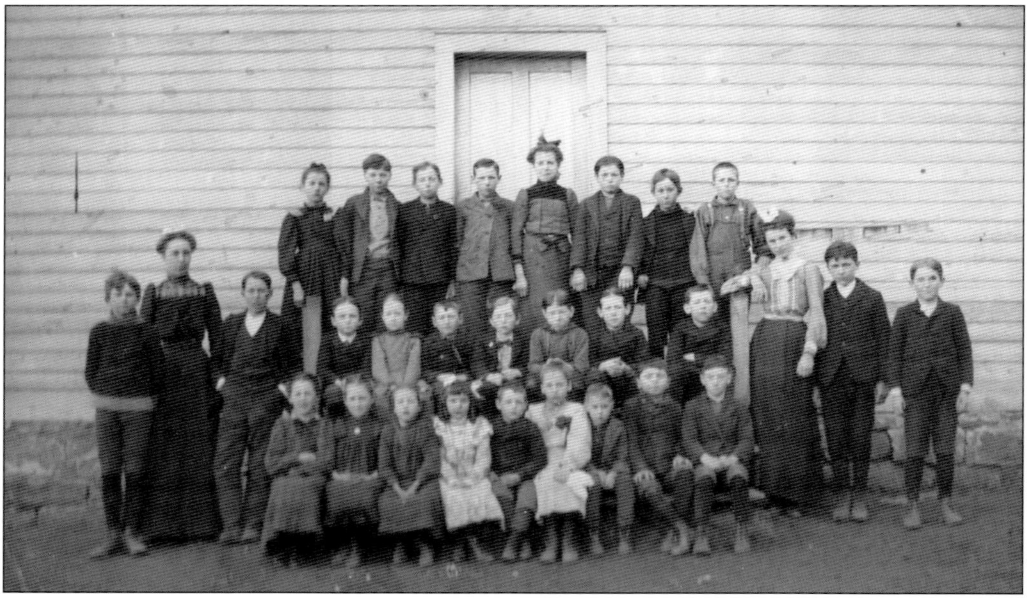

At one time, there were as many as six schoolhouses in South Kersey and Boones Mountain. These South Kersey schoolchildren posed for this school photograph with their teacher, Margaret Meredith Whammond. Some of the students' surnames were Lipsey, McMeeken, Huston, Sidlinger, Menod, and McKluskey. Most of the students are young, as there was not as much need for a higher education beyond learning to read, write, and do basic math. (Courtesy of Ken Meredith.)

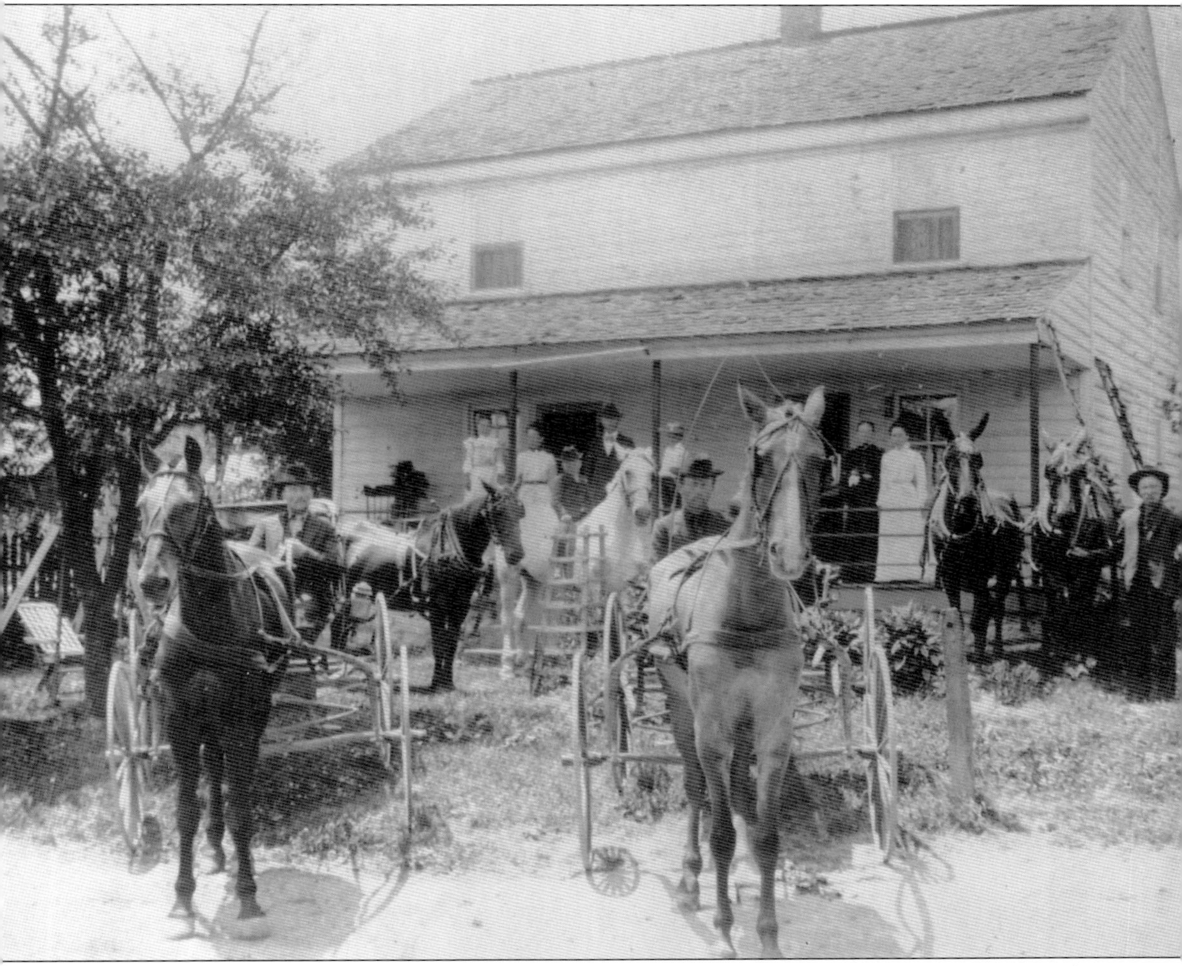

Taken in 1906 at the Meredith homestead on Chicken Hill in South Kersey, this photograph shows descendants of two of the oldest families in the township. Holding the mules on the right is James Reesman Meredith, and his wife is in black to his right. In the buggies are Will (left) and Harry Meredith. The Elijah Meredith family arrived in 1813–1814. Elijah, who may have been as old as 50 at the time, arrived with nine nearly adult children. They cleared and made farms of most of the South Kersey area, just outside of present-day Kersey and Dagus Mines. His descendants have lived in the township longer than any other family, and still own and farm some of the land, though most of it has been sold. The Reesman families arrived in 1818, settling near the present Koch farm, at the intersection of South Kersey and Boones Mountain Roads. (Courtesy of Ken Meredith.)

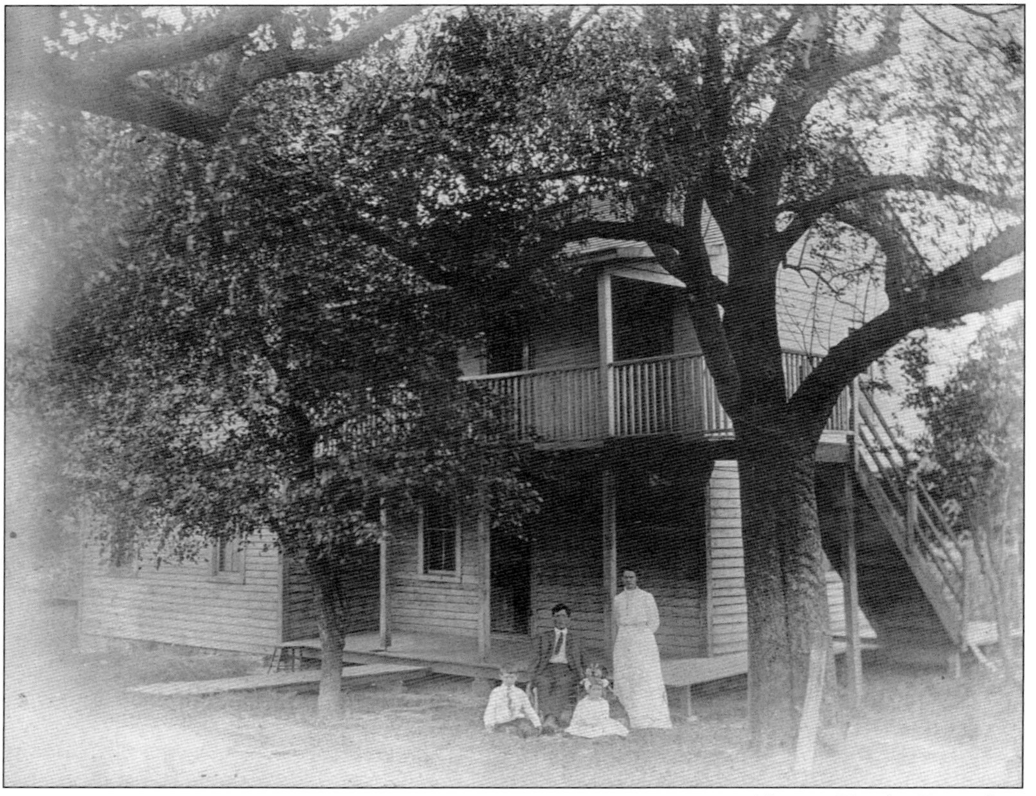

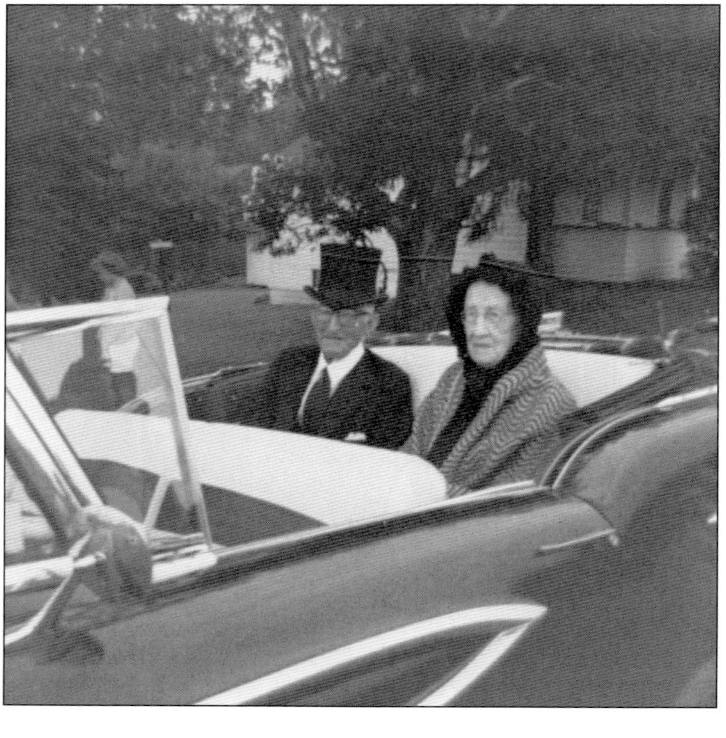

Above, Charles R. and Mabel Huston Meredith pose with their children Percy and Helen outside their home in South Kersey around 1910. The farm, which was later sold to local dentist Dr. James Higgins, was between South Kersey and Greens Roads. Charles Meredith was the great-grandson of Elijah Meredith. During the 1963 Fox Township sesquicentennial celebration, he was the oldest living direct descendant of Elijah Meredith, and was an honorary grand marshal in the parade (left). Mabel died in 1964 at age 83, and Charles died in 1970 at age 96. (Both, courtesy of Ken Meredith.)

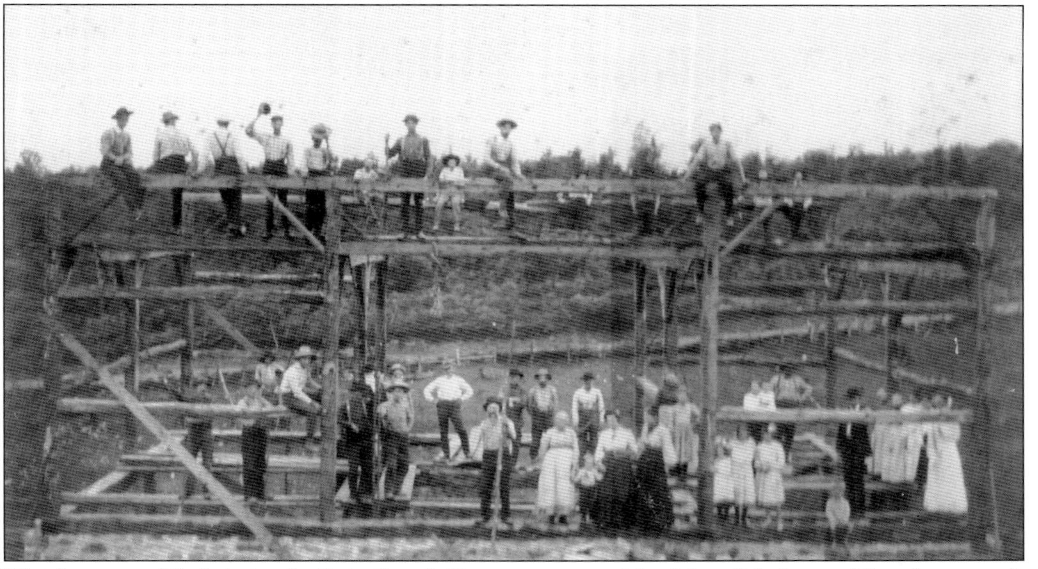

This barn was likely being built in South Kersey on one of the Meredith farms. The photograph above shows the hand-dug basement and the freshly laid, hand-cut sandstone foundation. The photograph below illustrates the post-and-beam construction and the use of mortise and tendon joints. There is also a temporary floor for building the top of this Dutch-type barn. The corner posts appear to be at least 10 inches square and 20 feet high. The front and rear side frames of the barn were raised using long poles called pikes. The women would have created a feast for the workers in this neighborhood effort, which is typical of the kind of cooperation needed to survive in the township. That civic pride and cooperation still exists today. (Above, courtesy of Chris Casey; below, courtesy of Ken Meredith.)

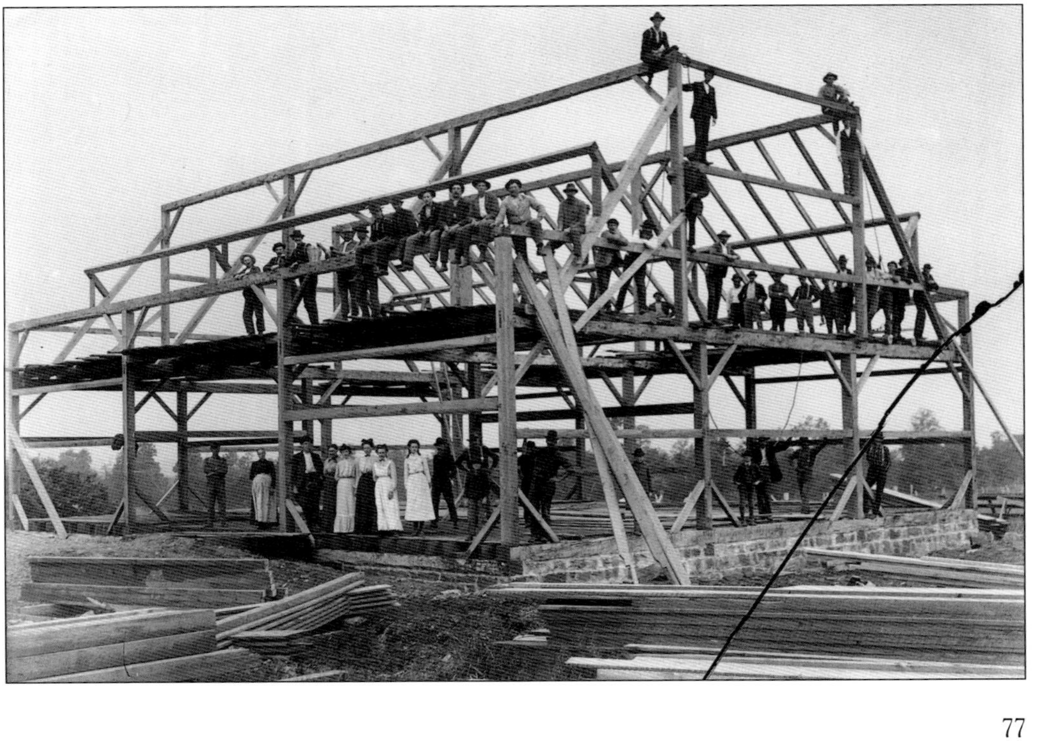

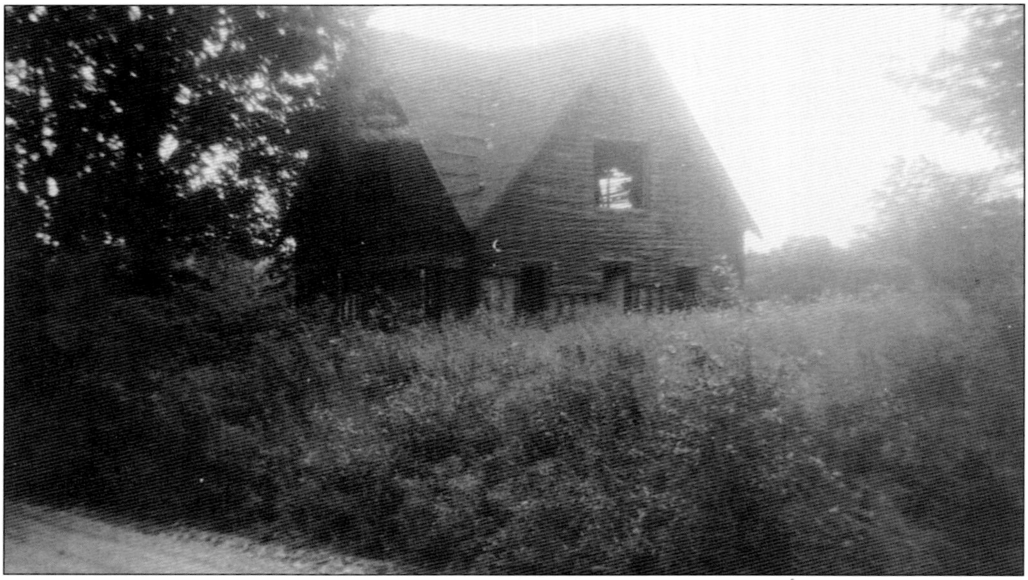

This photograph shows the Calvin Meredith farm in ruins. It was one of the many Meredith family farms in the South Kersey area. Today, most of the land has single-family homes on it. Calvin Meredith, Elijah Meredith's grandson, died in 1861. Elijah's great-great-grandson, who also owned this farm, died in 1974. (Courtesy of Barb Pistner.)

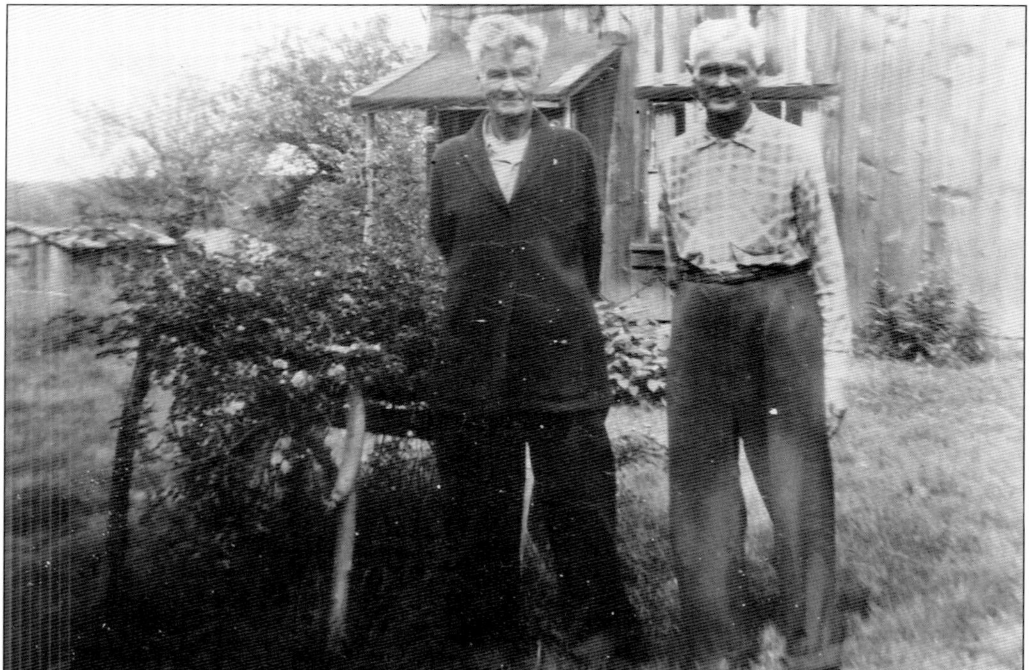

James Huston (left) bought this South Kersey farm in 1912 from Kersey merchant R.W. Beadle. A descendant of Huston has lived on the farm ever since, for more than 100 years. Dorothy Huston Mertz, a direct descendant, has contributed much to the collection and writing of the history and genealogies of Fox Township. (Courtesy of Barb Pistner.)

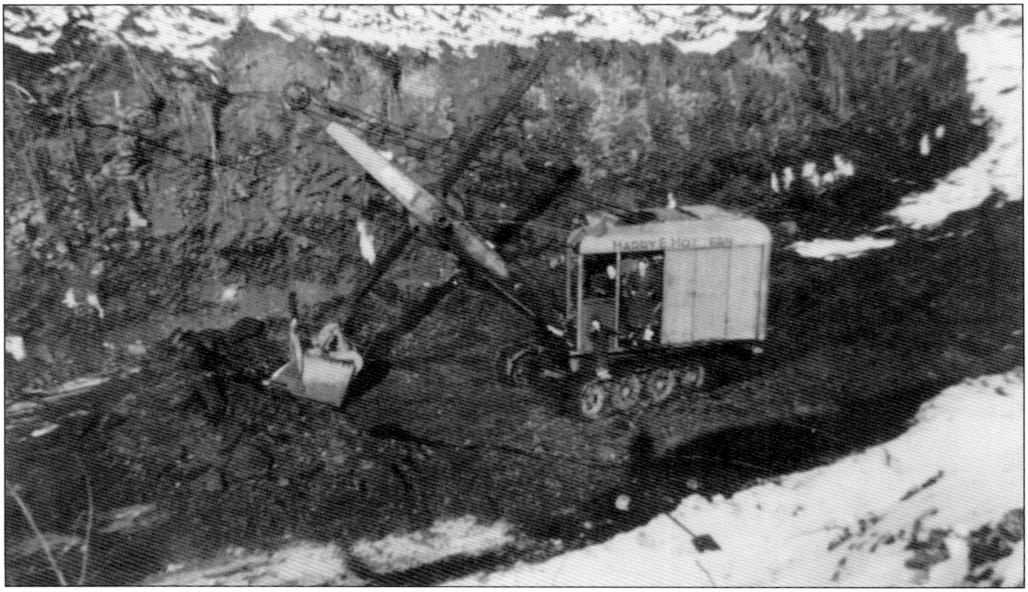

With the development of modern heavy equipment such as bulldozers and steam shovels, it became economically feasible to strip-mine coal near the surface. In 1938, South Kersey's first surface mine (above) was opened by Harry Mottern on the Sidlinger farm, near the Huston and Scolari farms. The Mottern Coal Company still exists. Among the legacies of strip mining are the large lakes, like the one below, often left behind after the mining. Though the highly acidic water was bad for the environment, many of these became great swimming holes for the youth of the township. They had immense high walls to dive from, and most were very deep. Many a township resident learned to swim in the holes. This photograph is of the Sidelinger farm. Today, most of these mines have been reclaimed. (Both, courtesy of Barb Pistner.)

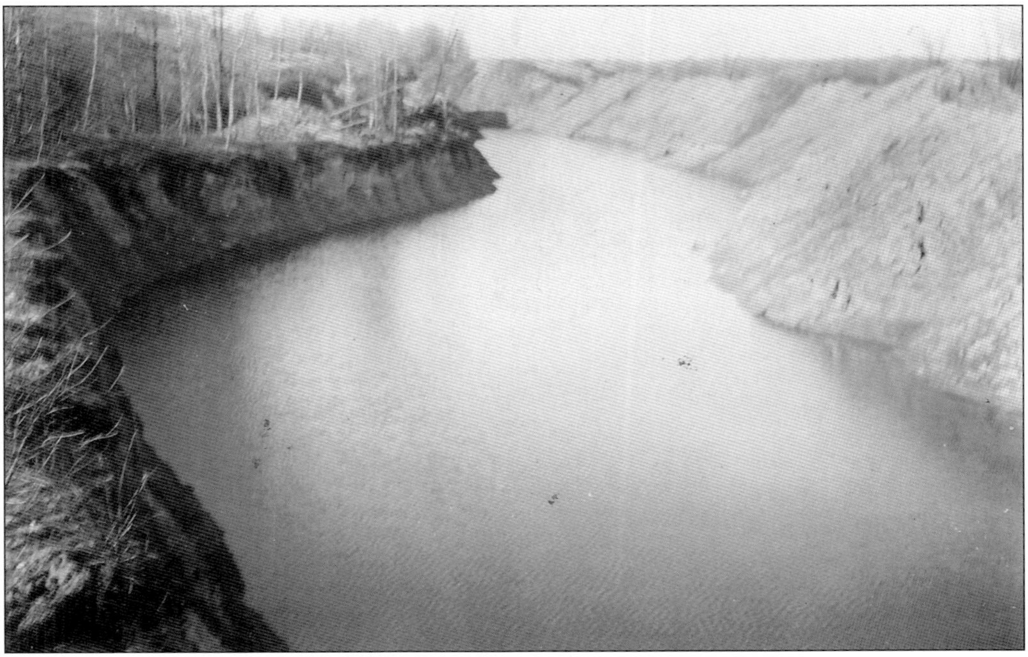

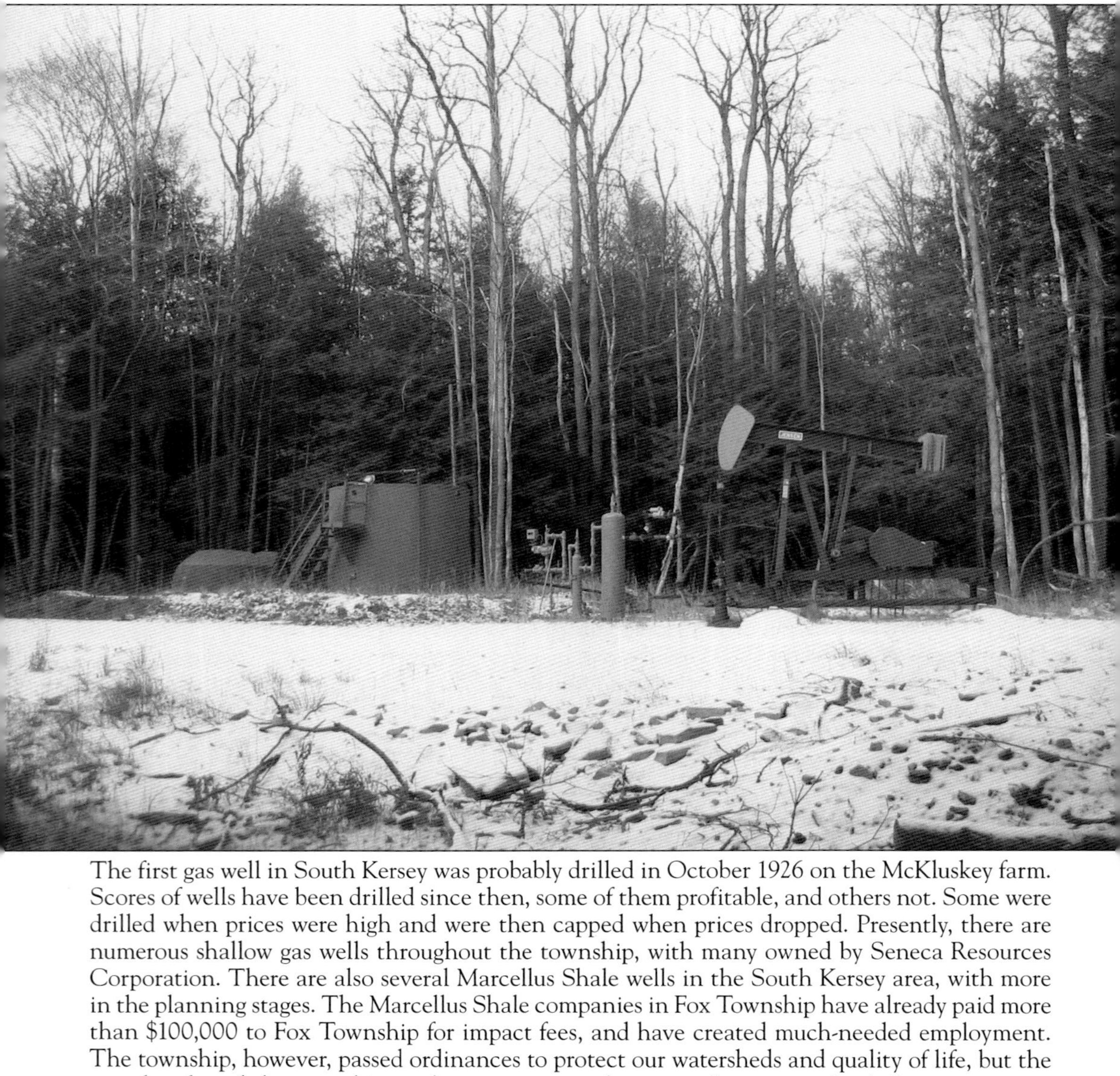

The first gas well in South Kersey was probably drilled in October 1926 on the McKluskey farm. Scores of wells have been drilled since then, some of them profitable, and others not. Some were drilled when prices were high and were then capped when prices dropped. Presently, there are numerous shallow gas wells throughout the township, with many owned by Seneca Resources Corporation. There are also several Marcellus Shale wells in the South Kersey area, with more in the planning stages. The Marcellus Shale companies in Fox Township have already paid more than $100,000 to Fox Township for impact fees, and have created much-needed employment. The township, however, passed ordinances to protect our watersheds and quality of life, but the state has forced the township to change its zoning laws to make it easier for drilling companies to drill in areas that the community wanted free of wells, including watersheds.

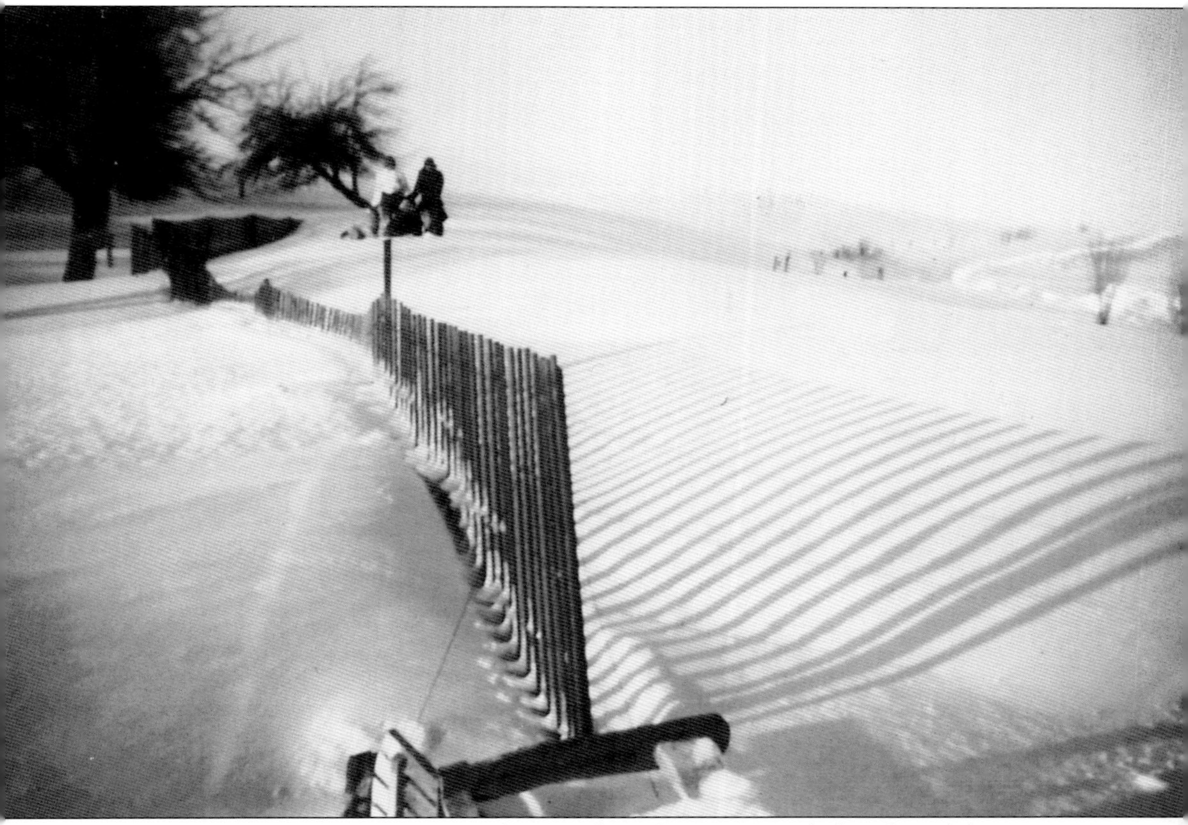

Farming is not easy in this part of Pennsylvania. The soil is not particularly rich, and the growing season is just over 120 days. To survive, early pioneers had to rely on hard work and each other. In 1816, because of the 1815 eruption of Mount Tambora in Indonesia, Fox Township, and much of the globe, suffered what is known as "the year without a summer," as the volcano's eruption lowered global temperatures significantly. There was snow, ice, and frost every month. Even today, nature is tough on farmers, as seen in this photograph on Chicken Hill Road in 1963. For years, "snow fence" was a common term along the highways of Fox Township. Farmers and township workers put up miles of it across fields and near roadways in the fall, and then removed them in the spring. The goal was to prevent snow from drifting across the road, in an era when roads could not be plowed as efficiently as they can be today. (Courtesy of Ken Meredith.)

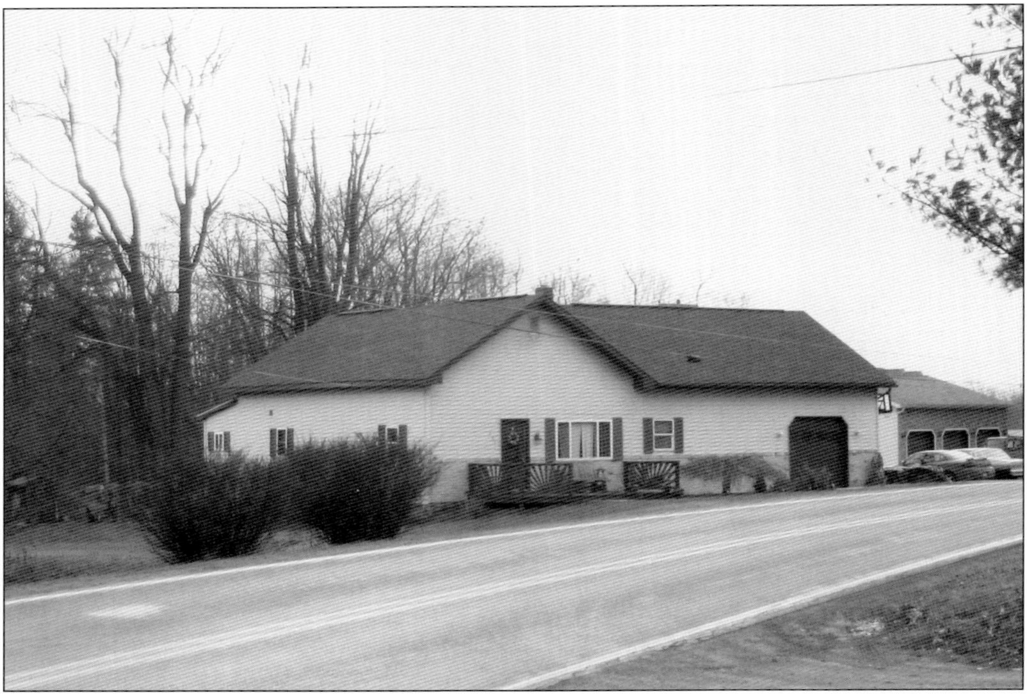

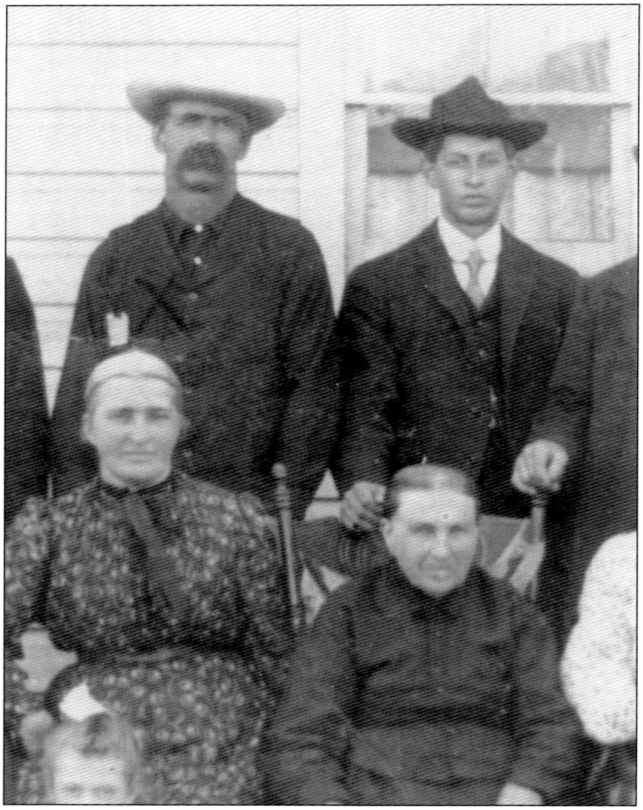

The former Ridge schoolhouse, seen above, was more commonly called the Graveyard schoolhouse because of its location beside Ridge Cemetery. It is now a private residence. It was used between 1934 and 1947, and it is typical of the 20 or so small schools in the township. It is located at the corner of Ridge and Brandy Camp Roads.

The Auman farm was near the Jay Township line, by Red Hill Summit. Seen here in 1902 are, from left to right, (seated) Sara Smithbauer Auman and her mother; (standing) Wolfgang Auman Jr. and the Aumans' son George. Wolfgang Auman Sr. came to America in 1846, and Auman Jr. was born three years later.

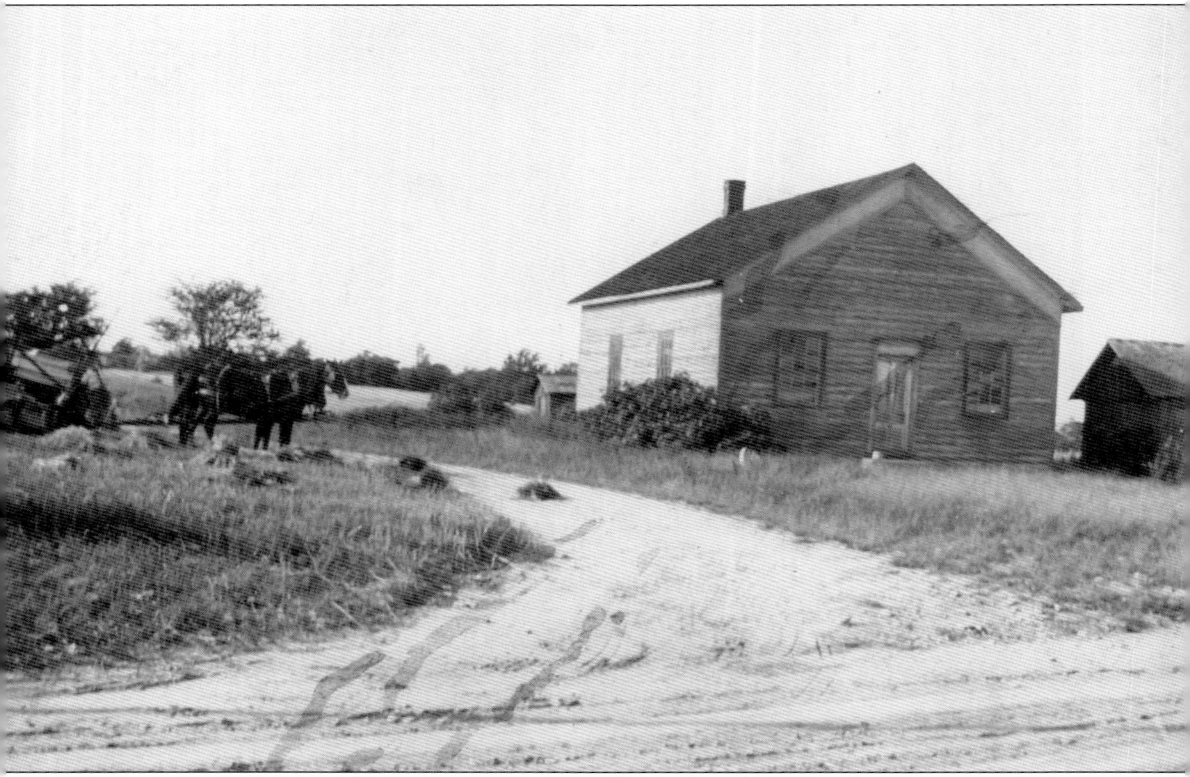

Irishtown may have been the first small village to become established in Fox Township. The first Catholic church, either Immaculate Conception or St. Michaels, was located near the intersection of Browns and Old Kersey Roads. A cemetery with many graves marked only by stones and undulations is still there, but records of the early pioneers who are buried there cannot be found. This photograph shows a newer school built on the site of the first school in Fox Township. On the corner of Browns and Irishtown Roads, it served the community from 1823 to 1912. The first teacher was Dr. William Hoyt. The earlier structure may also have been used for Catholic services. The building was later moved to Bootjack Hill, and the locals took the foundation stones and used them for their own structures. Note the farmers mowing hay on the left. (Courtesy of William and Janice Haller.)

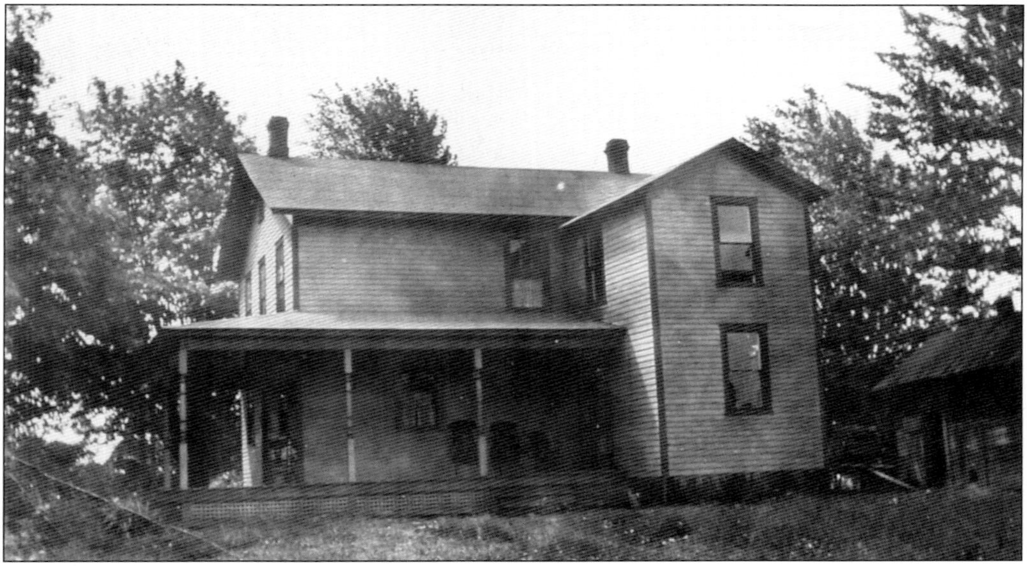

Located on Browns Road, the Brown homestead was destroyed by arson in 2007. The Browns were a very prominent Irishtown family since the mid-1800s. Irish immigrant Michael Brown built this house in 1854. Hector Brown, the last resident, was famous as a woodsman and for his walking abilities. The wing on the right was added later, as the family grew. Some of the outbuildings behind the residence are seen below in 1973, when the property was no longer a working farm. The size and quality of the structures testify to the hard work, skill, and success of the Brown family. (Both, courtesy of William and Janice Haller.)

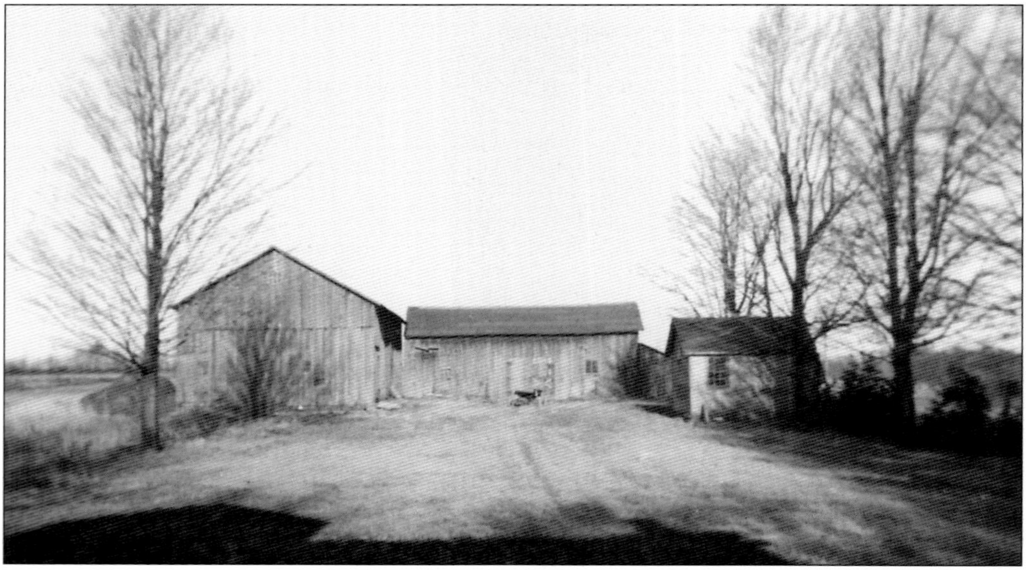

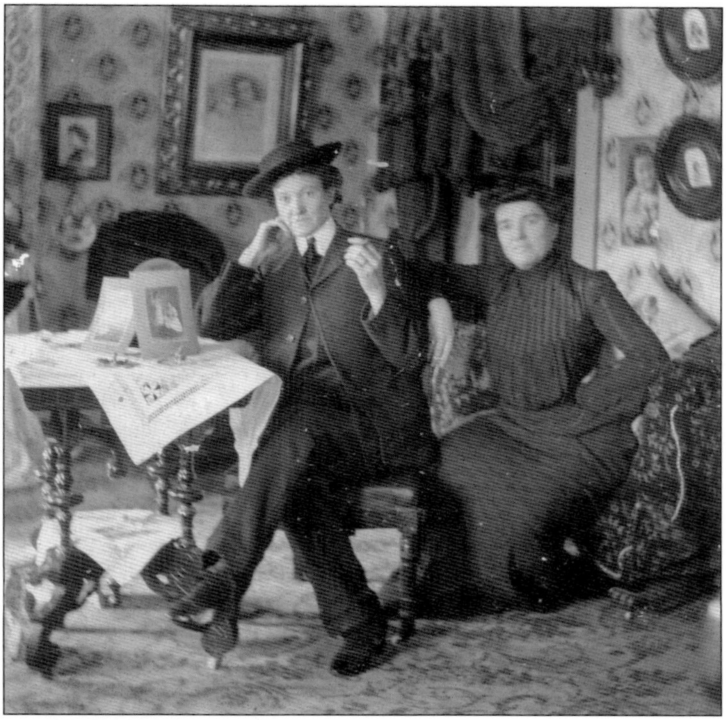

Jim Avery and Margaret Brown pose in the parlor of the Brown residence in the early 1900s. Note the fine carpet, ornate wallpaper, and the quality furniture and picture frames, which testify to the family's prosperity at the time. (Courtesy of William and Janice Haller.)

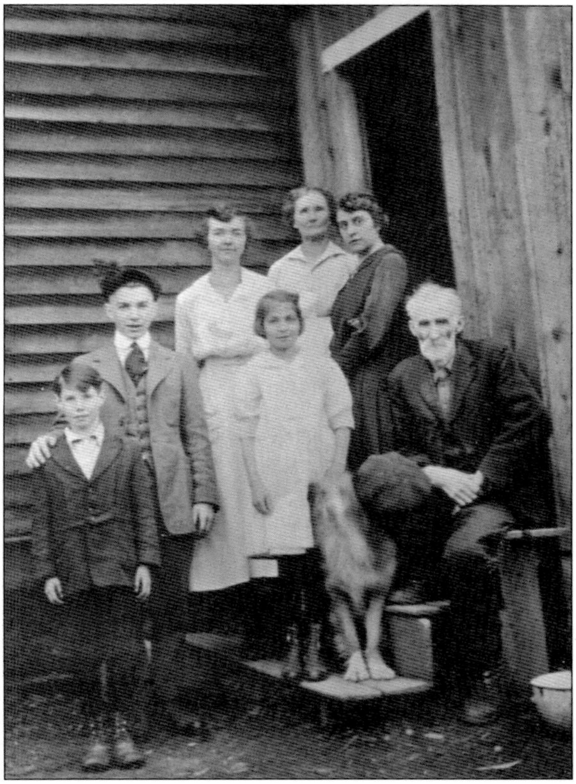

The Brown family poses for a family photograph in 1917. They are, from left to right, Hector, Terry, Helene, Vivian, mother Rose Adams Brown, Anna, and father Terrence Brown. In all, the Browns had 13 children. Terrence Brown died a year after this photograph was taken, quite possibly during the Spanish Flu pandemic. A new baby also died of the flu. (Courtesy of William and Janice Haller.)

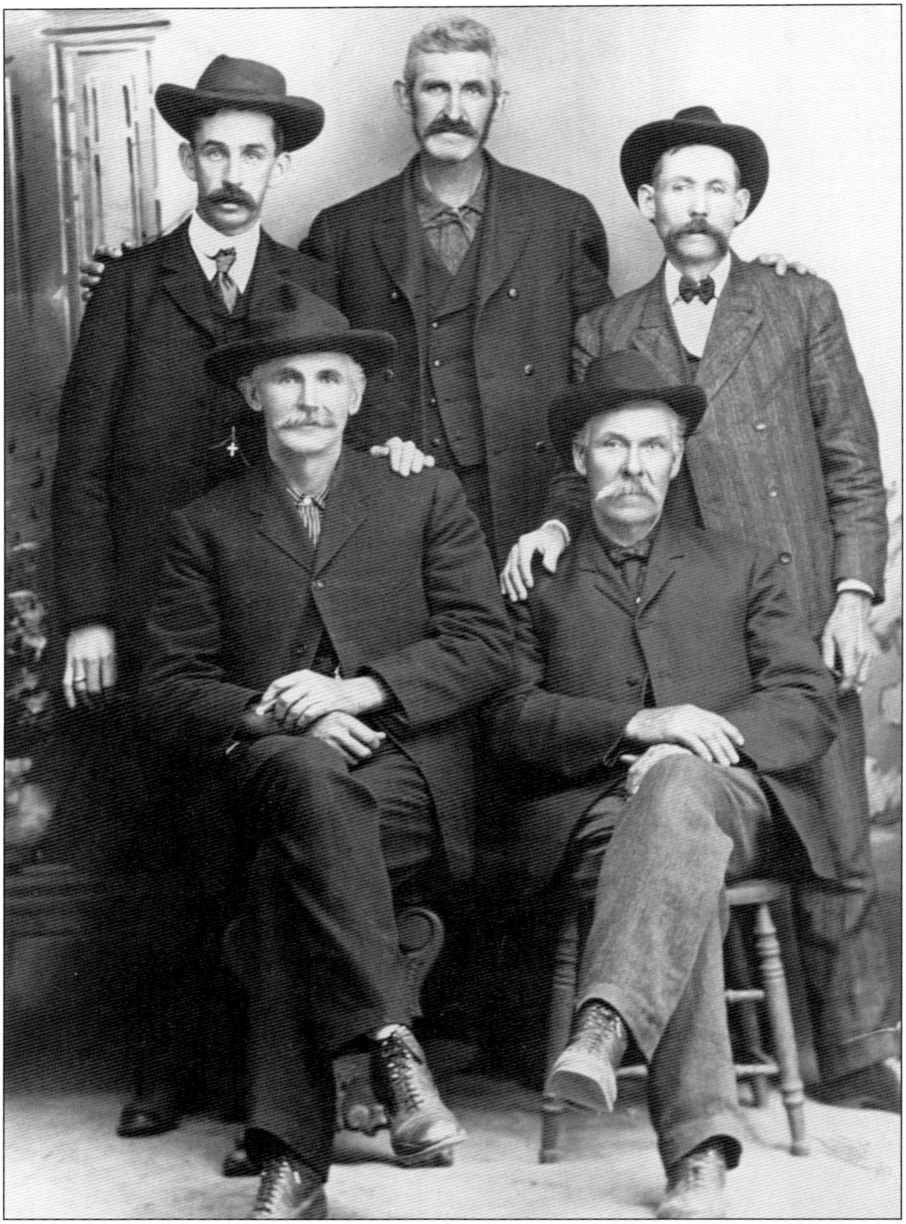

Except for Irish native Bernard Canavan (seated, right), these men were the sons of early Irish immigrants to Fox Township. Seated on the left is William Callahan, and standing are, from left to right, Patrick Jerden, Patrick Callahan, and Patrick Largey. Canavan, Callahan, and Largey were farmers in Irishtown. Canavan's wife was killed in an unsolved murder in June 1903, while picking strawberries. The papers called it a "Murder Most Foul." She was found near the PS&N railroad tracks in a state of unconsciousness. Her skull had been split open by an 18-inch-long, 3-inch-thick hemlock knot found nearby covered with hair, and she had several teeth knocked out. The 50-year-old died the next morning, leaving behind her husband and a daughter. Several desperate-looking characters, or tramps, were seen in the area and suspected, but nobody was ever apprehended. (Courtesy of Joan Verbka.)

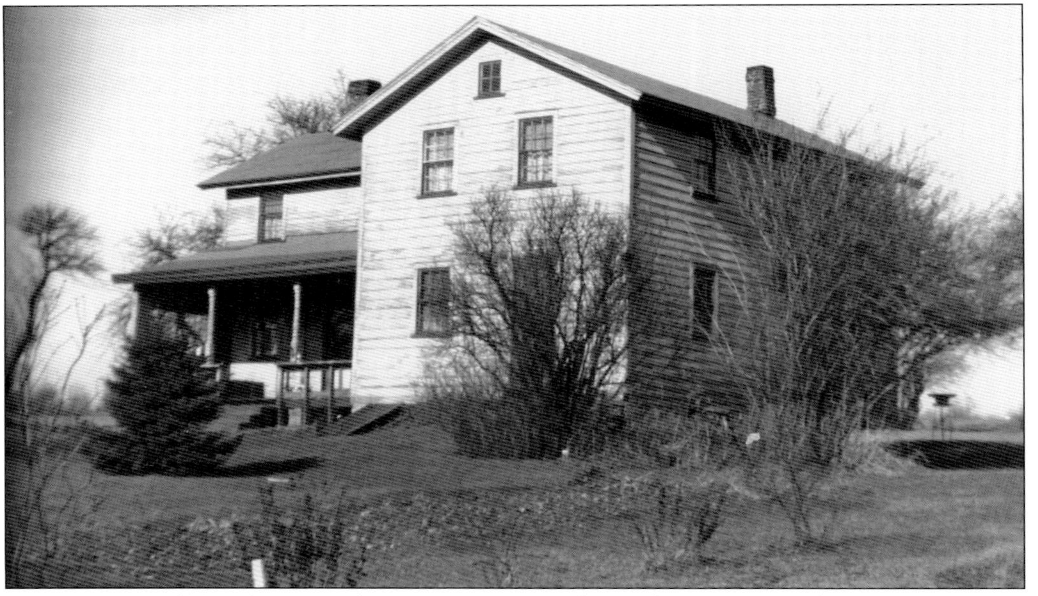

The William Callahan homestead, on Raven Run Road in Irishtown, is seen above in the 1960s. It was destroyed by fire in the 1970s, when the Seigel family owned it. The late summer photograph below shows a harvest table at the farm. Enjoying the picnic are, from left to right, George and John Eberl, Mrs. Callahan, Joe, Ann, Martha, and Margaret Callahan, Joseph Pieltz, and Patrick Callahan (far right, between the horses). They proudly display their crop yields, including corn, potatoes, cauliflower, cabbage, pumpkins, and rutabagas or turnips. A cultivator also sits on the table. Although the growing season is short in Fox Township, farmers still display their wares at the annual Elk County Fair, held in late August since 1975. (Both, courtesy of William and Janice Haller.)

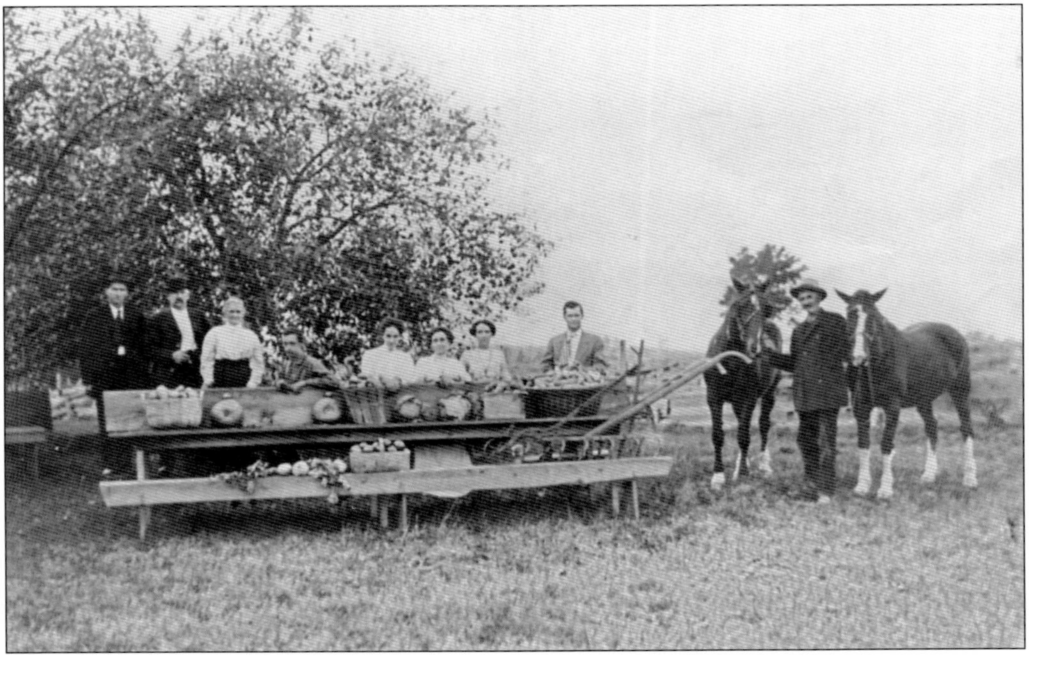

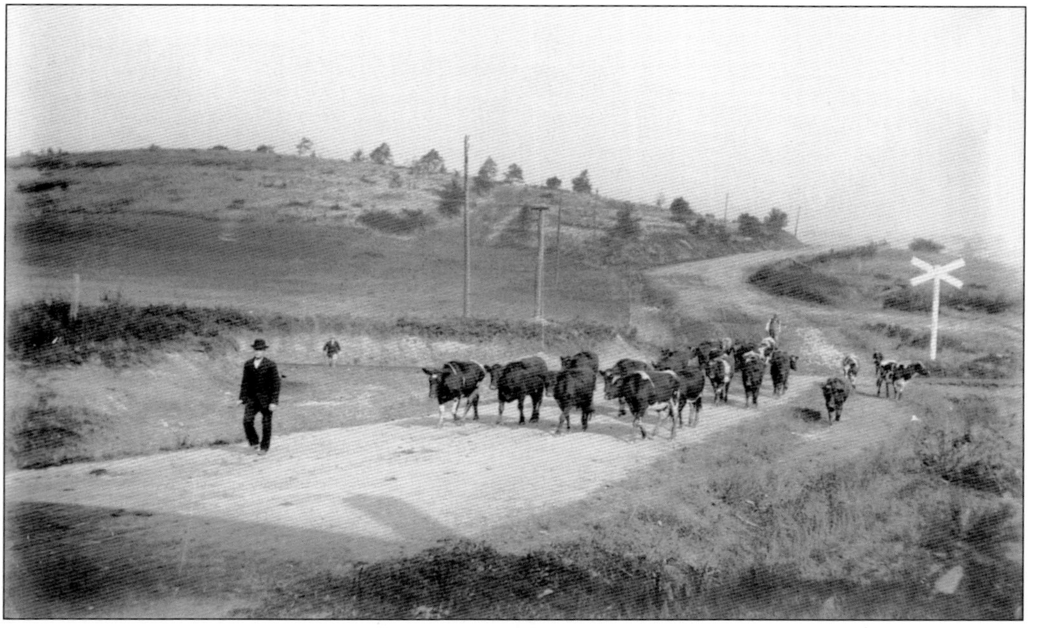

This cattle drive comes into town on Irishtown Road at the PS&N crossing, near the present township building. Perhaps it was headed to Straessley's meat market, or to his slaughterhouse on Main Street. Straessley peddled meat door-to-door and delivered to the various hotels and taverns. In a time before refrigeration, meat had to be fresh, especially in the summer, when the only refrigeration came from stored winter ice in icehouses. (Courtesy of Chris Casey.)

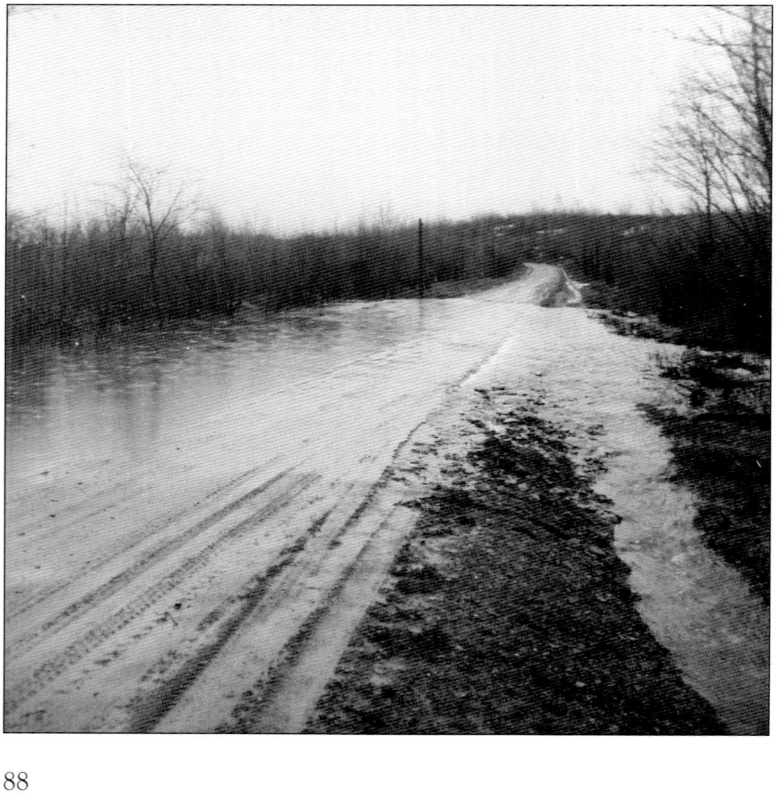

Irishtown Road is seen here at the low, swampy headwaters of Beaver Run. In the early 1900s, Mr. Urmann had a pond here that residents ice-skated on in the winter. The road was still dirt in this 1963 photograph, much of it what was known as "red dog," a coal-baked shale waste product. The bridge and culvert over the stream were replaced in 2012 in hopes of alleviating flooding. (Courtesy of William and Janice Haller.)

An early resident of Challenge, in Fox Township, Jacob Silas Himes moved to Irishtown in 1938, and, with his sons, built a farm, which ceased operation in 1960. He was a township supervisor in the 1940s and 1950s. He is seen here in 1958 at his home. The farm is still in the family, and his descendants live throughout the township.

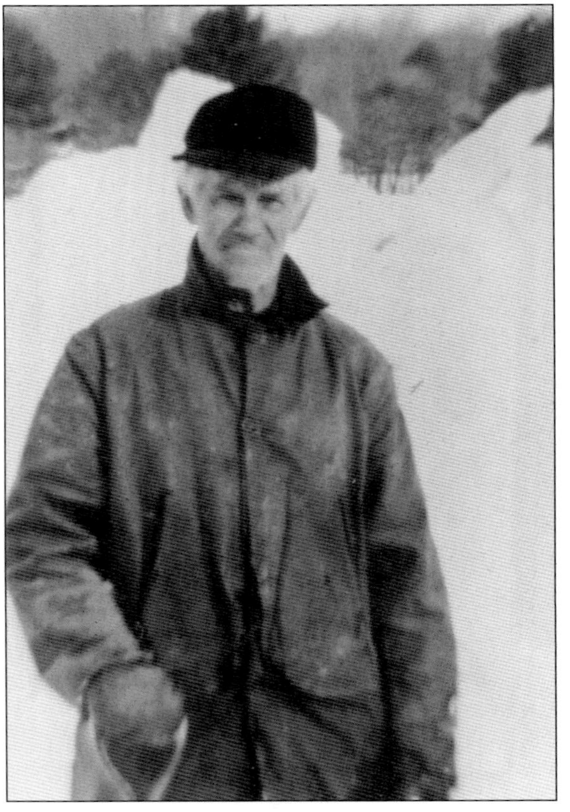

Christina Edwards Musselman Thompson lived in Dagus Mines, near the railroad tracks (below). Once, as she sat on her porch peeling potatoes, a man who was trying to shoot a dog accidentally shot her. The bullet ricocheted off the railroad tracks and hit her in the stomach. She got up from the porch, walked into the parlor, and fell over dead.

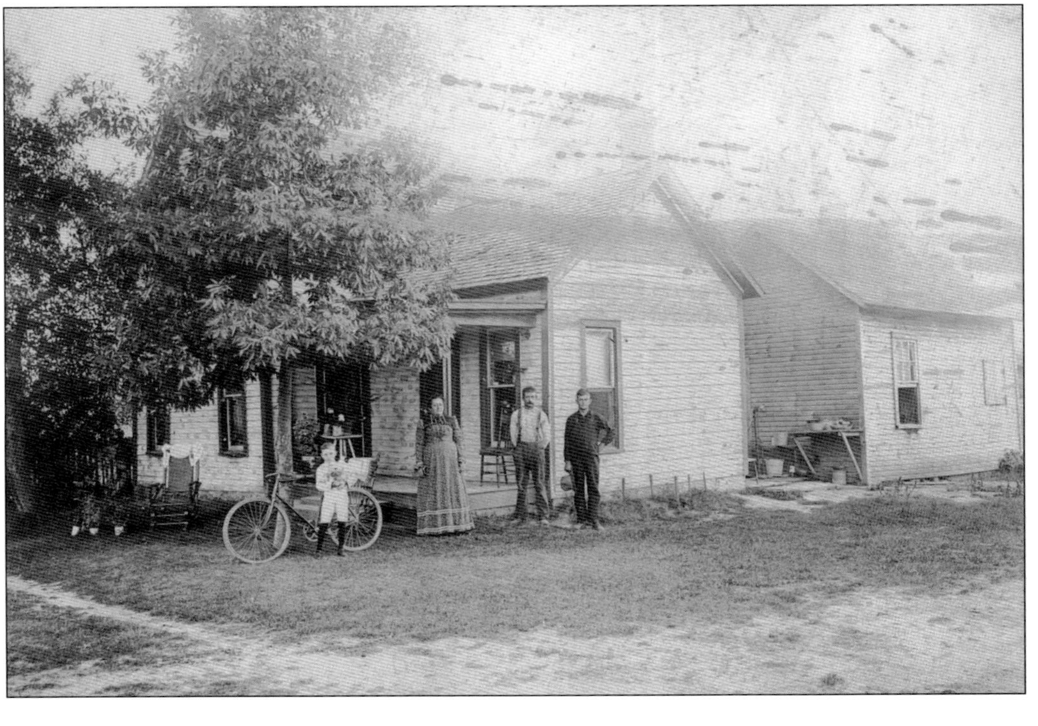

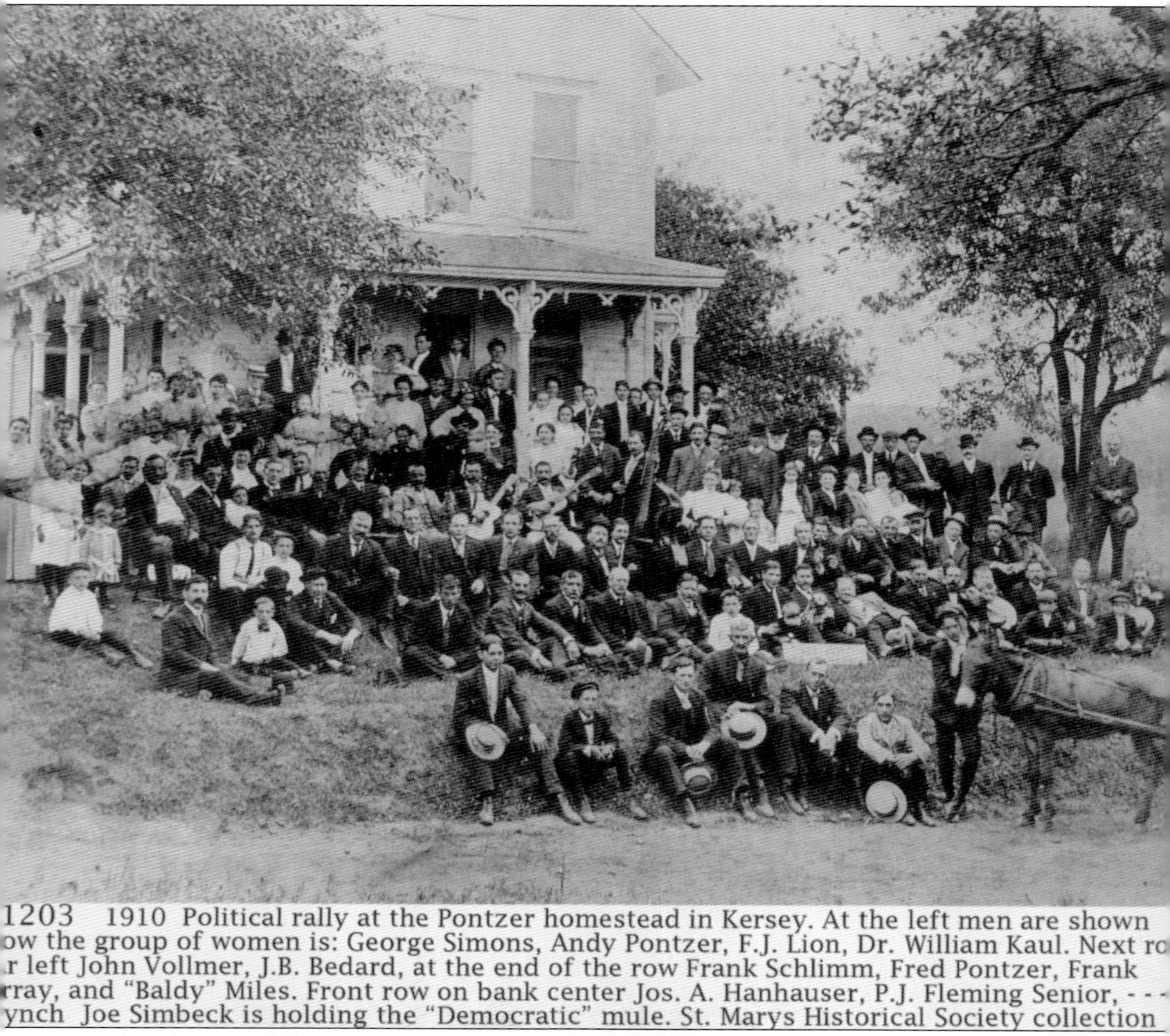

This photograph was taken of a 1910 political rally at the Joseph Pontzer homestead, on Dietz Road in Fox Township. Pontzer emigrated from Germany in 1846 with three sons, four daughters, and their families. Clearing the land that is now the Elk County Fairgrounds, the family quickly prospered. Their descendants became businessmen, doctors, lawyers, teachers, and other contributing citizens. Much land in the township is still owned by the Pontzer estate. This is a Democratic rally—note the donkey—which is fitting because, in recent years, Elk County has been a rare island of Democrats surrounded by Republican counties. The development of unions was a contributor to the area's Democratic support, but the county has Democrat roots going far back, even voting against President Lincoln. The county also always voted against Prohibition, even though there was a temperance hall and society in Toby, and always voted against women's suffrage. (Courtesy of the St. Marys Benzinger Township Historical Society.)

Five

Fox Township at Work

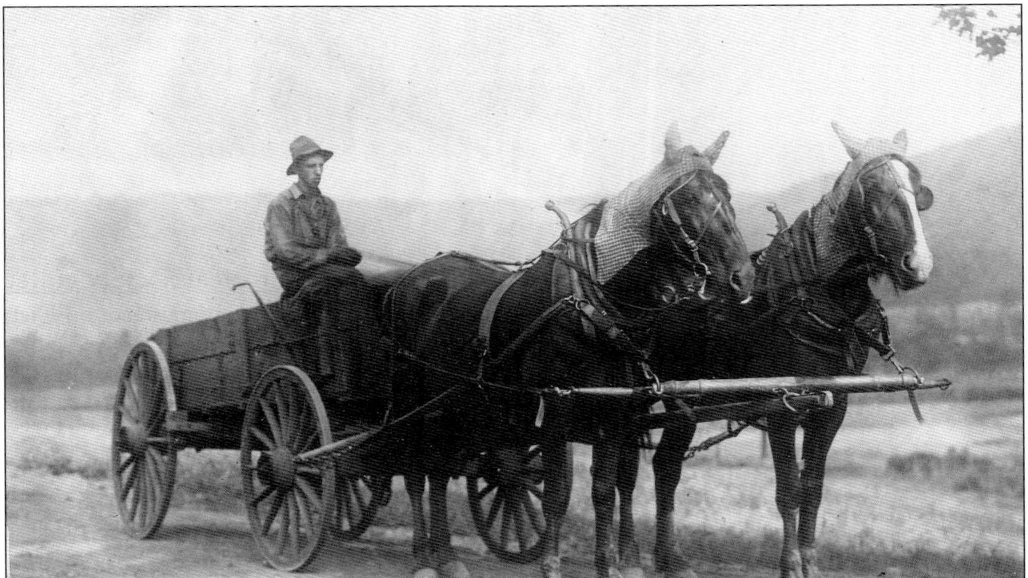

Arther Beck of South Kersey pulls a Studebaker wagon with a team of horses in June 1920. The horses must have been a little skittish, as both have blinders on. The coverings on the horses' heads are to ward off flies, which might account for their skittishness. Descendants of Beck still live in Boones Mountain and Bennett's Valley. (Courtesy of Barb Pistner.)

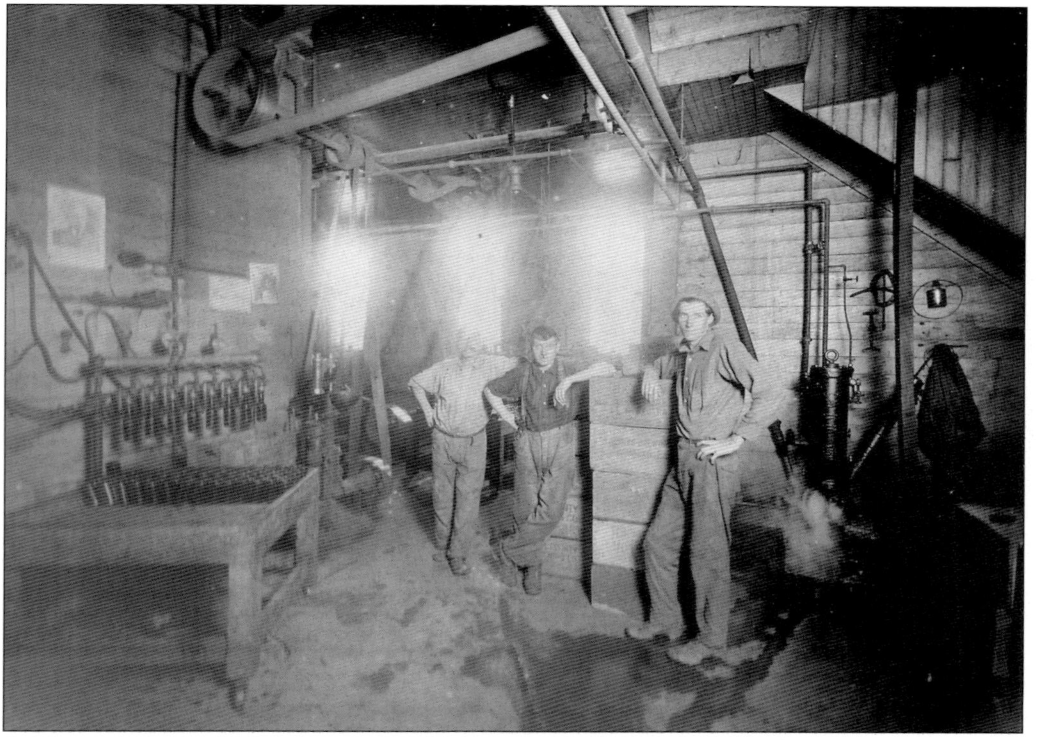

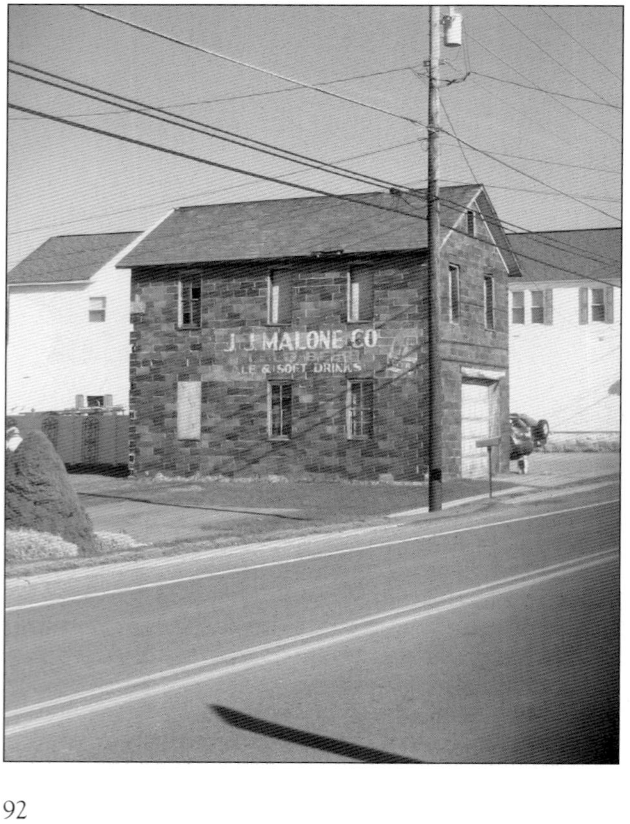

Ray Mosier (center) and Larry Brown (right) are at work in the M.J. Hackerl bottling works on Main Street in Kersey. Formerly Urmann's bottling, it was sold to J.J. Malone in 1933. The leather belts used for turning the machinery are visible at top.

J.J. Malone was a distributor for Koehler beer, brewed in Erie, and Anita pop, from Flecks Beverage, which was bottled near Punxsutawney. In the late 1930s, Malone became the chairman of the Elk County Democratic party. His trucks were often seen at mine entrances on election days to take miners and others to the polling places. The bottling works is now a residence, and the building in this photograph is now a storage garage.

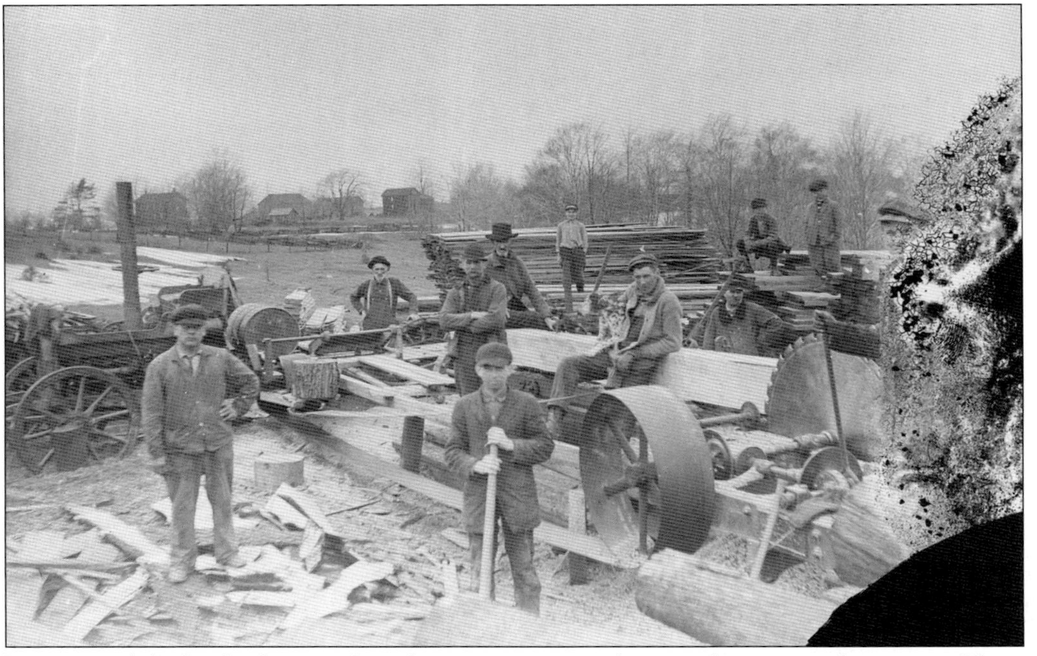

Logging and the lumber business have been important in the township since its beginning. These photographs show a mobile standard-stick rotary sawmill. The boards are stacked without spacers for drying, which would indicate shipment to another location. Aside from making lumber for building construction, much went into the mines for shoring and to the railroads for ties. Farmers had their woodlots cut either for personal use or to sell for cash. Lawrence Glass moved this sawmill from place to place, cutting lumber for local individuals. These 1916 photographs were taken on the north side of Browns Road, across from the Brown homestead. Below, from left to right, are Larry Brown, Lawrence Glass, Terry Brown, Pete Ireinmiller, John Hau, Pat Callahan, John Glass, Larry and Clement Brown, Clement Klein, and Bill Weismiller. (Both, courtesy of William and Janice Haller.)

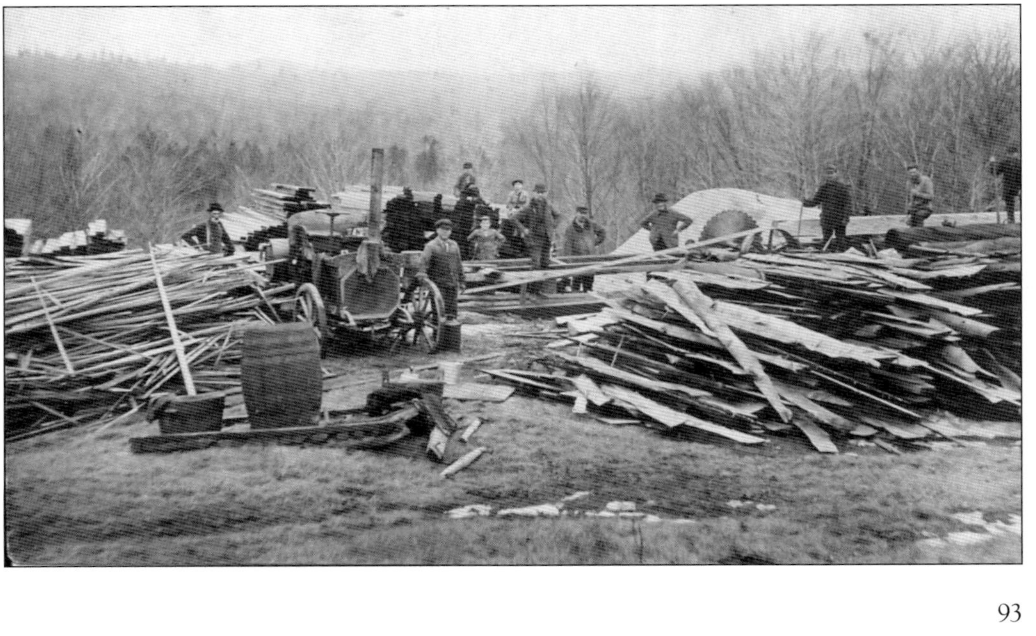

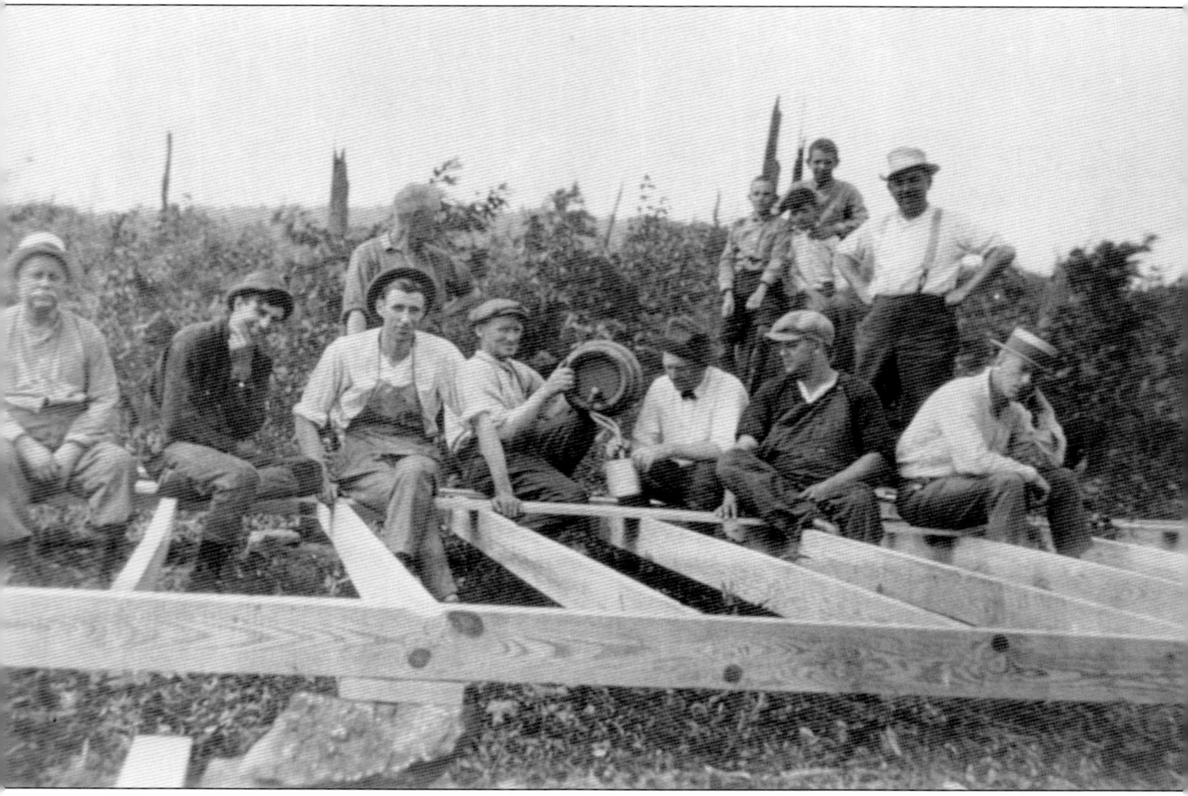

These men begin to frame a structure, probably in the Irishtown area. They are sitting on the floor joists, which are placed on a rock. The lack of a good foundation would suggest they are building an outbuilding or a camp. It appears that a forest fire has gone through the area within the last 10 years, as numerous burnt stumps are visible. Forest fires were common occurrences in those days, often starting as a result of sparks emitted from passing steam engines. The men are, from left to right, (seated) Mike and Ed Spangler, Larry Brown, Robert Dannie, John Spangler, Grechem Dowie, and Larry "Swan" Swanson; (standing) Chester Taylor, George Eberl, and Eberl's young sons. (Courtesy of William and Janice Haller.)

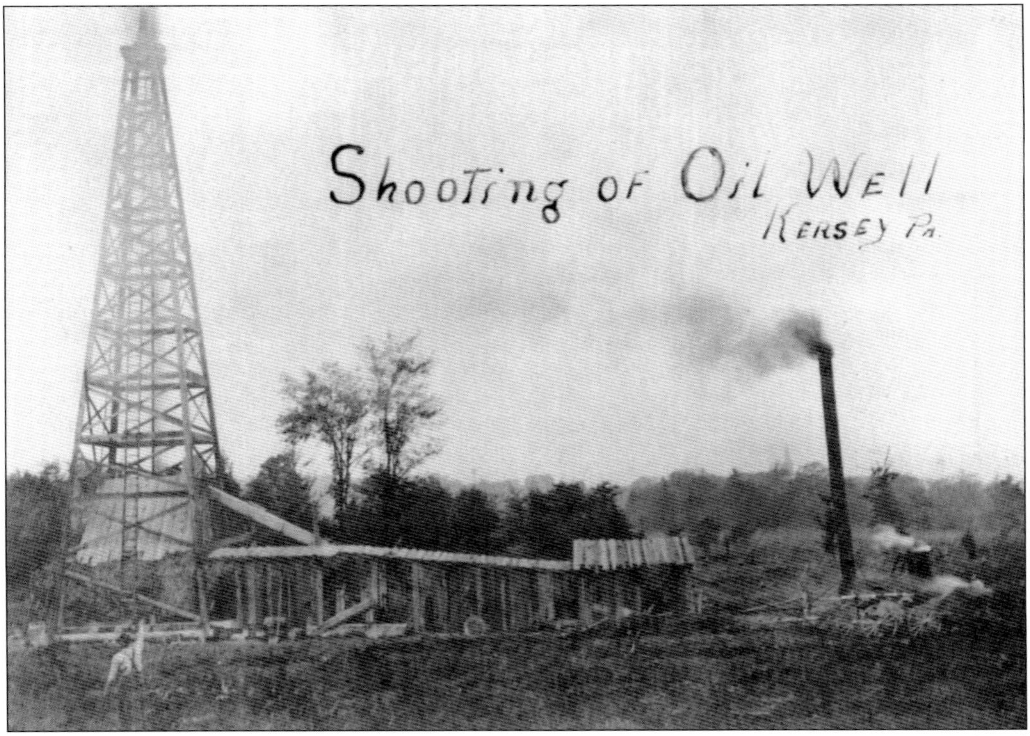

Gas and oil exploration has gone on in the township since the 1860s. The Toby Creek Oil and Gas Company was incorporated in February 1865. This well was on the Kersey Flats, near the current Fox Township Park. The photograph was taken after 1894, as the St. Boniface Church steeple is just visible in the center-right distance.

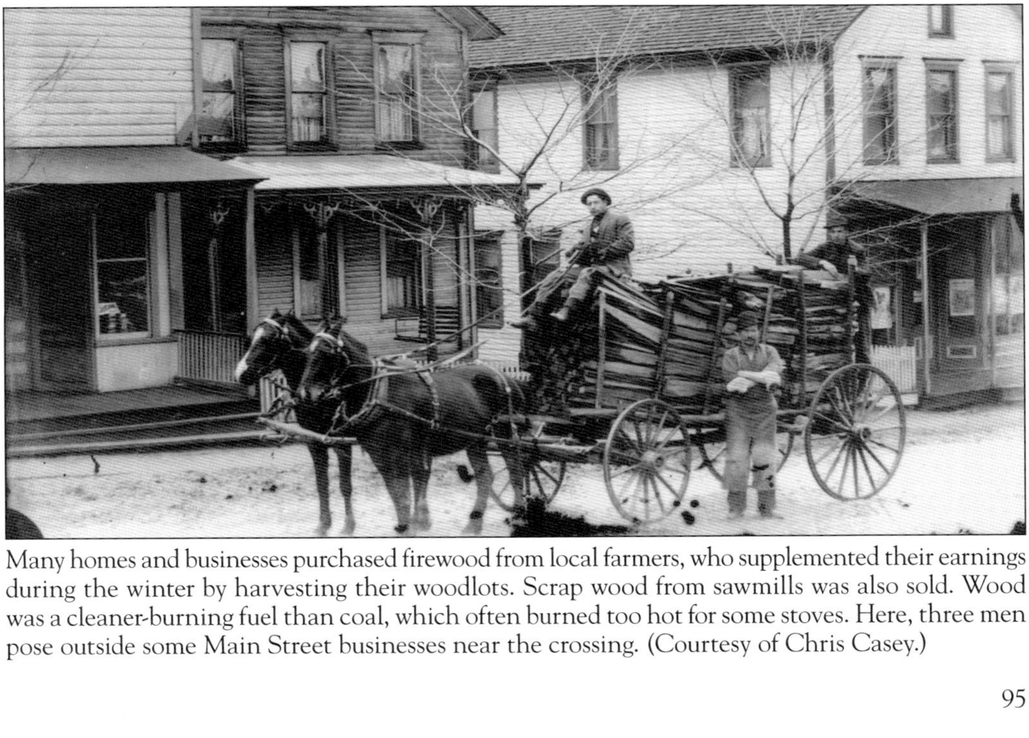

Many homes and businesses purchased firewood from local farmers, who supplemented their earnings during the winter by harvesting their woodlots. Scrap wood from sawmills was also sold. Wood was a cleaner-burning fuel than coal, which often burned too hot for some stoves. Here, three men pose outside some Main Street businesses near the crossing. (Courtesy of Chris Casey.)

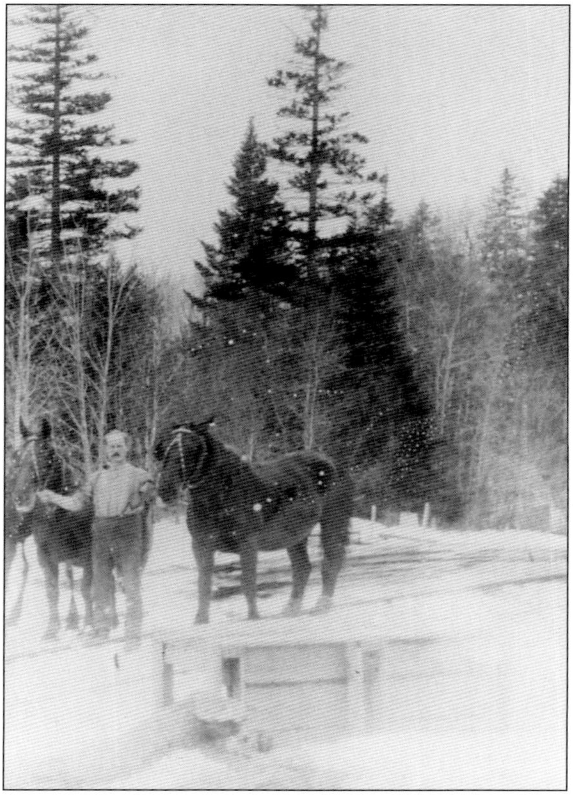

As winter made growing things impossible, it was the time to do non-farming activities and to catch up on other work. The frozen ground made skidding easier. Here, John Michael Schreiber moves lumber with some nice-looking workhorses at his Greens Road property around 1900. Schreiber had a blacksmith shop on Main Street, but also farmed at this location.

Charles Uhl began the Ayrshire dairy farm on Old Kersey Road in 1921. For about 30 years, the dairy was home to the only tourist attraction in the township, known as the "Queen of the Herd." Billed as the world's largest fiberglass cow, she reigned until she was sold when the dairy closed and its owners retired. Casey and Tony Mattivi are seen here with the Queen of the Herd in 2000. (Courtesy of Mary Mattivi.)

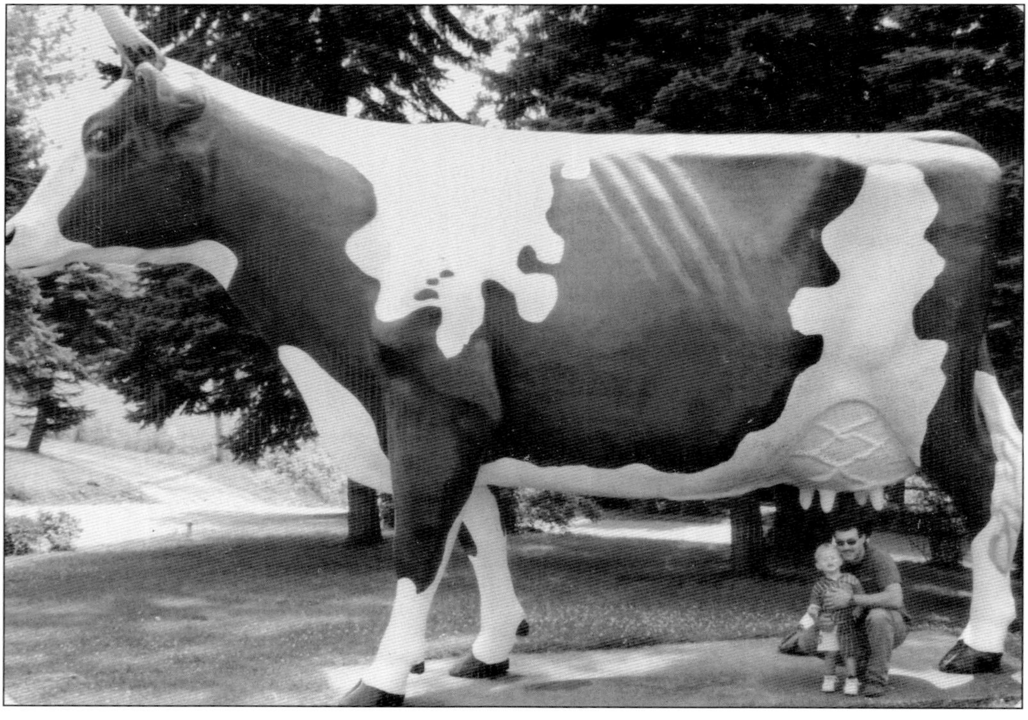

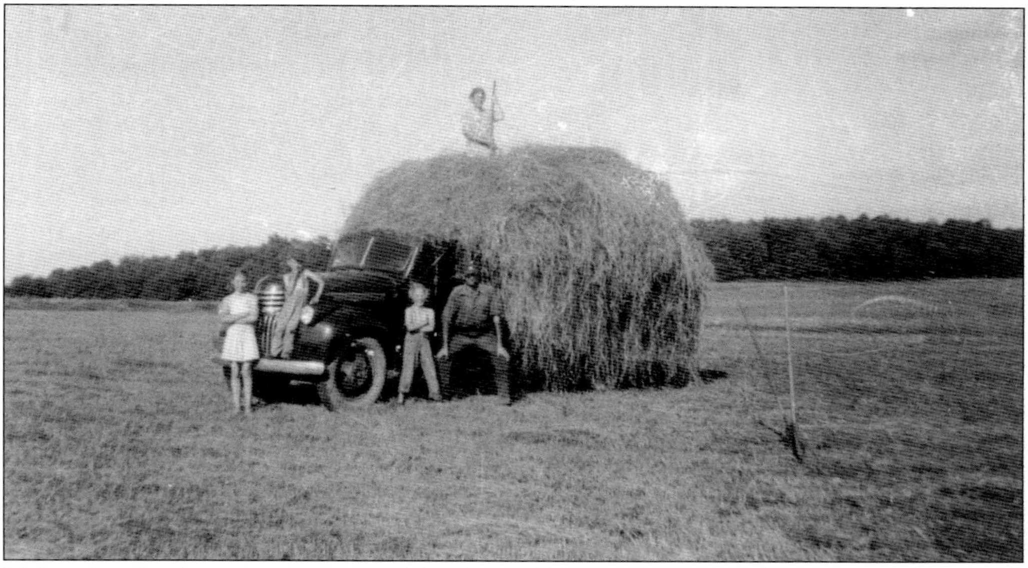

Making hay has been a summer ritual for almost 200 years for men and women, young and old. Water never tasted so sweet as after a hot July day in the hayfield. Because hay needed to be dry when it was stored, it was usually harvested in the hottest days of summer. Loose hay was thrown by pitchfork onto the hay wagon, or as in this 1940s photograph, onto a truck.

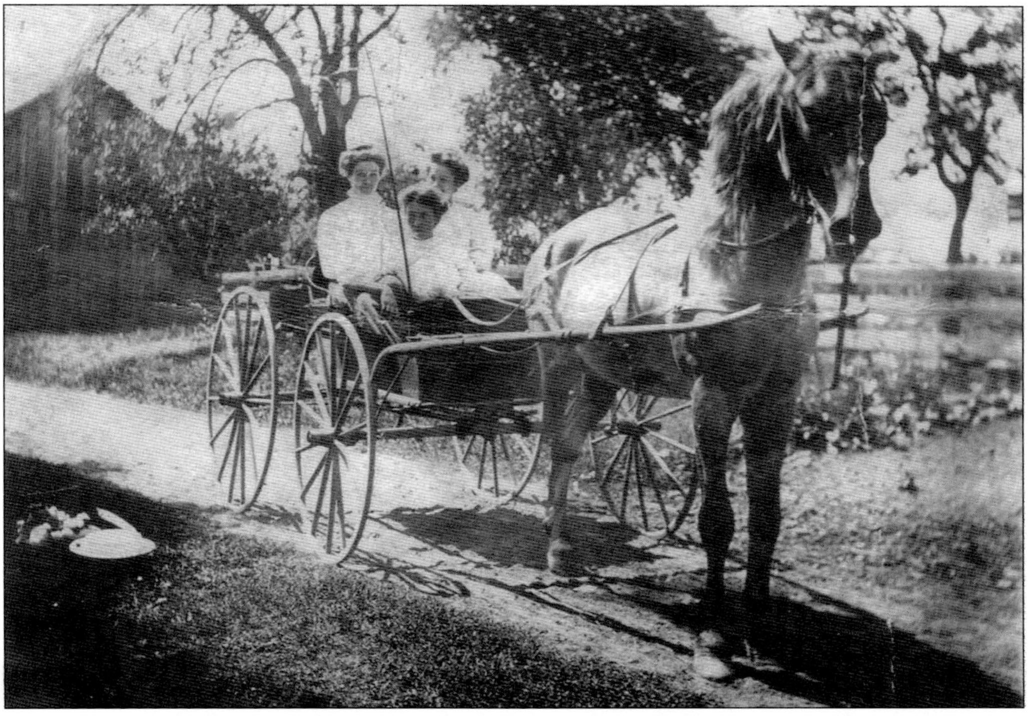

Here, Gladys Delo (front), Mabel Huston (back, left), and Maude Huston are out for a ride in a very expensive buggy on the Meredith farm. These thin-wheeled rubber tires and what appears to be a Tennessee Walker were not common. The buggy also has central support springs and a cover for added comfort. Maude Huston went on to marry Charles Meredith. (Courtesy of Barb Pistner.)

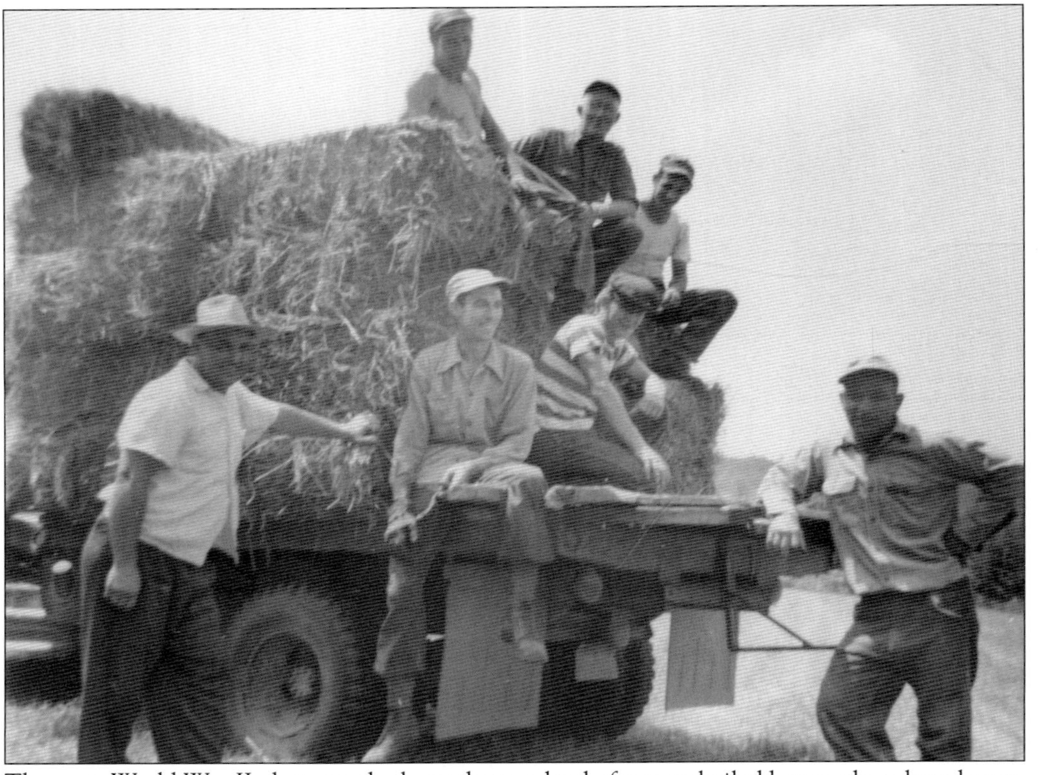

The post–World War II photograph above shows a load of square-bailed hay ready to be taken to the barn on the Luchini farm in South Kersey. The men, nearly finished with their day's work, are, from left to right, (first row) Ralph DeVivo, Louis Luchini, unidentified, and Angelo DeVivo; (second row) Johnny Luchini, Paul Meredith, and Josie Luchini. Prior to bailing, the hay must be raked into rows, which both aides in drying and enables the bailer to take in the hay or straw. Below, one of the Luchini brothers does the raking. (Both, courtesy of Hazel Luchini.)

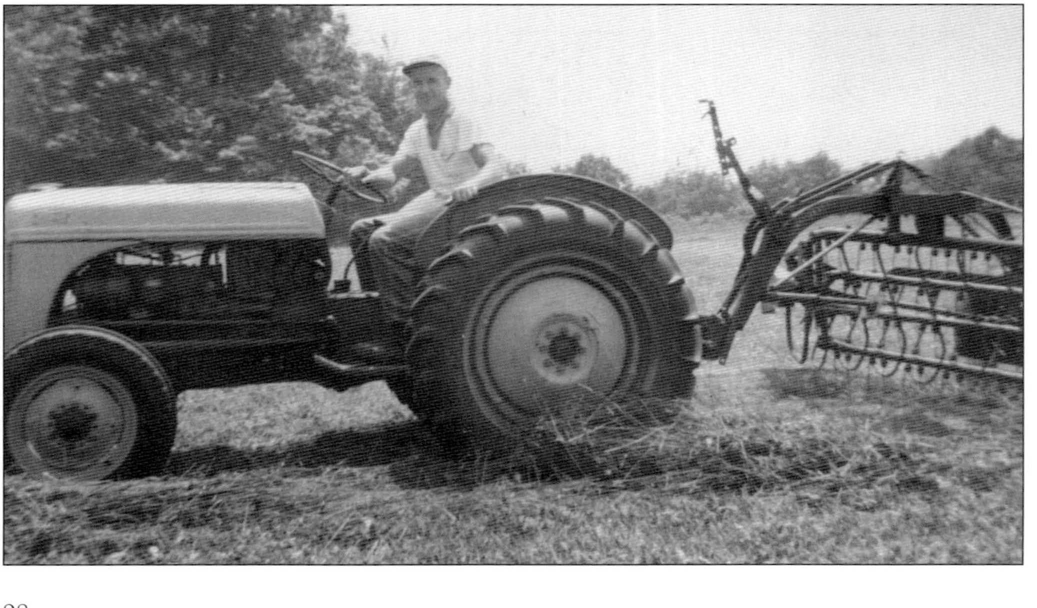

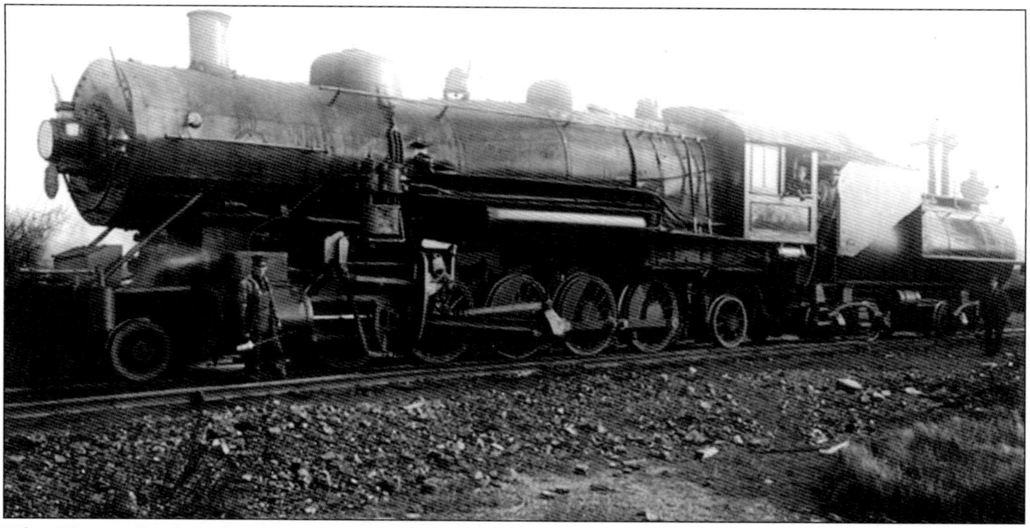

The Kersey Railroad, a Pittsburgh, Shawmut & Northern subsidiary, carries coal up the steep grade from Byrnedale to Paine Station, just outside of Kersey. It required a large, powerful engine. Engine No. 98 was bought specifically for this route, but it weighed 235,000 pounds and needed 8,000 gallons of water to make the short trip, making it too heavy for the bed and rails, so it was only used for a short time. (Courtesy of the Allegheny County Historical Society.)

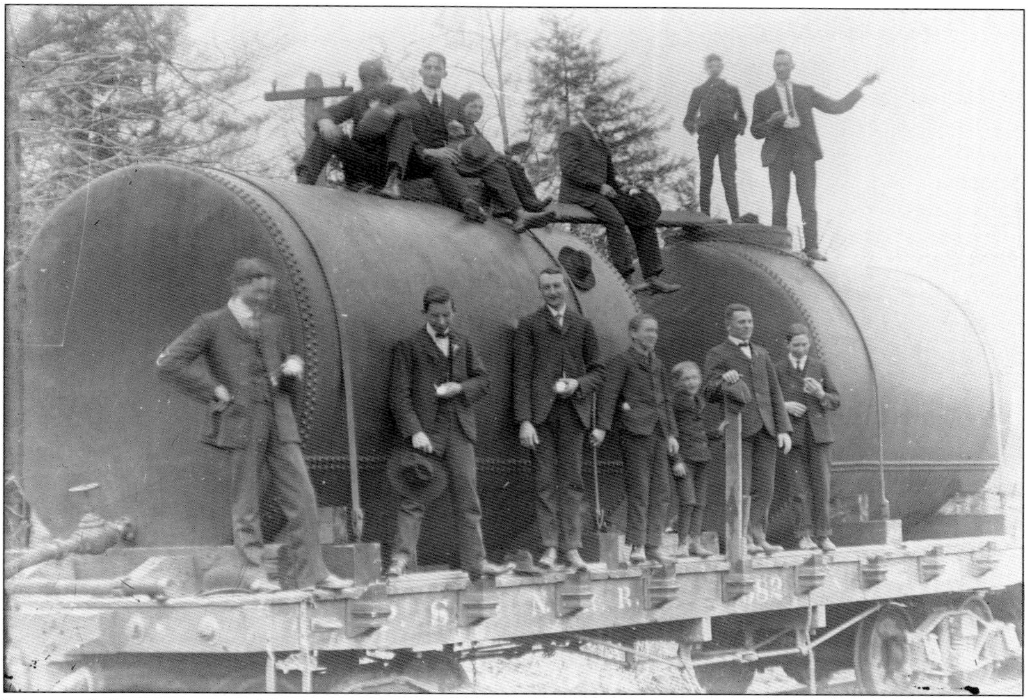

Many of these men and boys are checking their pocket watches, as if waiting for the tanks to empty. The valve on the left, with the hose connected to it, looks open. This is the only known photograph in the PS&N files showing such a tank arrangement. (Courtesy of Chris Casey.)

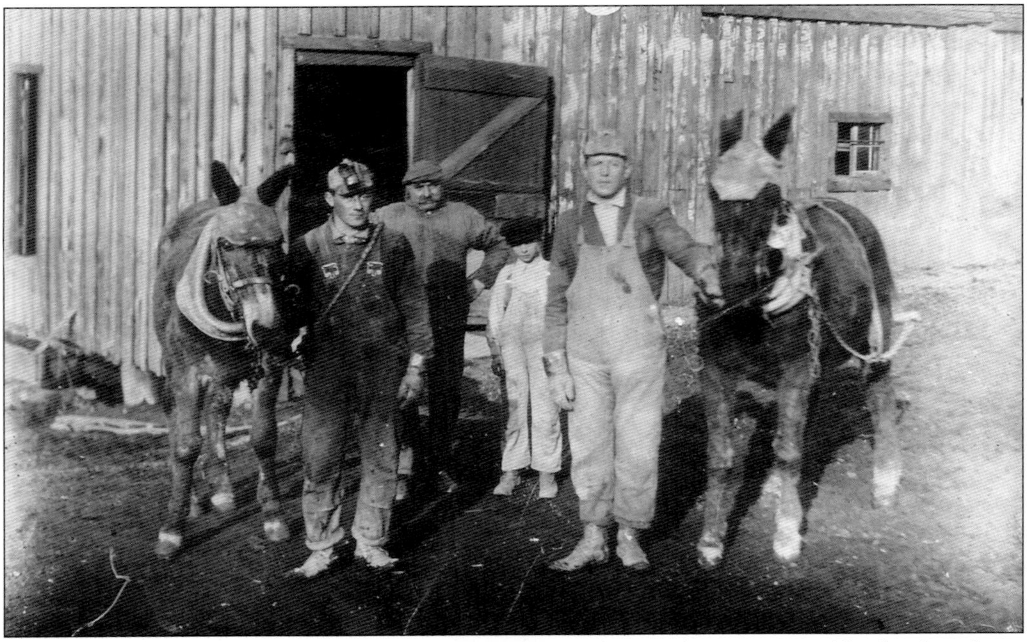

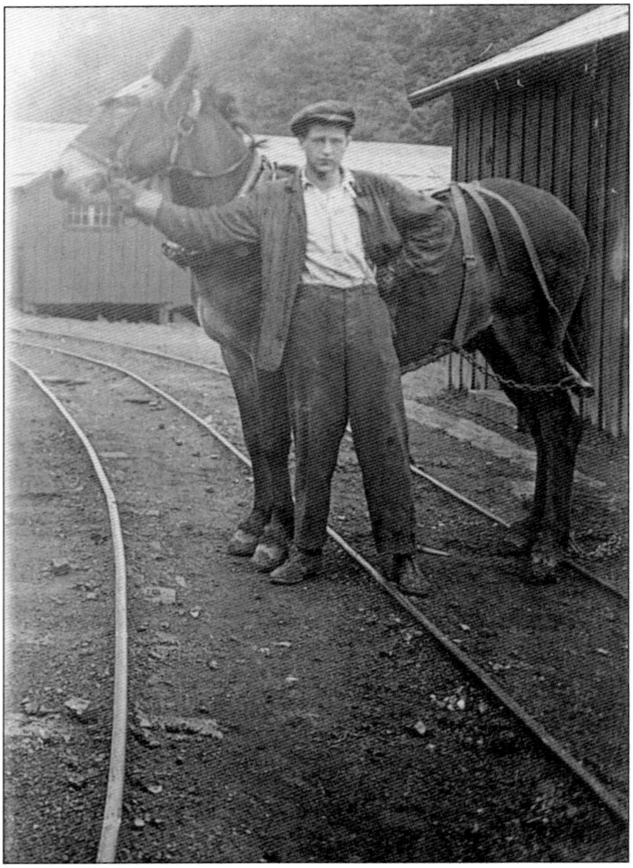

Above, miners Charles Angelo (left) and Victor Lavella (right) pose with the mules used to haul coal from the mines before electric cars came into use. The mules have a tin covering on their heads to protect from rock falls. Although they were stubborn, as mules are, their endurance and sure-footedness made them indispensable in the mines. Victor Lavella later owned a farm and slaughterhouse near Fairview. There were mule barns in Kersey, Dagus, Coal Hollow, and Toby, and the barn boss played a vital role in the health and cooperation of the animals. Often, boys would drive the animals to the mines early in the morning and then back home at night. At left, Joseph Mark Mosier readies a mule for the day's work. (Both, courtesy of Joan Verbka.)

At right, some of the last Coal Hollow and Toby miners and United Mine Worker officials pose on September 16, 1971. The mine workers had a long struggle with the local mines for better conditions and wages. Beginning in the 1880s, there were numerous strikes and slowdowns in the coal fields of Elk County. This group includes, from left to right, (first row) Gust Johnson, Guirine Dallason, John Shuttleworth, and Harry Caimi; (second row) Tony Cesa, Abe Johnson, and Santo Cesa; (third row) John Swanson, Florendo Facetti, and Tom Beveridge; (fourth row) Harry Mitchell, Ed Sheeley, Ray Gornati, and Edwin Hallgren; (fifth row) Walter Meredith and Joseph Cesa; (sixth row) John Glance and Mario Parmi; (seventh row) David Johnson and Guido Magistrelli. Below is one of their adversaries, Pat Harrington, the superintendent of the Coal Hollow mine.

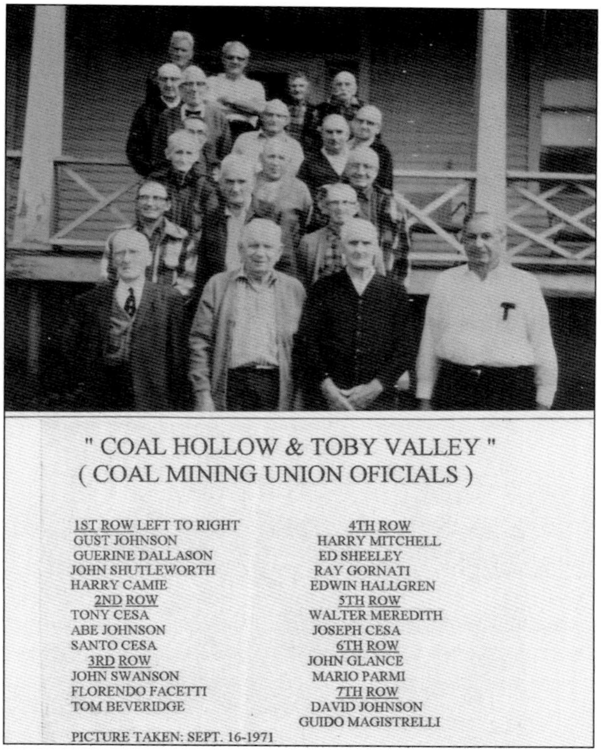

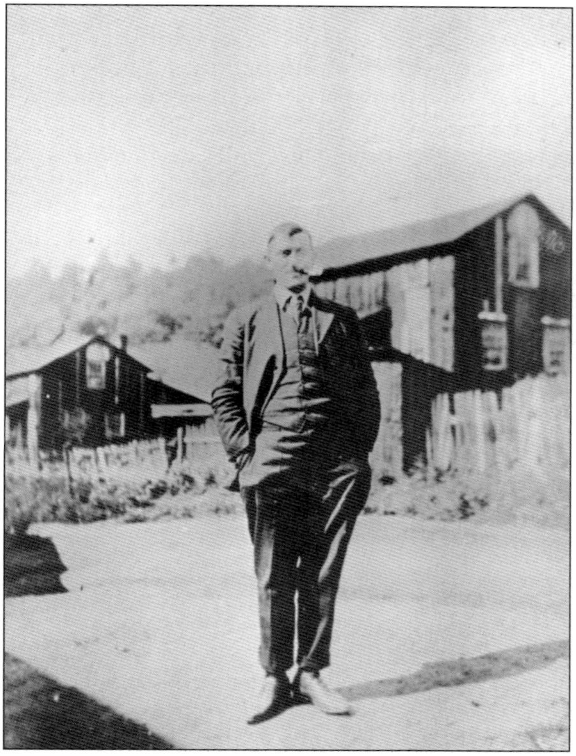

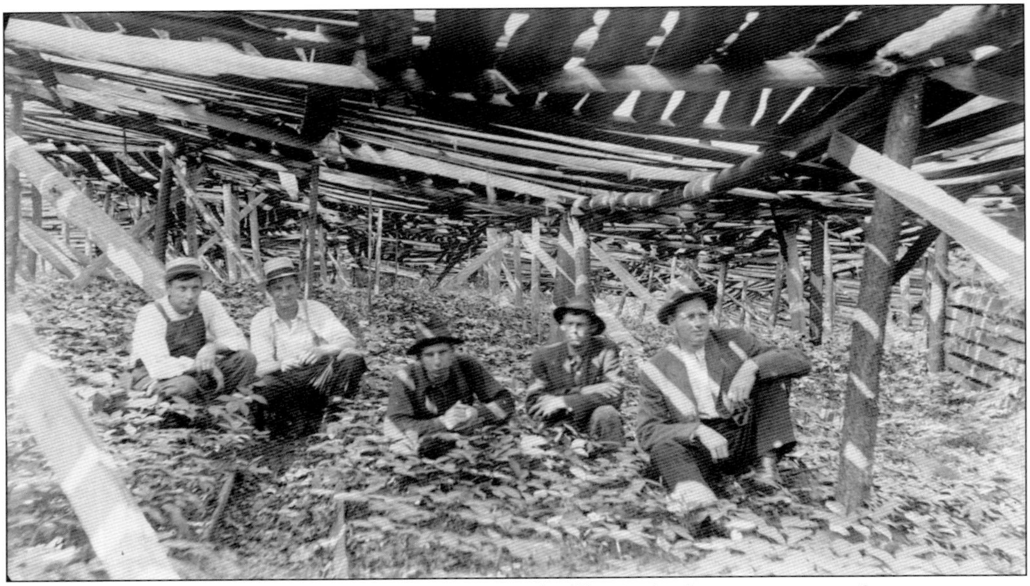

This lathe house was just west of Kersey, near Earlyville. Lathe houses were used as nurseries to protect young plants and seedlings from scorching sun or heavy rains. Though sometimes used for vegetables, they were most often used for the young trees needed to replace the denuded hillsides, which had been left bare from fire, farming, and mining. (Courtesy of Chris Casey.)

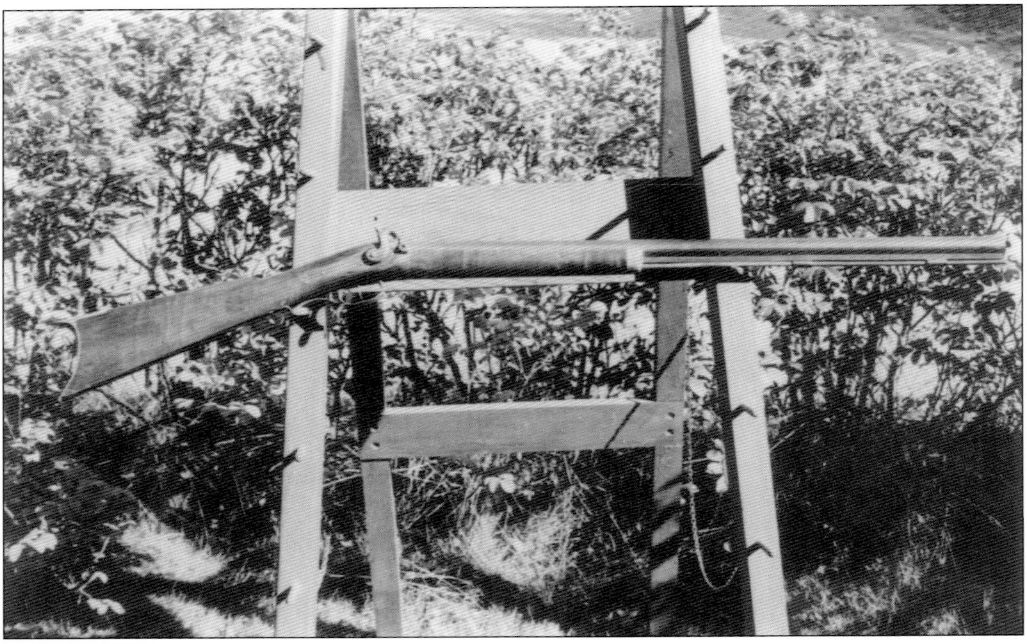

John Bonham, a gunsmith in the Green/Koch building, handcrafted this Hawkin-style muzzleloader. It is a percussion, or caplock style, making it easier and faster to load as well as more reliable. It was probably between 50 and 60 caliber. In 1862, at the age of 41, Bonham enlisted in the 135th regiment of the Pennsylvania Volunteer Infantry. He was married three times, first to Elizabeth Green, the daughter of John Green. (Courtesy of Barb Pistner.)

Six

Service to All

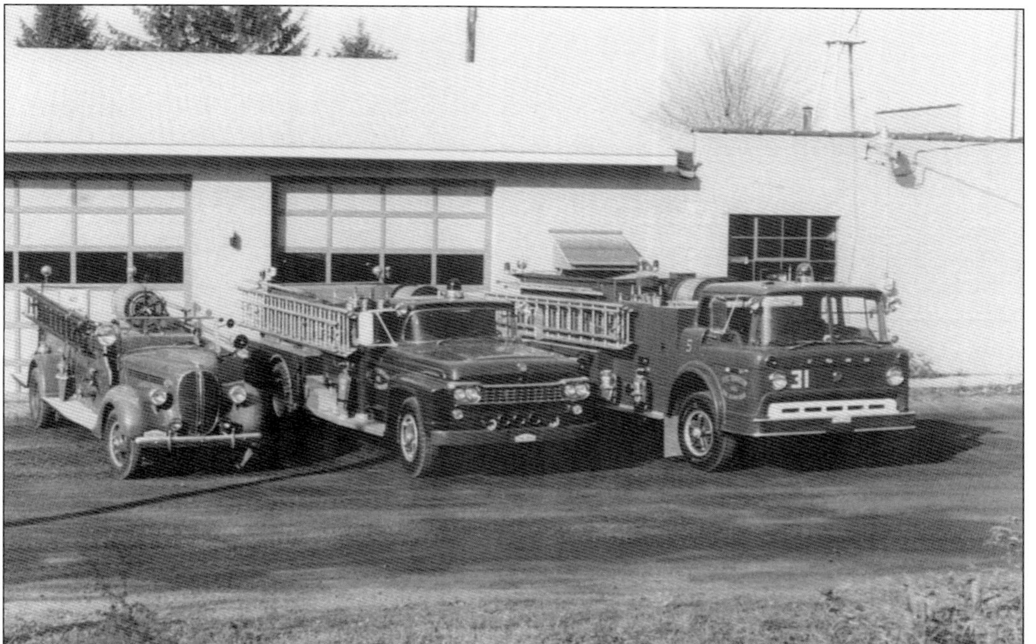

Although the forerunner to the Kersey Hook and Ladder Company was established in 1897, the current Fox Township Volunteer Fire Department was begun in 1937. These three trucks served as the main fire protection in the township for 68 years, from 1938 to 2006. They are, from left to right, a 1938 Ford, a 1958 Ford, and a 1973 Ford Maxim. The 1938 was a mainstay in parades for decades after its retirement. (Courtesy of Paul Neureiter.)

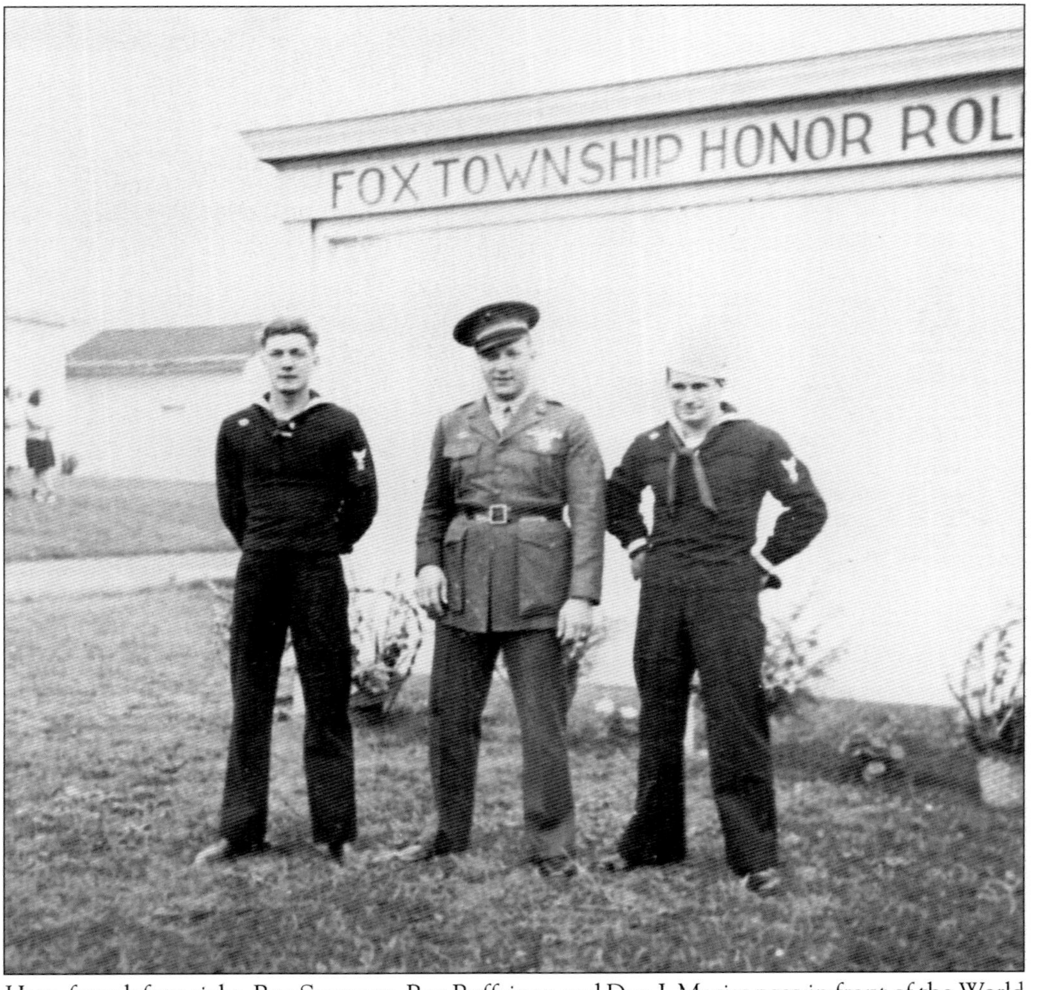

Here, from left to right, Ray Swanson, Ray Raffeiner, and Dan J. Mosier pose in front of the World War II Honor Roll sign on the grounds of the St. Boniface School. The sign listed the names of the more than 400 men and women from Fox Township who served in the war, including nine men who gave their lives. The men and women of our communities have served in all the wars and conflicts of this nation, and in all branches of the military. Men fought at Saratoga, Gettysburg, Antietam, Atlanta, the Argonne Forest, Normandy, Iwo Jima, New Guinea, Korea, Vietnam, Iraq, Afghanistan, and more. Some are buried at Gettysburg, at Flanders Field, and in North Africa, Normandy, Honolulu, and Arlington. They marched with Washington, Grant, and Sherman. They flew bombers over Germany, fought naval battles in the Pacific, and struggled in the jungles of Vietnam. No sign of those who served can do justice to the sacrifice and courage of our veterans. (Courtesy of Joan Verbka.)

Although many medals and decorations were won by Fox Township veterans during World War II, the highest medal awarded to a township resident was the Silver Star, won by Sgt. George Heigel for his service in France. The Silver Star is next to the Medal of Honor in importance. Sergeant Heigel was also a German prisoner of war and a Purple Heart recipient. (Courtesy of Jamie Dowie.)

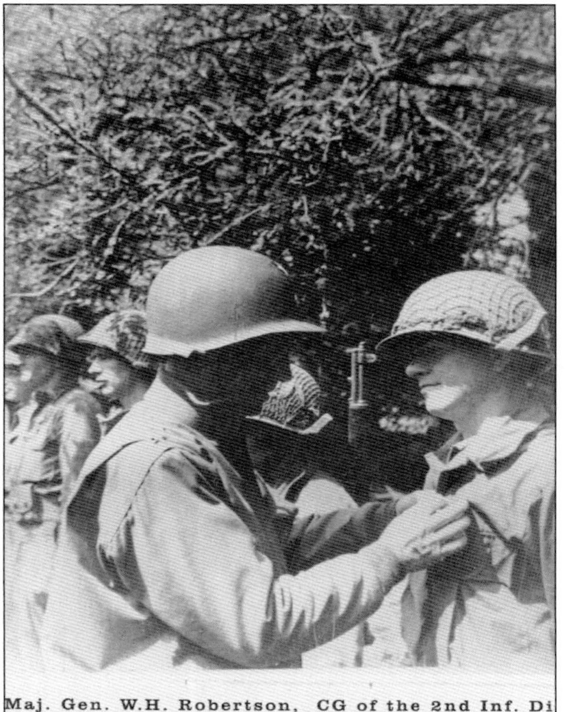

Maj. Gen. W.H. Robertson, CG of the 2nd Inf. Di presents the Silver Star to Sgt. G. Heigel of St. Marys, Penna.

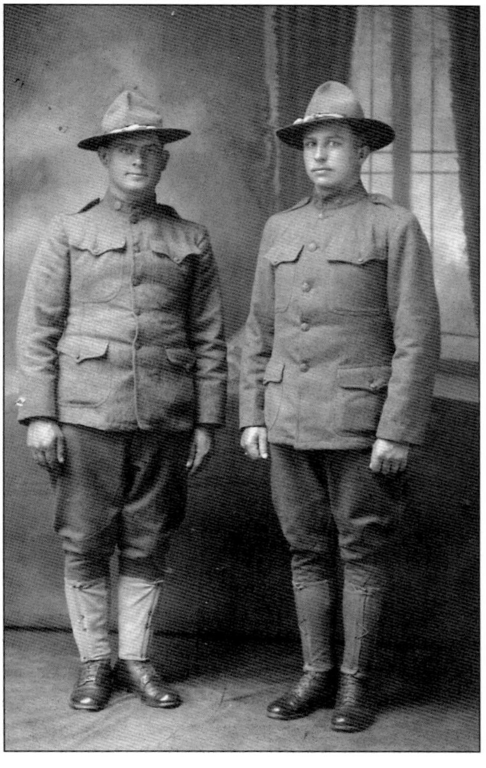

Charles Angelo (left) was one of nearly 120 township men and at least one woman—nurse Jane Leary—to serve in World War I. He was a member of the 106th Infantry, 27th Division, and saw action in France in 1918. Upon their return, the local World War I vets began American Legion Post 511. (Courtesy of Hazel Luchini.)

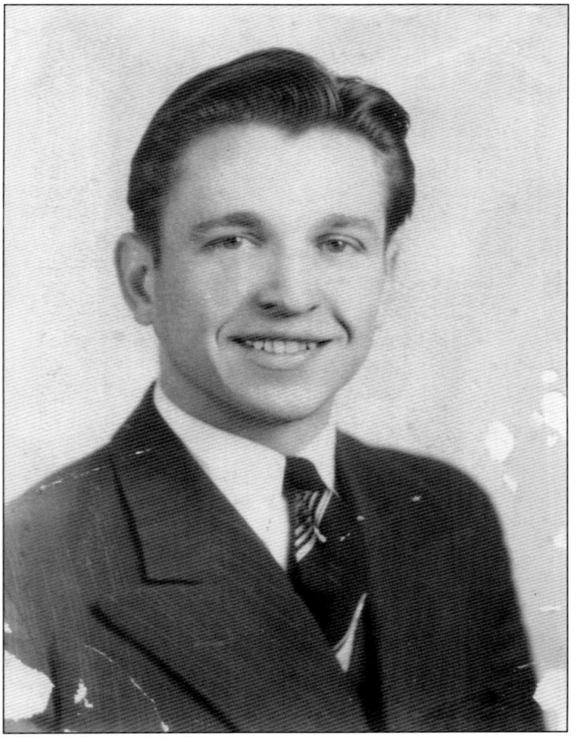

Albert Surra (left) was the first of at least 10 Fox Township casualties in World War II. A music teacher, glider pilot, and aerial forward observer, he was killed on February 12, 1942, over Rabat, Morocco, in North Africa, in an airplane crash during training. His two brothers, Mario and Leo, also served in the military during the war. Jerome "Tag" Dollinger (below) stormed ashore as part of the D-Day Normandy invasion, but was killed on June 19, 1944, when his body, according to sources, was "riddled with machine gun fire." He is buried in the military cemetery at Gettysburg. Floyd Ehrensberger also made it through the invasion, but was killed on October 10, 1944, farther inland. (Left, courtesy of Catherine Surra; below, courtesy of Jamie Dowie.)

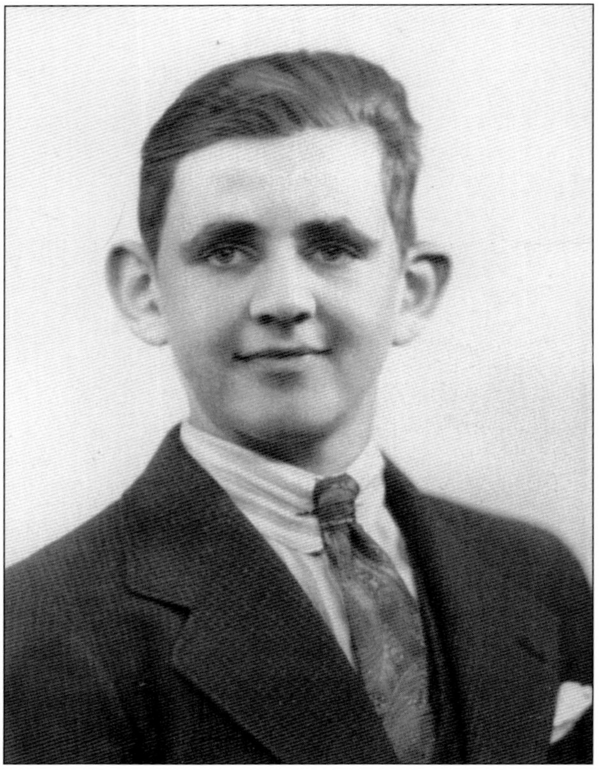

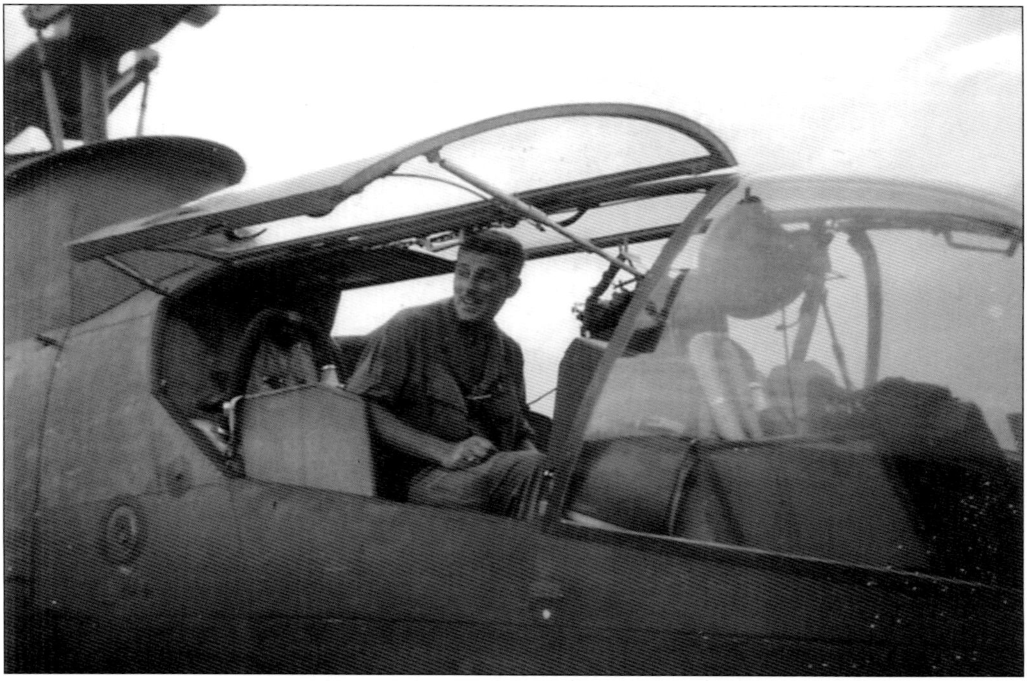

During the 1960s and early 1970s, scores of Fox Township residents served their country in the Vietnam War. This is Sgt. Craig Singer of Brandy Camp Road in 1969. He received a Purple Heart and was awarded the Bronze Star. He was also Boy Scout Troop 94's first Eagle Scout. Singer has been serving the veterans of the area since his return and is very involved with Fox Post 511 of the American Legion. (Courtesy of Ralph C. Singer.)

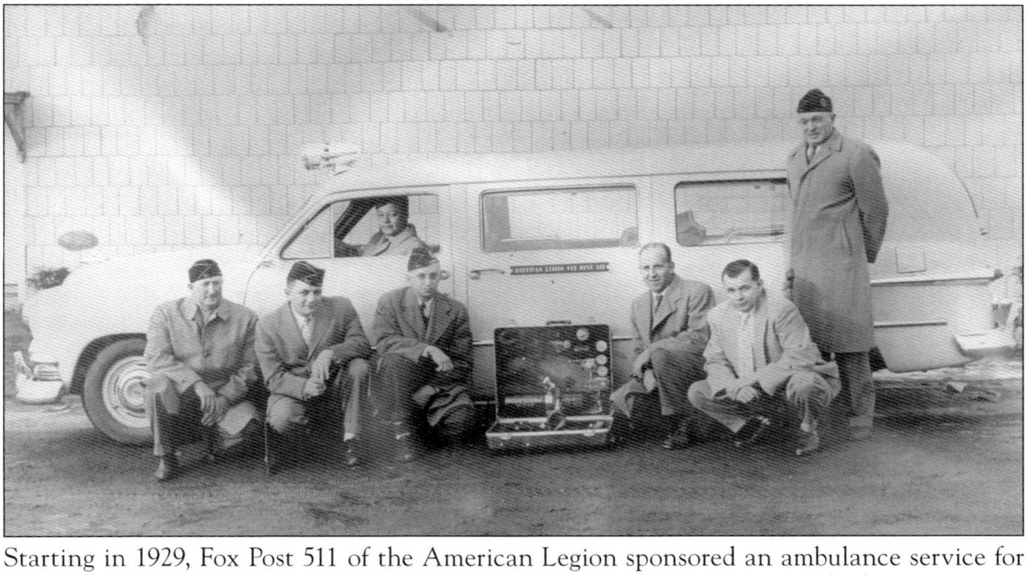

Starting in 1929, Fox Post 511 of the American Legion sponsored an ambulance service for township residents. Today, the service, on Main Street, is self-supporting. The legionnaires in this 1959 photograph are, from left to right, Art McConnell, George Dallason, John Ohlin (in ambulance), John Caimi, Cornelius Dietz, Tom Holtzhauser, and Gus Sicheri. (Courtesy of George Mosier.)

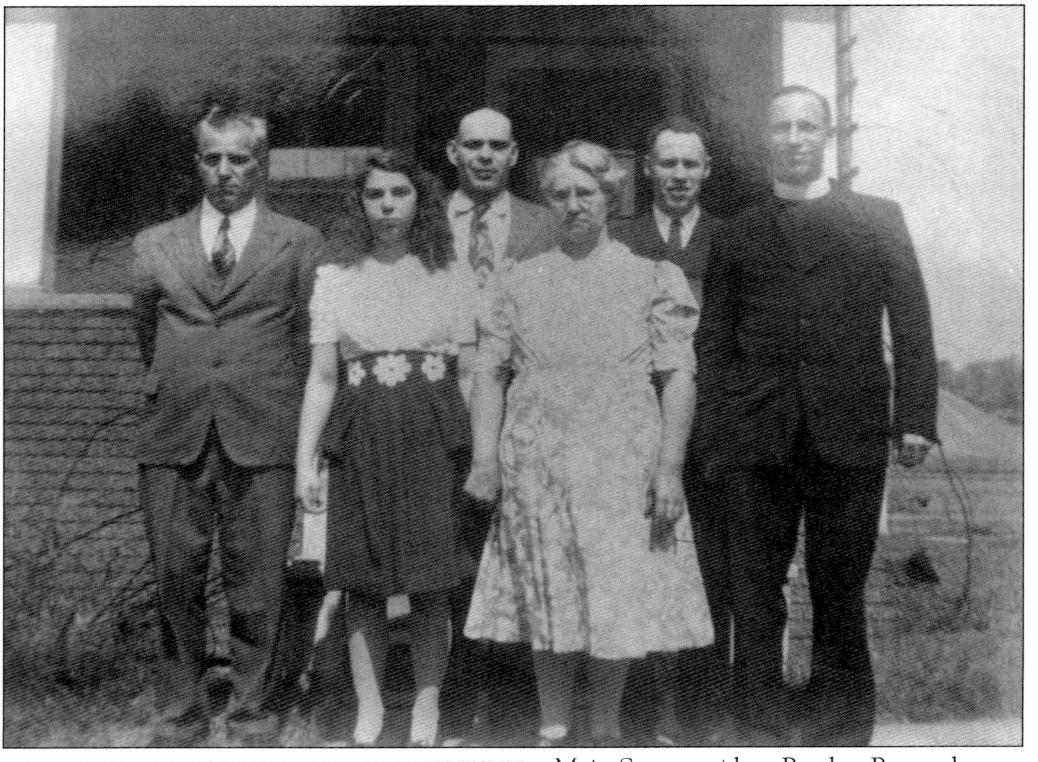

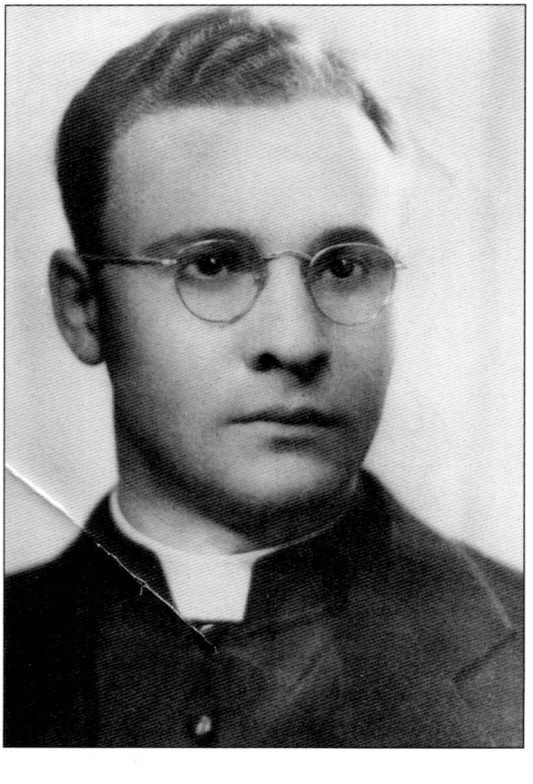

Main Street resident Brother Bernard "Fred" Mosier, CSC, was born in 1908 and joined the brotherhood in 1926. He served the poor of Bangladesh for 10 years, where he had a personal meeting with Gandhi. He continued to serve the poor and troubled in the United States until his death in 2002. He is seen here on the far right with his family; his mother, Mary, is next to him.

Msgr. Geno Monti, a Coal Hollow native, built Our Lady of Fatima, a school, convent, and chapel in Farrell, in 1960. In recognition of his efforts, he was named monsignor in 1970 by Pope Paul VI. The school was renamed for him in 1980. He is seen here in his 1937 ordination photograph. He was born in 1909 to Battista and Esther Monti.

Seven

SPORTS, RECREATION, AND LEISURE

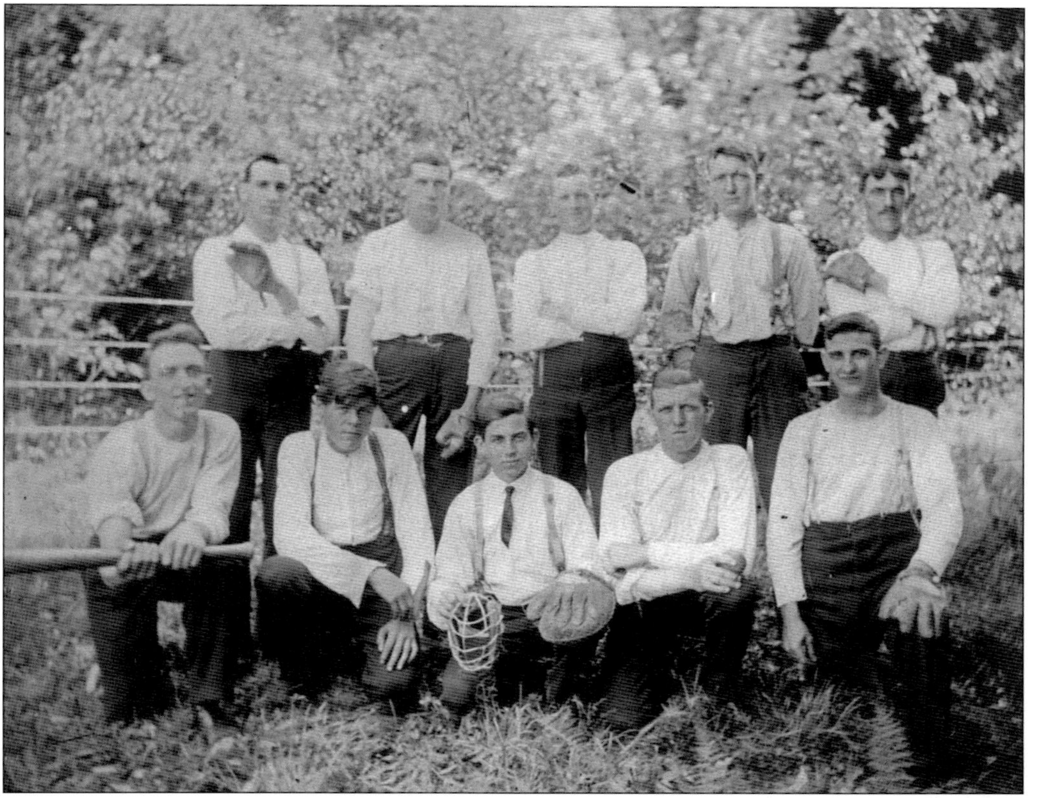

Baseball has been the most important sport in Fox Township since at least the Civil War. Scores were recorded in early newspapers for the Earlyville Nine and the Centreville Unknowns. An early score has the Unknowns defeating the St. Marys Lonestars 58-47. Notice the small size of the baseball gloves in this photograph.

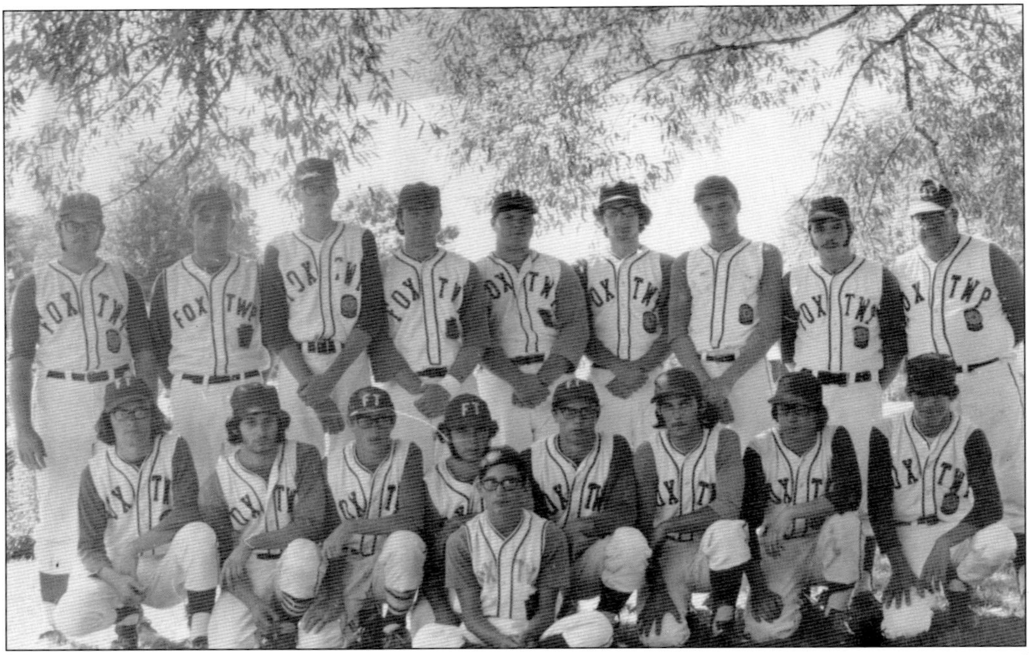

Between 1962 and 1972, Les Pionelli managed the Fox Township American Legion team to 9 of the 14 Elk County League titles. The team also went to two Western Pennsylvania state finals and two Pennsylvania state finals. The Junior Legion team was fourth in the state in 1974. The 1970 Legion team is seen here, with coach Pionelli at back right. (Courtesy of Anna Mae Short.)

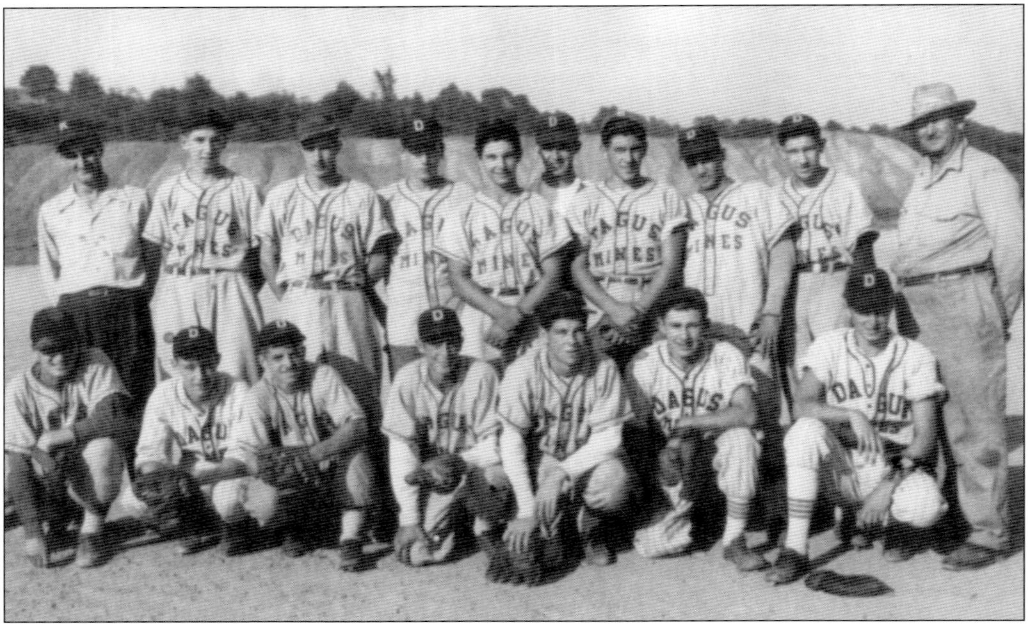

Dagus Mines had outstanding teams prior to World War I. They were 26-5 in 1913, with a 20-game win streak. They lost only twice in 1914 and 1915, to teams from larger nearby towns. The 1949 team is seen here in front of the rock dumps at the Dagus field. Some of the player surnames were Dacanal, Heigel, Pasquinelli, Petrocchi, Longhi, and Mosier. (Courtesy of Fox Township.)

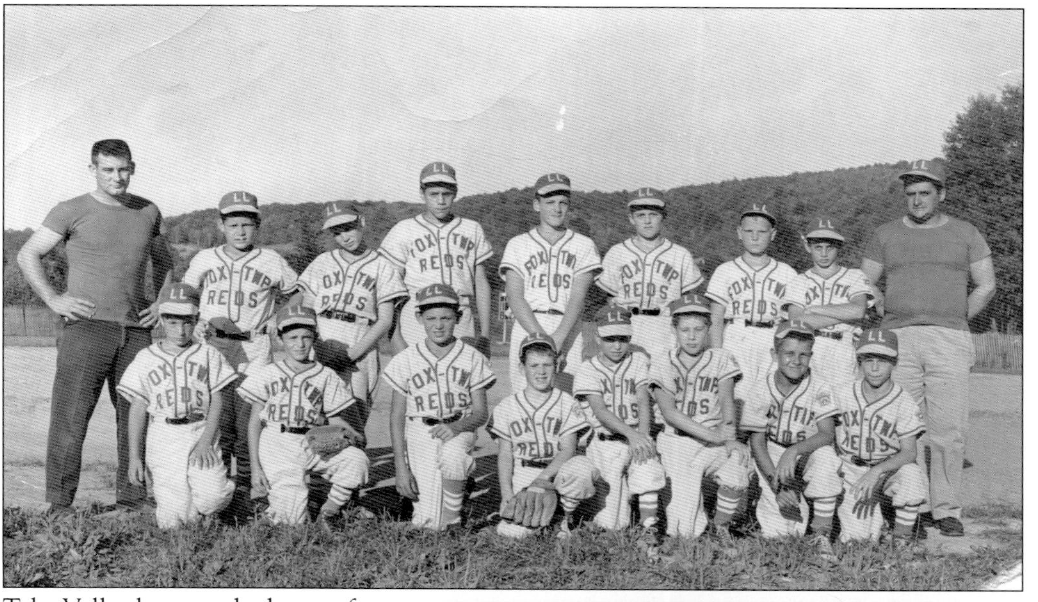

Toby Valley became the home of Fox Township Little League in 1961, and the field is still used today. Thousand of young athletes have played there. Today, girls can also play Little League baseball. The Reds, the first league championship team, are seen above. Ralph Iorfido and Emery Vanhorn were the managers. New fields at the Fox Township Park are also used today. At right, on this 1907 postcard, young George Johnson wrote his Aunt Agnes to show off his new Toby Valley baseball uniform. Interestingly, the writing is in Swedish. (Courtesy of Joan Verbka.)

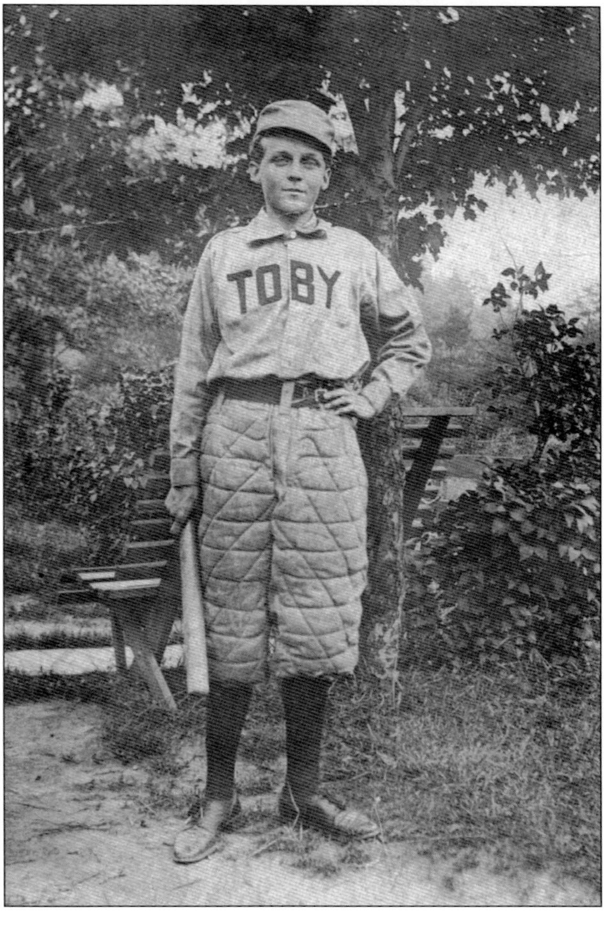

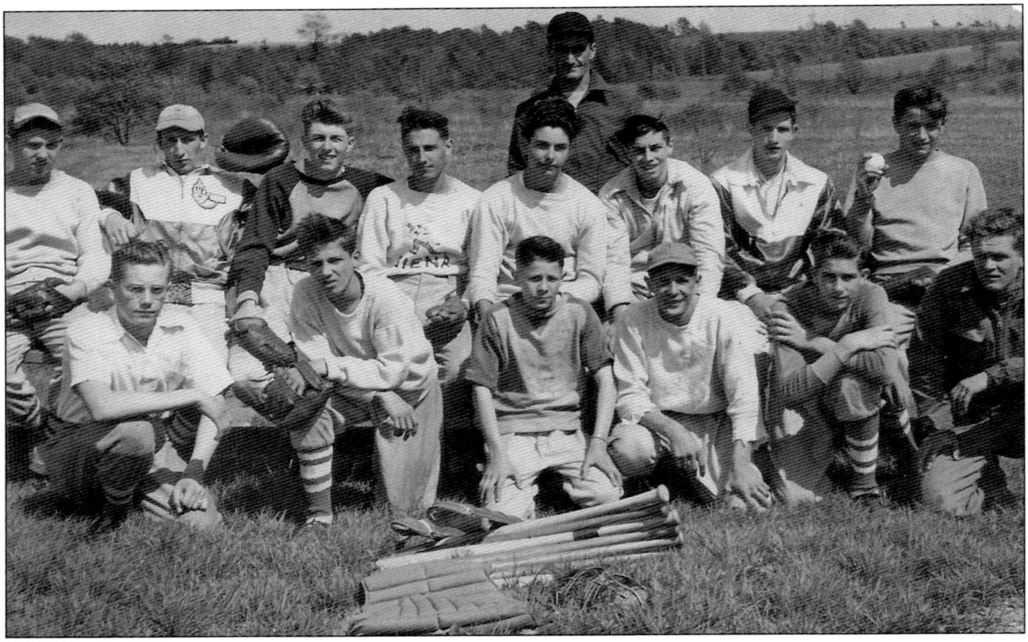

From 1945 to 1951, Kersey High School dominated the area baseball leagues, winning four Elk County League titles and three AML League titles. The undefeated 1948 County League champions are seen above after practice. They played St. Marys, Ridgway, Johnsonburg, Wilcox, Bennett's Valley, and others. The team includes, from left to right, (first row) Dick Halgren, Jack Mosier, Sam Luchini, George Lavella, Edward Heigel, and Ray Weidow; (second row) Frances Mosier, Joe Neureiter, Art McConnel, Vic Lavella, Aldo Pasquinella, Jim Beimel, Leo Biladeau, and Bob Longhi; (third row) Tom Carpin. Below is another championship team from around 1950, which included, from left to right, (first row) Carl Beimel, Joe Petrocchi, Jack Moyer, Sam Luchini, and unidentified; (second row) Tom Carpin, Bill Freeburg, John DaCanal, Bill Harvey, Skip Heigel, and Aldo Pasquinelli.

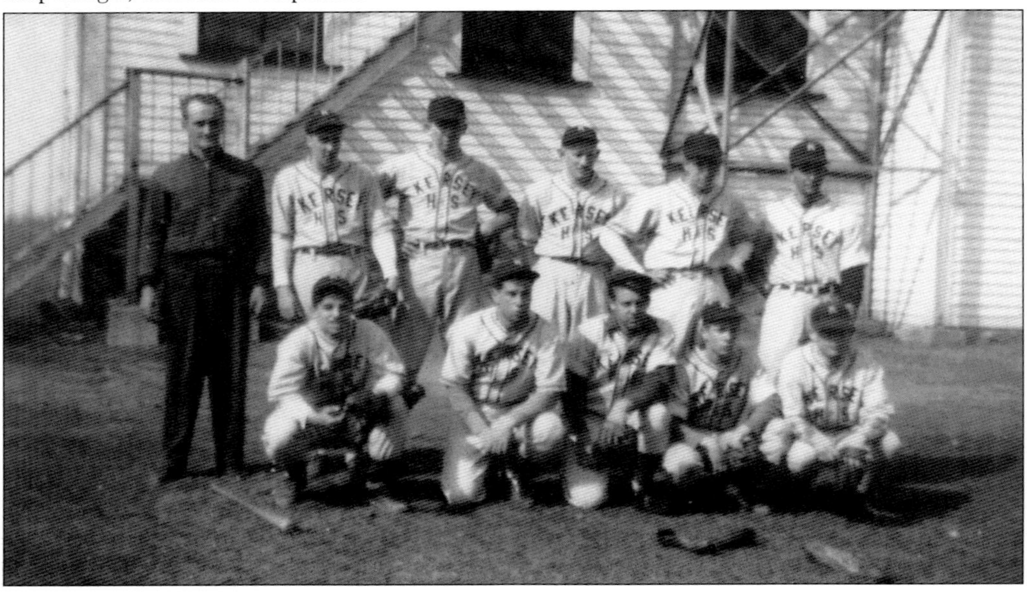

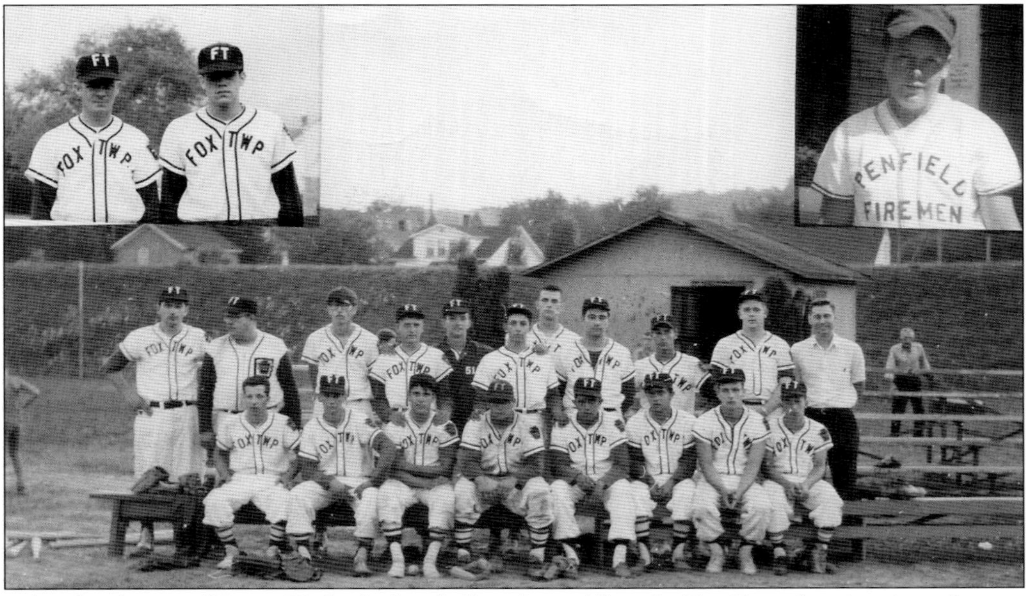

After the closing of Kersey High, the baseball tradition fell to the Fox Township American Legion teams. In the late 1960s, the Legion baseball teams were Pennsylvania state contenders, annually making it to the playoffs. The 1966 team (above) went all the way to states, and finished in the top eight. The team included, in no particular order, Sam Luchini, Wes Pionelli, Mike Shutika, John Rio, Larry Kunes, Denny Iorfido, Mickey Murray, Fred Porco, Fran Coccimiglio, Vic Gregori, Frank Zambenini, Bill Neureiter, Louis Mattivi, Jim Steinbiser, Bill Tami, and Doug Butterfuss. The 1967 team, who were undefeated league champions at 16-0, are seen below. They are, from left to right, (first row) D. Farley, Mickey Murray, Fred Porco, Fran Coccimiglio, Vic Gregori, F. Zambenini, B. Neureiter, and Jerry Tamburlin; (second row) Sam Luchini, Mike Shutika, John Rio, Brent Pasquinelli, Larry Kunes, Denny Iorfido, Les Pionelli, and Vic Straub.

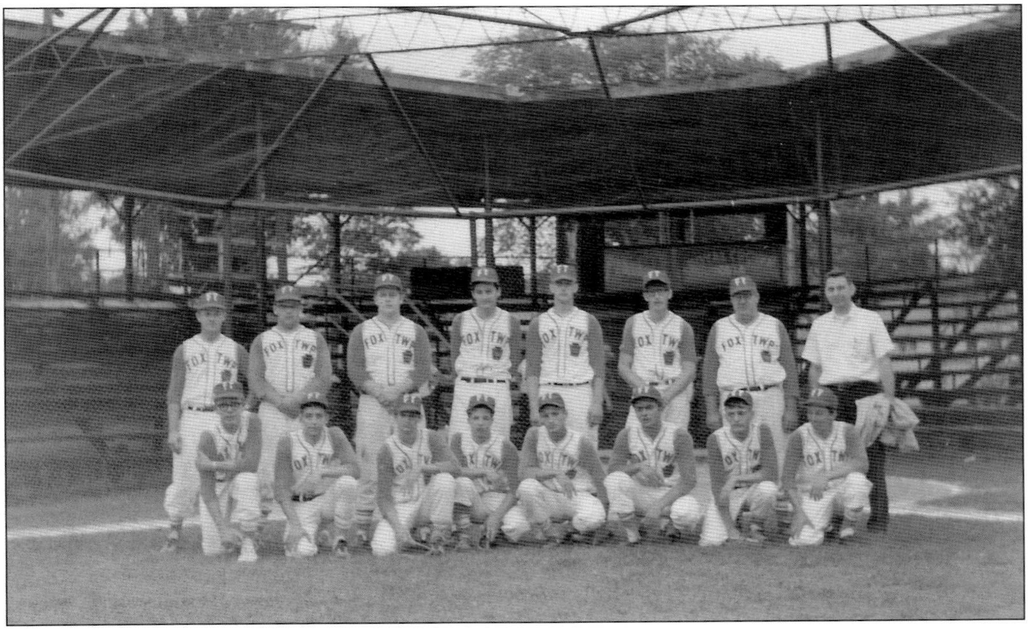

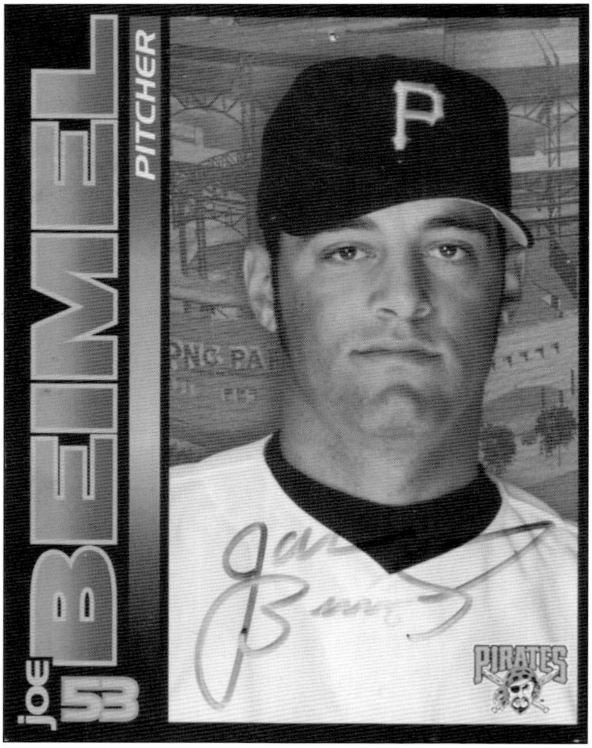

Joe Beimel was drafted by the Pittsburgh Pirates in 1998. In his career, the left-handed pitcher played for the Pittsburgh Pirates, Los Angeles Dodgers, Colorado Rockies, Tampa Bay Devil Rays, Minnesota Twins, and Washington Nationals. He was a relief specialist for most of his career. It was said that he "owned" Barry Bonds, because of his success against the great slugger. (Courtesy of Ron Beimel.)

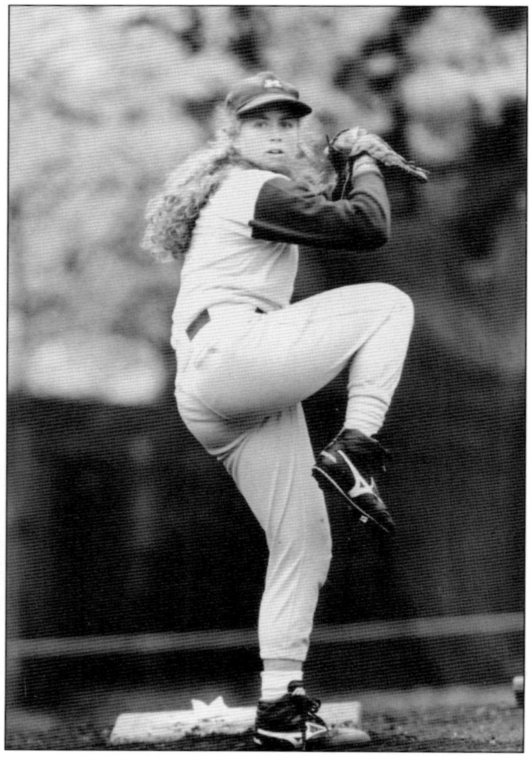

In 1991, Jodi Haller was the first woman in the United States to pitch in a college baseball game, for St. Vincent's College in Latrobe, Pennsylvania. In 1995, after accepting a scholarship to Meiji University in Tokyo, she became the first woman to pitch in Japan's college ranks. (Courtesy of William and Janice Haller.)

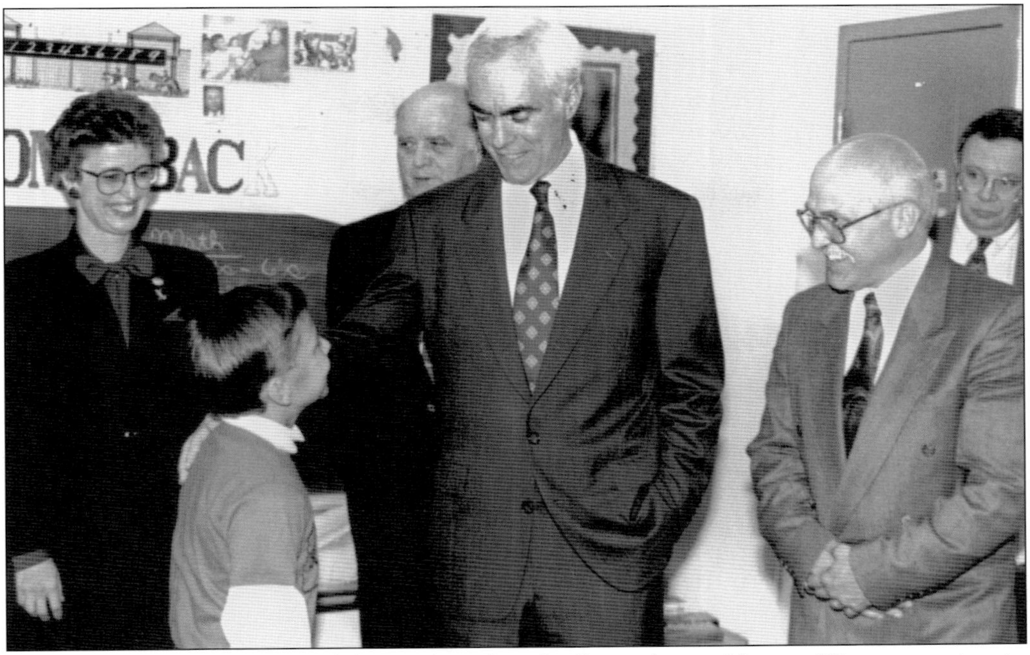

Kersey resident Dan Surra (right) was elected to the Pennsylvania House of Representatives in 1991. He served the 75th legislative district until 2008. Surra served the area with distinction and battled against the urban-area legislators who dominated the assembly. He was known for bringing back local tax dollars, especially in fair funding for schools. He also fought to protect the environment and for economic development. (Courtesy of Dan Surra.)

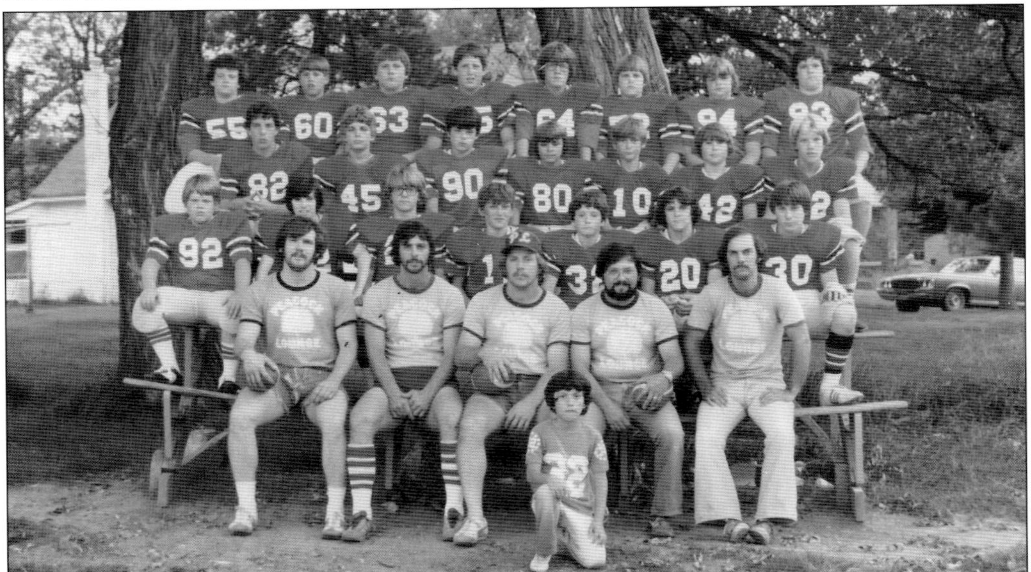

Beginning in 1973, the Kersey Comets became the township's team in the area midget football league. During its years of existence, the team won the league the majority of the time. The 1977 team is seen here. The coaches, in the first row from left to right, are Tom Young, Paul Powers, Jim Swanson, Gary Tamburlin, and Steve Shuttleworth. (Courtesy of Fox Township.)

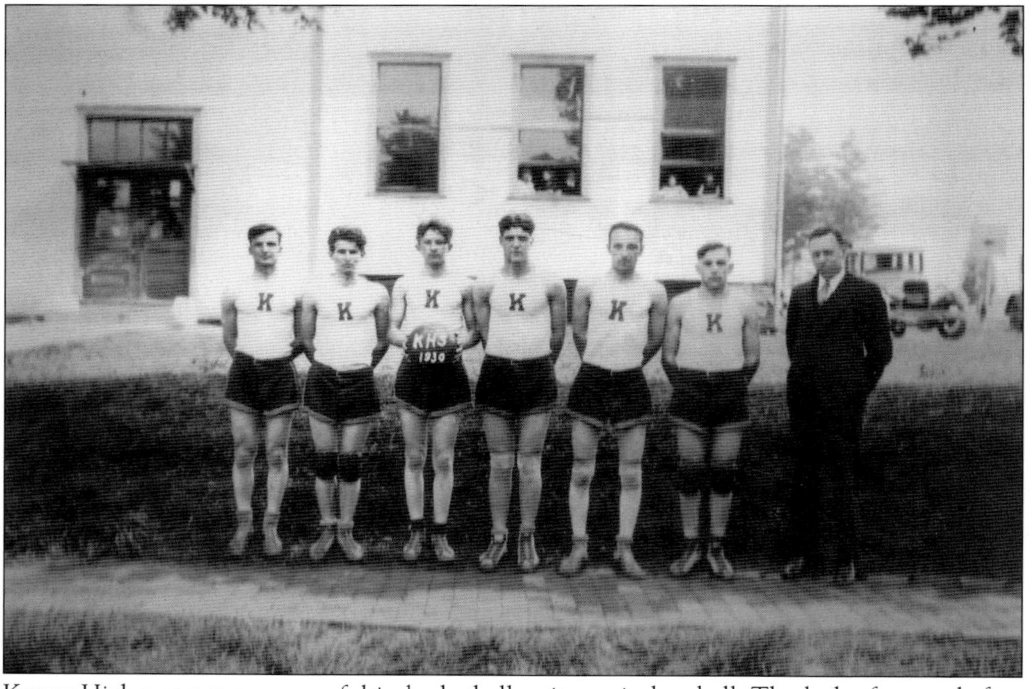

Kersey High was not as successful in basketball as it was in baseball. The lack of a gym before the construction the Community Building made it difficult to produce many winning seasons. The team played home games in the UMW hall. This 1930 team included, among others, Arthur Freeburg, Pat Swanson, Gelindo Gradizzi, and Charles Donovan.

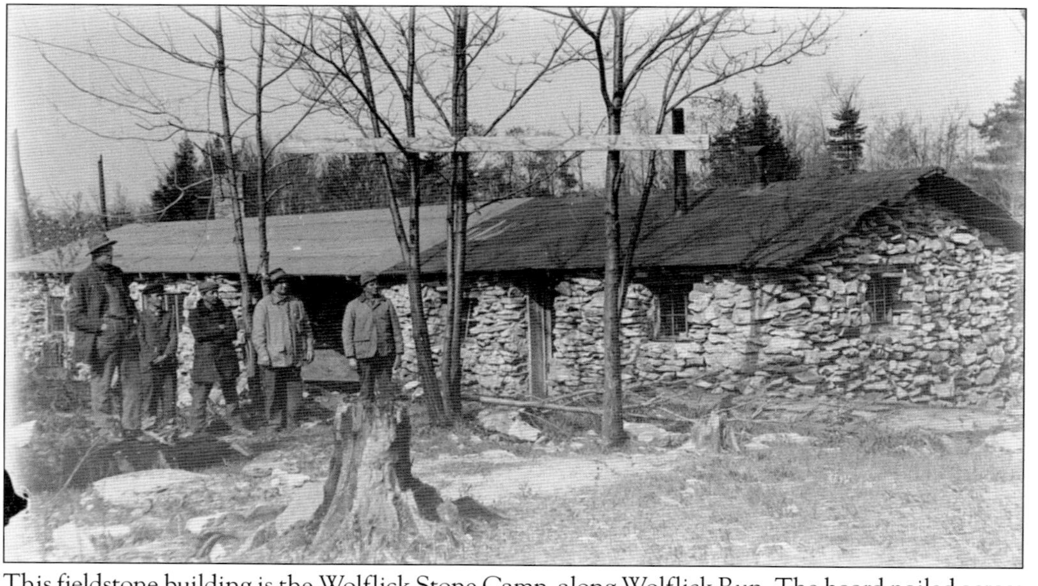

This fieldstone building is the Wolflick Stone Camp, along Wolflick Run. The board nailed across the trees is for hanging deer or bear caught during hunting season. The two men near the front are George Heigel (left) and Edward Spuller (right). Note the size of the stumps, which show how the land looked after it was denuded of trees. The smaller trees are the emerging, second growth forest.

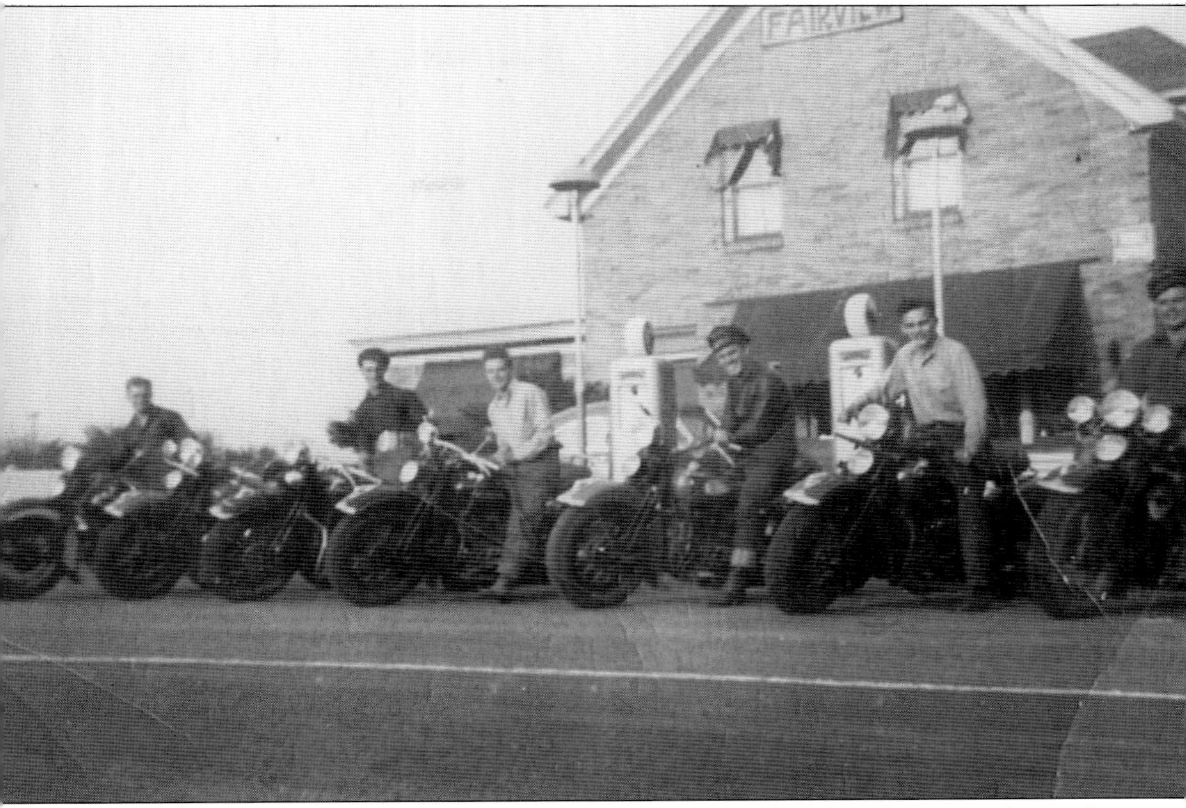

Following World War II, area young men began the first motorcycle club in the county. Some of the "saddle pals" are seen here at Tom Moore's gas station, at the intersection of Routes 255 and 948. The station was razed when Route 255 became four lanes in the mid-1970s. They are, from left to right, Fred Haller, Bud Silvis, Paul Hoffman, Dewayne Rorhbach, Gib Dippold, and Lajoy Newell. (Courtesy of Jim Catalone.)

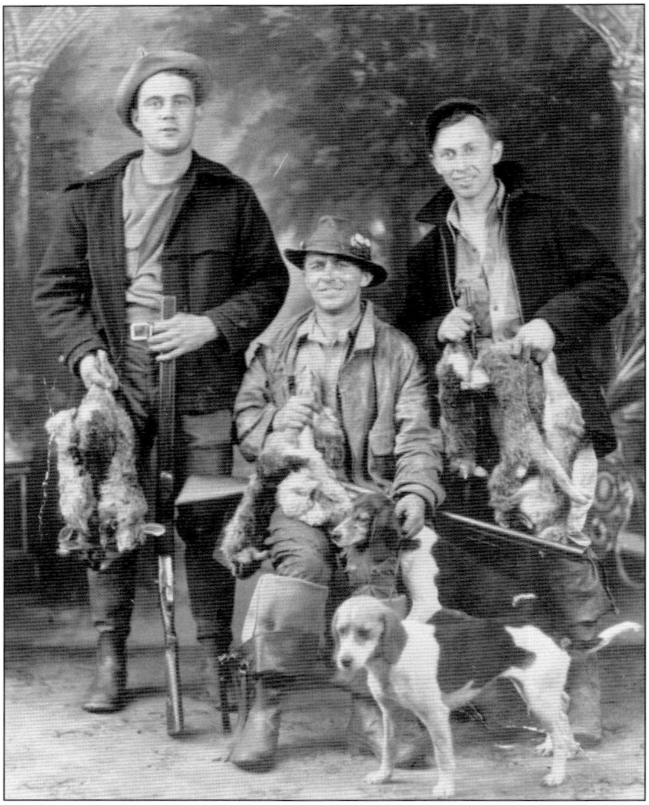

Rabbit hunting reached its peak between the 1940s and 1960s, as reforestation provided the kind of brushy habitat perfect for the animal. Seen here are, from left to right, Jim Cuneo, Maynard "Jiggs" Beimel, and Romaine "Shorty" Beimel, along with beagles Mack and Jack. They have caught their limit of rabbits. Jiggs Beimel's reputation as a skilled hunter was well known, and he passed his knowledge along to his nine sons. (Courtesy of Ginger Himes.)

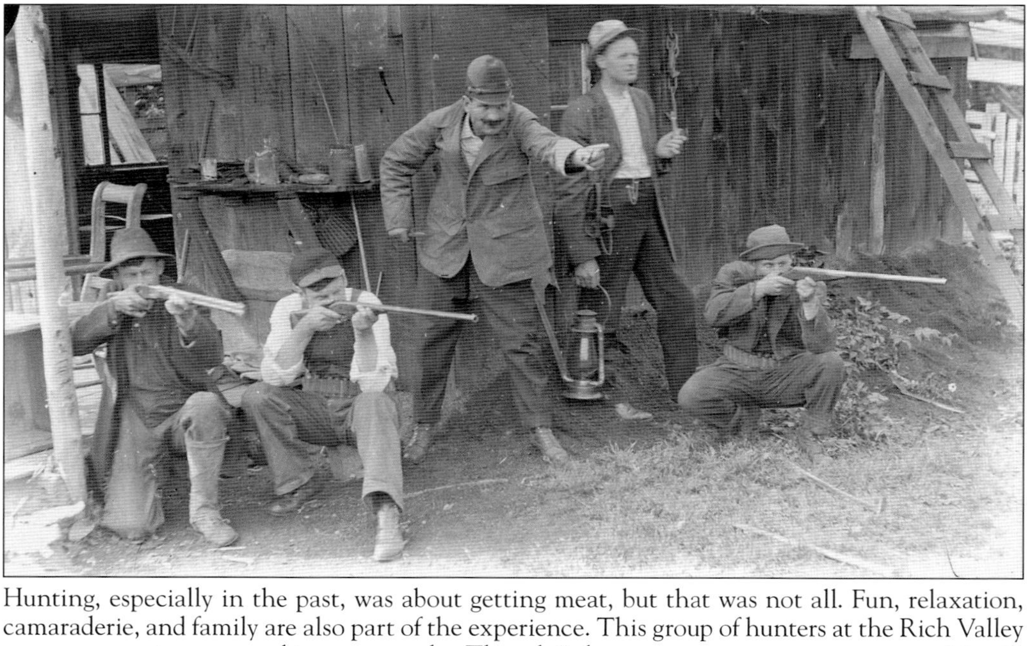

Hunting, especially in the past, was about getting meat, but that was not all. Fun, relaxation, camaraderie, and family are also part of the experience. This group of hunters at the Rich Valley camp appears to see some big game nearby. Though "what goes on at camp stays at camp" is still true, there is usually nothing to hide. (Courtesy of Chris Casey.)

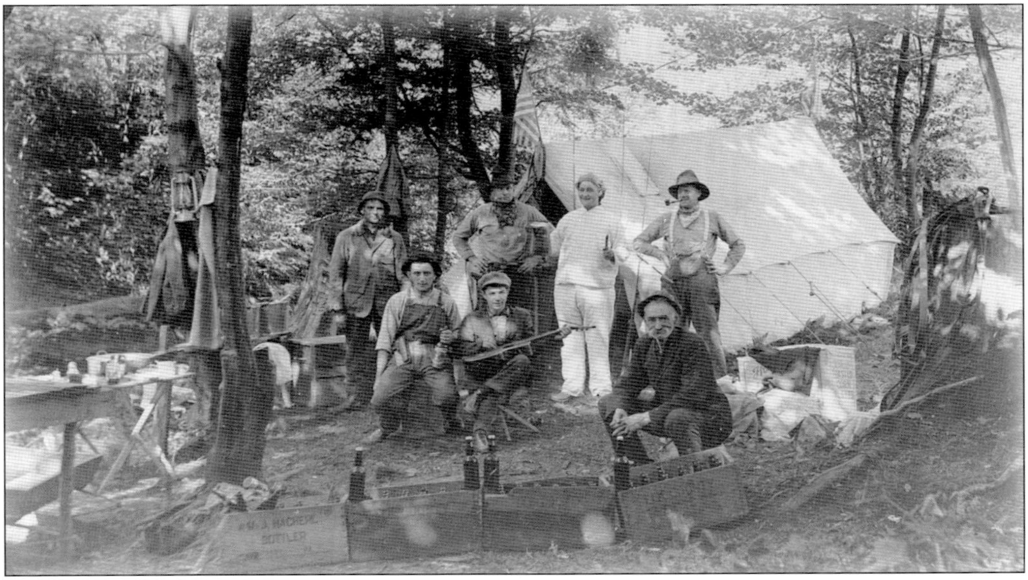

Hunting and fishing have always been leisure activities in the township. This fishing camp does not look much different than today. Four cases of Elk County beer bottled at Hacherl's, a guitar, a pistol, and an American flag are present. Notice the Kellogg's Toasted Corn Flakes box at right, and the buckboard seat under the table to the left.

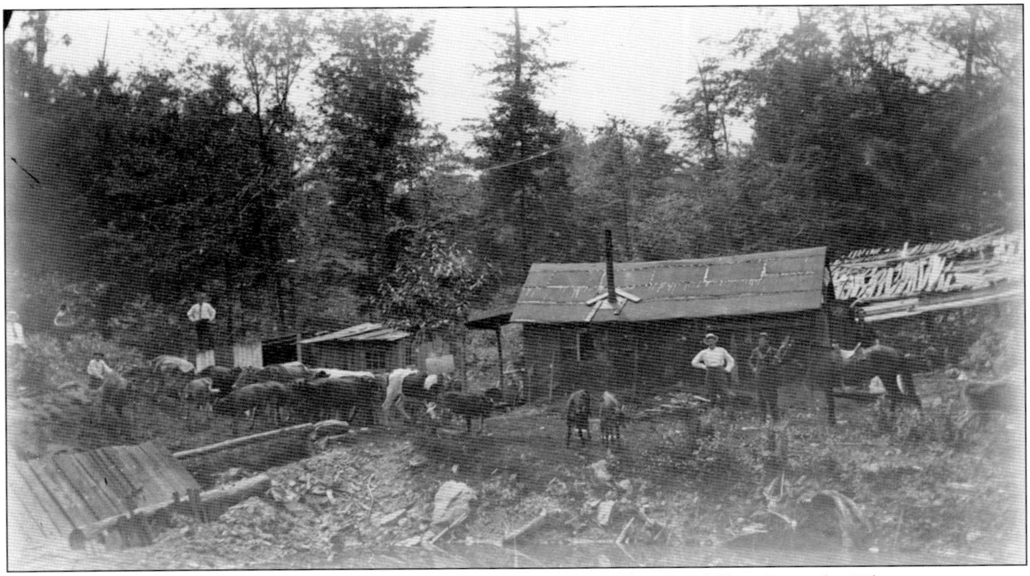

A herd of cows and perhaps a few oxen are driven past Birch Valley Ranch. There are many photographs of young men relaxing, drinking, and playing cards here, which suggests it was also a camp or a place to escape for some fun and relaxation. There appears to be a covered springhouse in the lower left corner. (Courtesy of Chris Casey.)

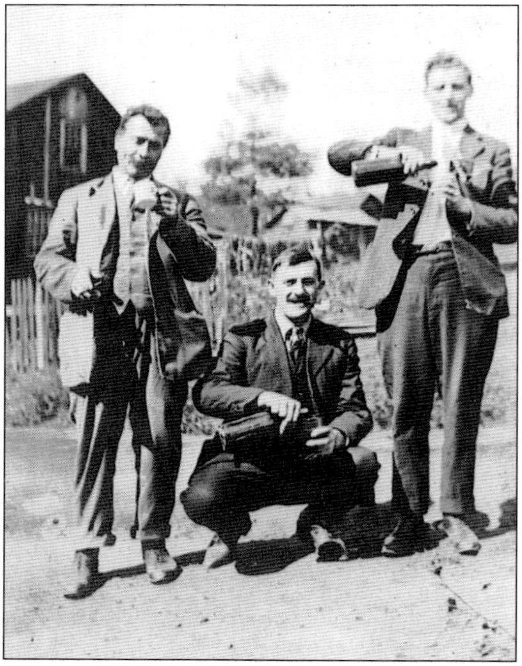

During Prohibition, there were many illegal stills and speakeasies in the area. These three gentlemen, who called themselves "the moonshine toppers," are outside a corn liquor and gambling saloon known as Slagers Shanty. John Pearson (right) managed the Coal Hollow establishment. John Cannera is on the left. (Courtesy of Joan Verbka.)

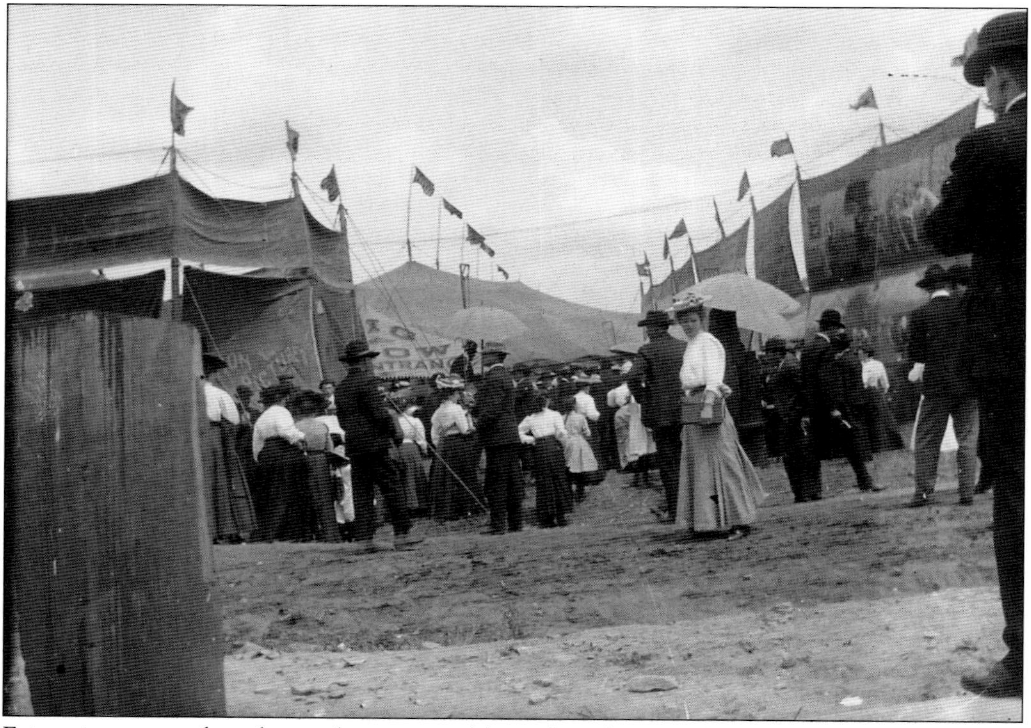

Fairs, circuses, and medicine shows arrived by rail to the township frequently. In June 1866, preeminent entertainer Dan Rice brought his show to Fox Township. Once, his train was chased from Centreville when some of his men were found waylaying township citizens. (Courtesy of Chris Casey.)

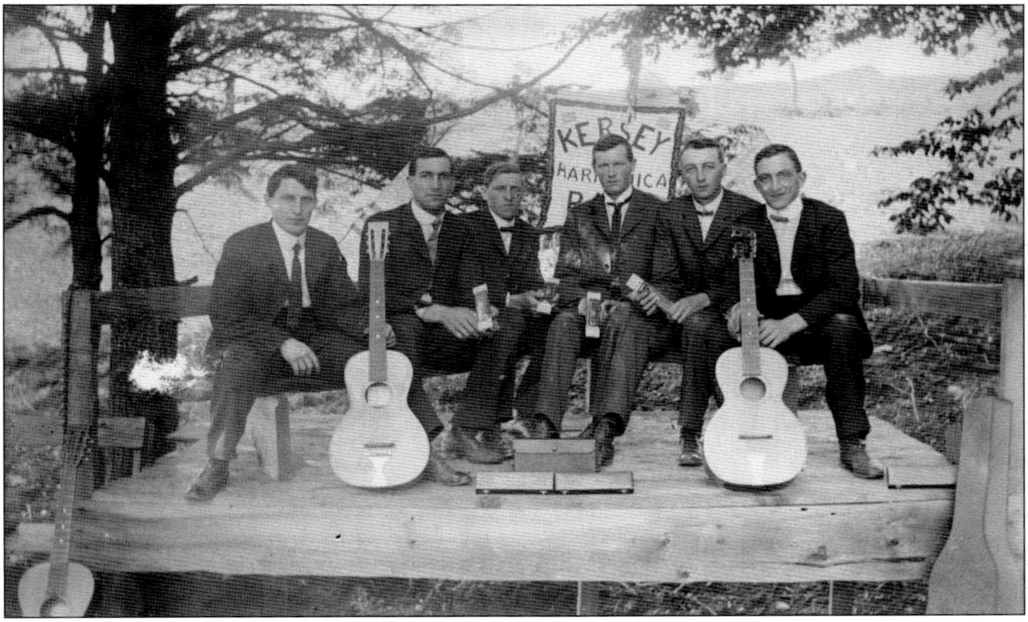

Holiday celebrations have been a part of the community's history since its creation. Annual Fourth of July picnics were held at Greens Grove, across Route 948 from the current Fox Township Park, for many years. Women would set a long table with delicious food, while the remainder of the celebrants would march with a band in a parade from Kersey. A notable person would read the Declaration of Independence, games would be played, and there would be music, dancing, and fireworks. The harmonica band and outdoor bowling alley in these photographs are typical of the festivities. Today, celebrations are held annually at the nearby Fox Township Park. The first indoor bowling alley in Kersey was owned and operated by Mose Harvey. (Both, courtesy of Chris Casey.)

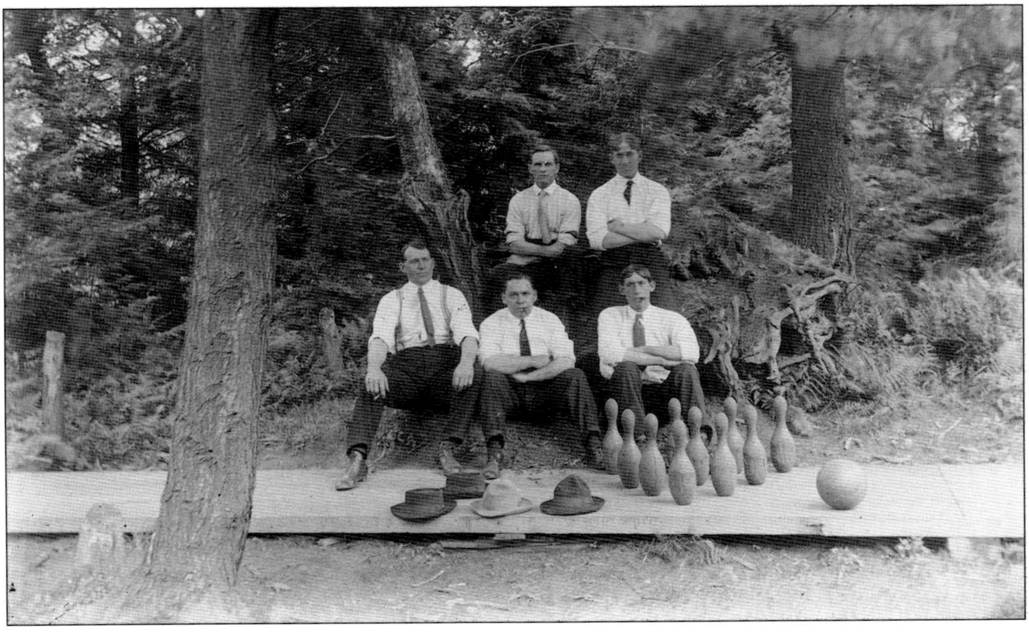

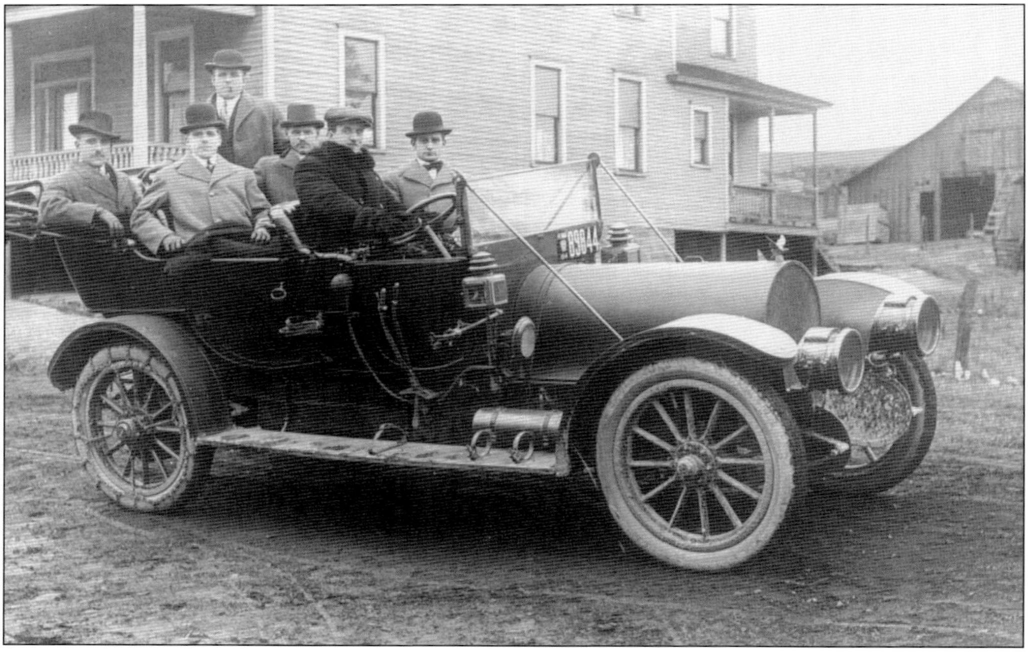

These men pose in brewer Alois Urmann's steam car in front of Herman Johnson's Eureka Hotel, which was later owned by Bill Hau, and then became the Last Chance. This was the first car in the township. Urmann even brought a chauffeur from Buffalo to maintain it. Notice the chains on the wheels because of the poor roads. The car was eventually destroyed in a fire. (Courtesy of Ken Anderson.)

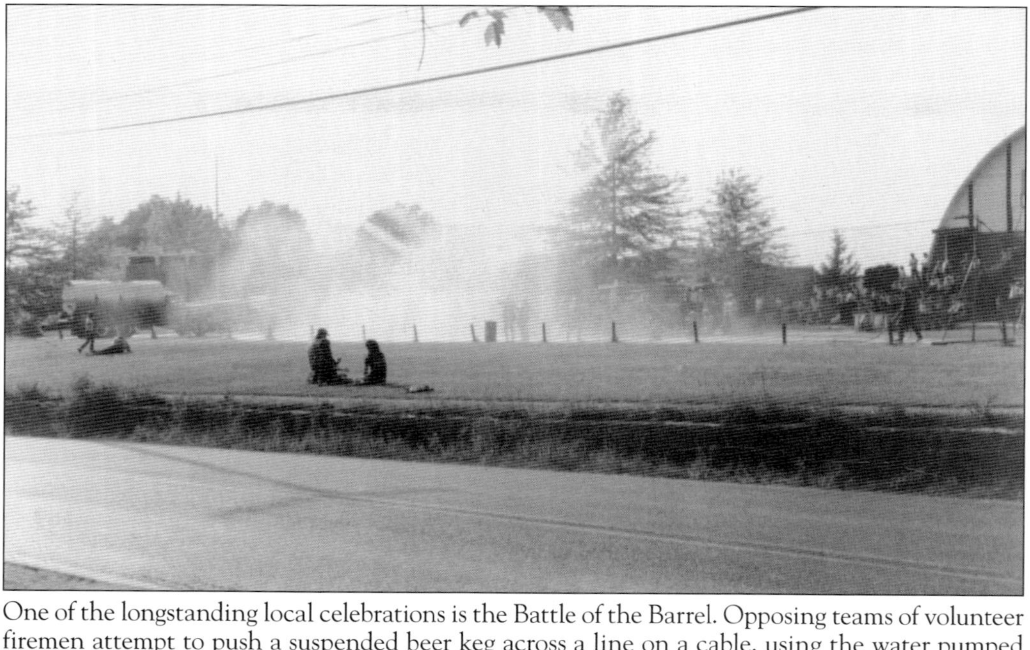

One of the longstanding local celebrations is the Battle of the Barrel. Opposing teams of volunteer firemen attempt to push a suspended beer keg across a line on a cable, using the water pumped through their fire hoses. This reverse tug-of-war continues until all teams are eliminated but the winner. Here, the battle takes place in front of the Community Building in the 1970s.

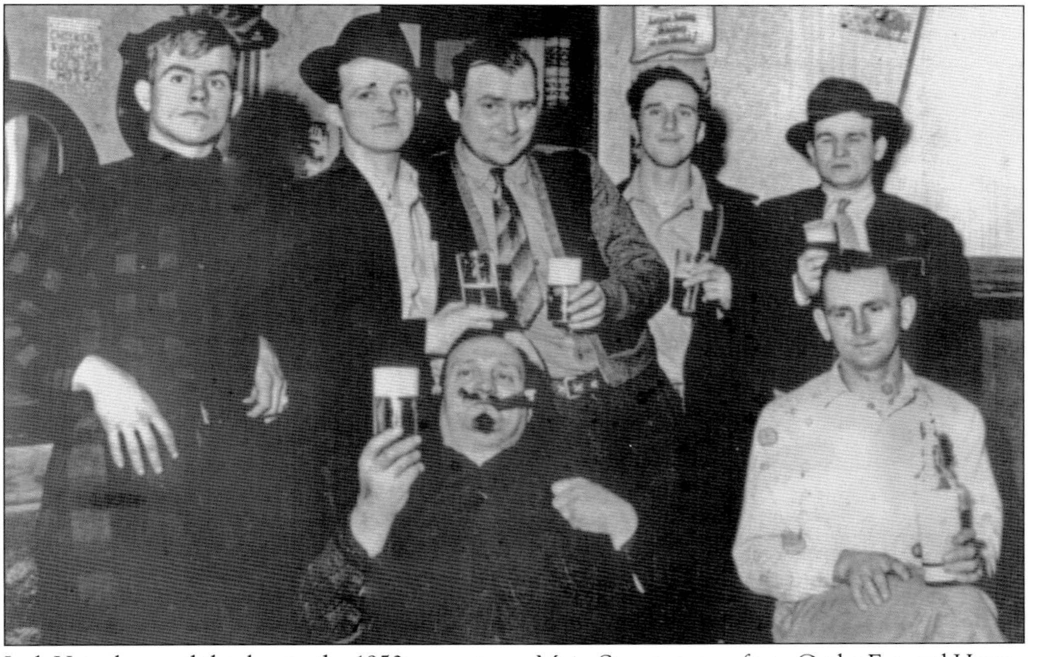

Jack Heigel owned this bar in the 1950s on uptown Main Street, across from Corbe Funeral Home. It advertised dancing and good food. This photograph shows the owner with some of his patrons. They are, from left to right, (first row) Andy Brem and Tim Heigel; (second row) George Heigel, ? Gustafson, Jack Heigel, Chickie Brem, and Chappy Weidow. (Courtesy of George Heigel.)

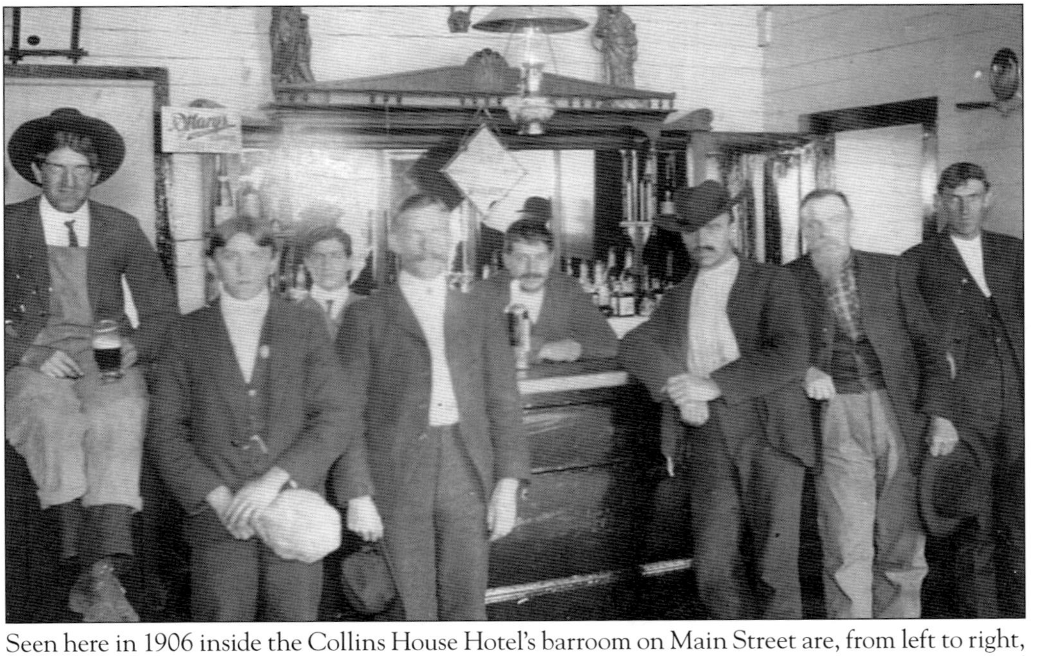

Seen here in 1906 inside the Collins House Hotel's barroom on Main Street are, from left to right, (first row) Wolfgang Pfilshifter, John Holtzhauser, Banty Schreiber, Matt Miller, Bosty Gahr, and unidentified; (bartenders) Jack and Joe Mosier. St. Marys beer is for sale, and just to the left of the kerosene lantern is a small, five- or six-point buck antler. (Courtesy of Pat McMackin.)

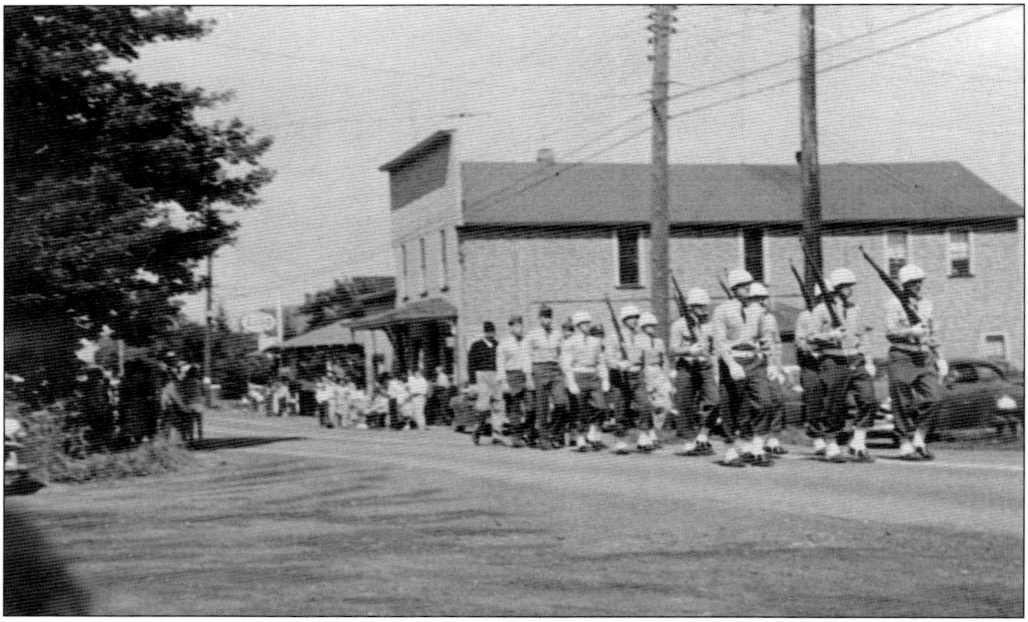

Parades have been a part of township celebrations since there were streets. In recent decades, there have been parades celebrating the country's bicentennial, the township's sesquicentennial in 1963, and numerous Pioneer Day and firemen's celebrations. Above, American Legion Post 511 leads a parade past the Elk filling station and the Eagles building during a Pioneer Day celebration in the 1950s. The proceeds were used to help pay for the new Community Building. The Lions Club float is seen below in the 1976 bicentennial parade. A grand parade is planned for the June 2013 township bicentennial, and it promises to be the largest and best ever. (Above, courtesy of Joan Verbka; below, courtesy of Hazel Luchini.)

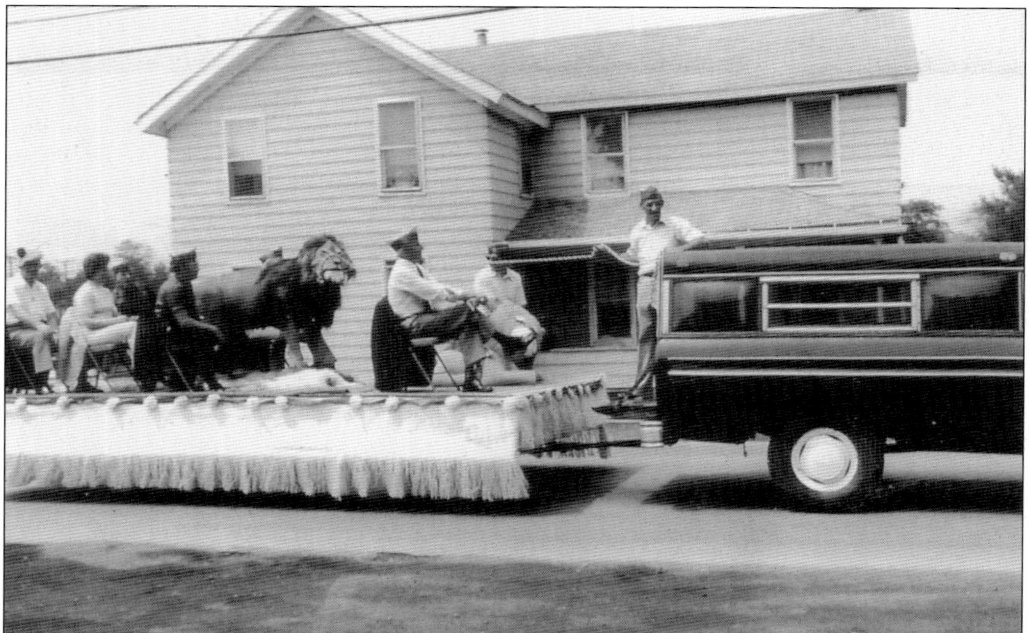

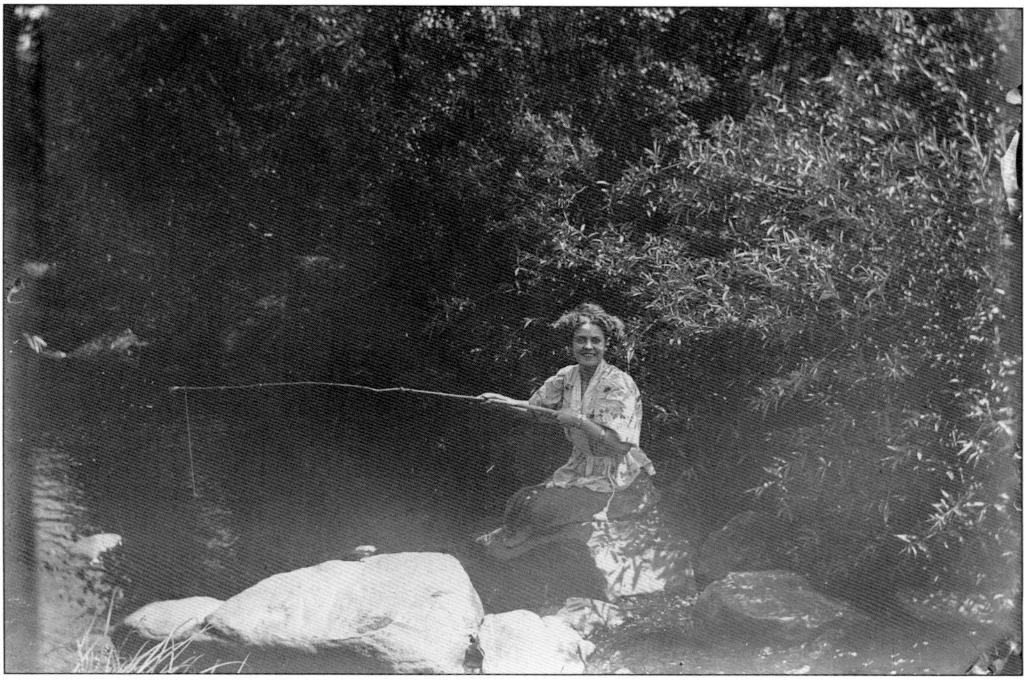

The women of the area also know how to have fun. Above, a woman fishes with a simple pole on a small stream, perhaps Wolflick, Byrnes, or Kersey Run. Below, a group of girls pose in costume for a Japanese Drill event around 1915. Girls usually stayed home and helped their mothers, but as time passed, organizations began allowing girls out in order to socialize and develop values promoted by the sponsoring organization. (Above, courtesy of Chris Casey; below, courtesy of Joan Verbka.)

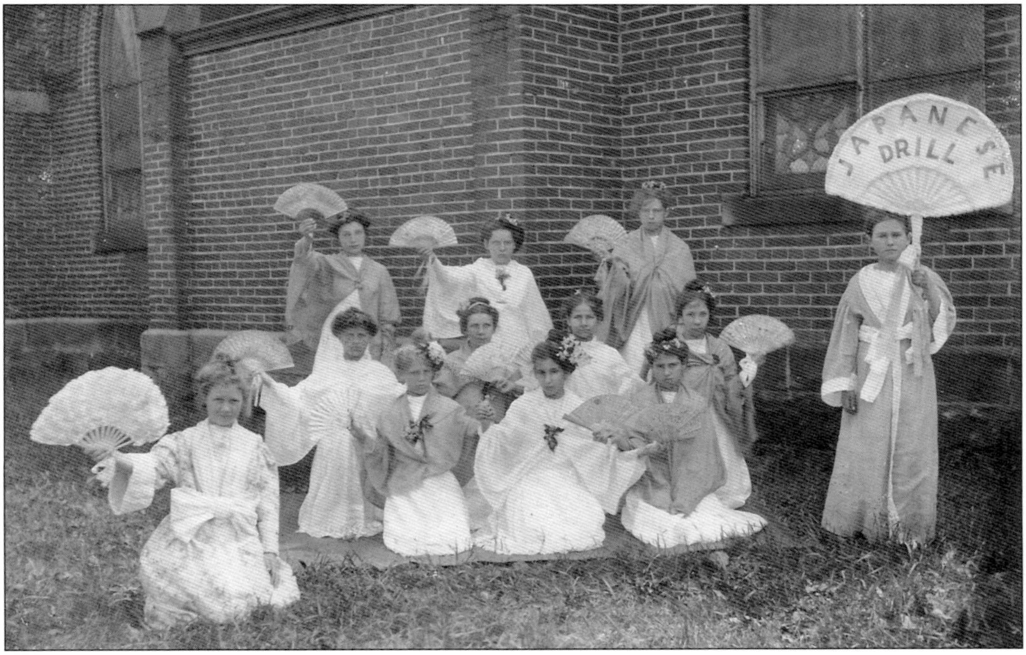

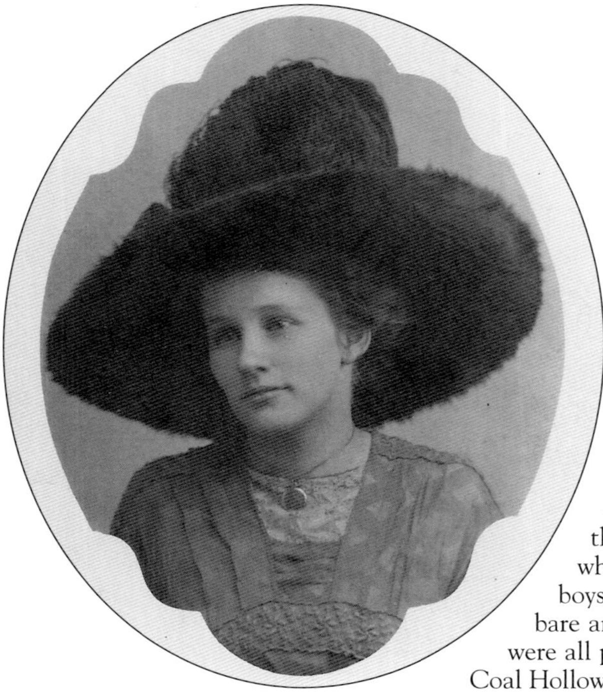

Fashion was also a part of a lady's leisure. Huge broad-brimmed hats were in style for evening wear in the first decade of the 1900s—sometimes they were even trimmed with feathers and stuffed birds. Hair swept up to the top of the head and tied in knots was also part of the style. Edith Schreiber of Main Street is seen at left in 1908. By the 1920s, the flapper style was in vogue, which tried to make girls look like young boys. Close-fitting flapper hats, short skirts, bare arms, and two- to three-inch high heels were all part of the style. Below, Mary Veoni of Coal Hollow poses in a stylish outfit.

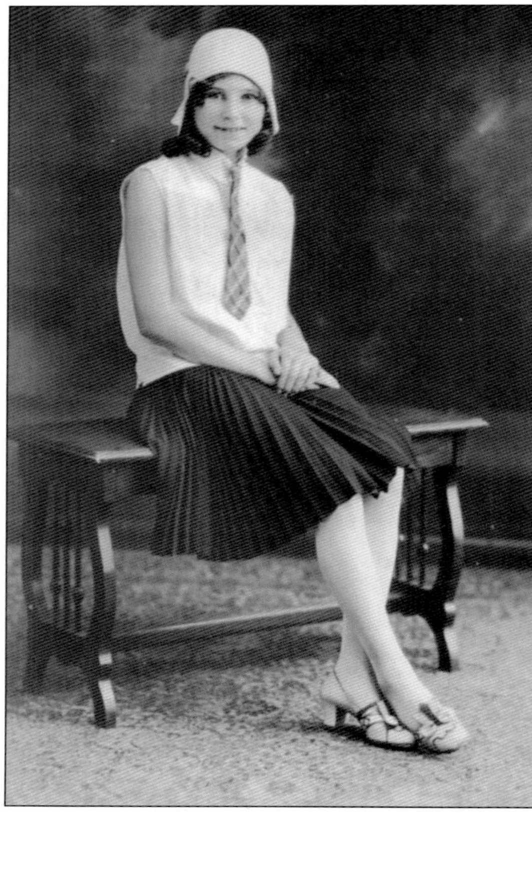

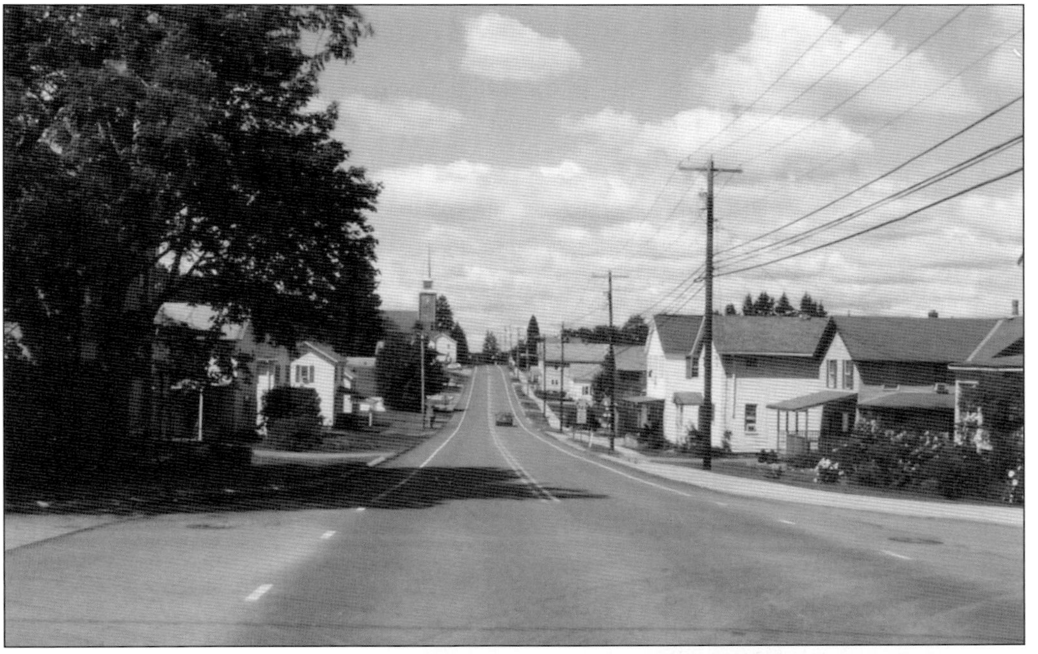

As Fox Township arrives at its bicentennial in 2013, much has changed, but much has stayed the same. Main Street in Kersey is no longer the retail center of the community. All the stores, shops, and offices are gone except one, the Corner Market. People must travel to St. Marys, the Million Dollar Highway, or DuBois to shop. The large employers are gone, replaced by many smaller factories and shops. The population of the township is growing slowly, but it is near its peak of about 3,700. These last two photographs of Kersey show buildings that are more than 100 years old alongside newer structures. Fox Township can take pride in its past during this next year, but it also looks forward with high expectations as it continues through the 21st century.

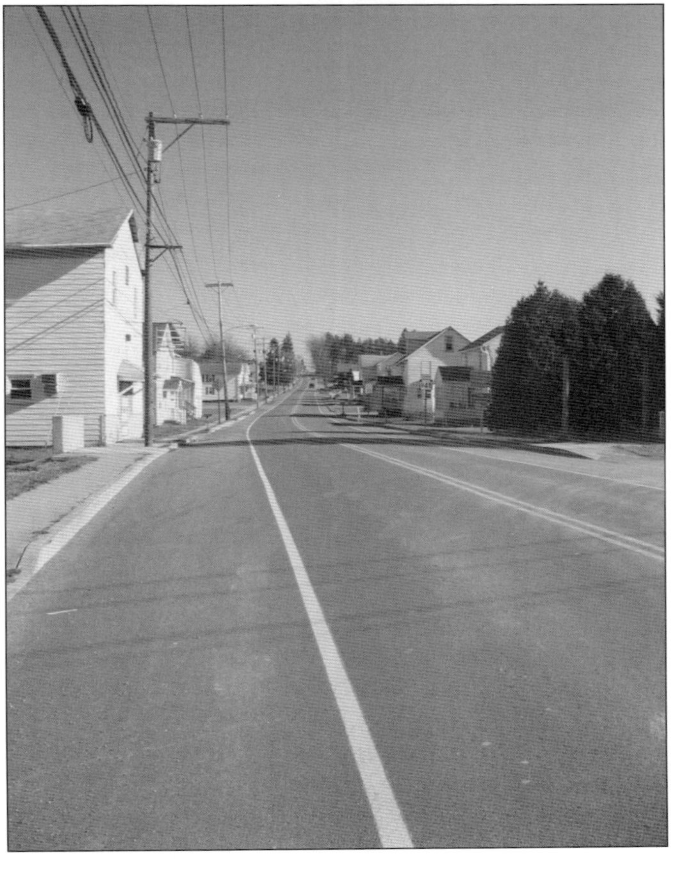